Discrimination and Disrespect

OXFORD PHILOSOPHICAL MONOGRAPHS

Editorial Committee

OTHER TITLES IN THIS SERIES INCLUDE

Discrimination and Disrespect

Benjamin Eidelson

OXFORD
UNIVERSITY PRESS

OXFORD
UNIVERSITY PRESS

Great Clarendon Street, Oxford, OX2 6DP,
United Kingdom

Oxford University Press is a department of the University of Oxford.
It furthers the University's objective of excellence in research, scholarship,
and education by publishing worldwide. Oxford is a registered trade mark of
Oxford University Press in the UK and in certain other countries

© Benjamin Eidelson 2015

The moral rights of the author have been asserted

First Edition published in 2015

Impression: 2

Published in the United States of America by Oxford University Press
198 Madison Avenue, New York, NY 10016, United States of America

British Library Cataloguing in Publication Data

Data available

Library of Congress Control Number: 2015940444

ISBN 978-0-19-873287-7

Printed and bound by
CPI Group (UK) Ltd, Croydon, CR0 4YY

Contents

Introduction

Hardly anyone disputes that discrimination can be a grave moral wrong. Yet this consensus masks fundamental disagreements about what *makes* something discrimination, as well as precisely why (and hence when) acts of discrimination are wrong. This book aims to develop systematic answers to those two questions. It offers a philosophical account of what discrimination is, and a moral theory to explain what is characteristically wrong with it.

That project has two central motivations. The first is theoretical: philosophical reflection, I hope, can help us to attain a clearer understanding of our own moral convictions in this vexed area of social and political life. The second motivation, however, is intensely practical. To confront hard cases in a thoughtful way, we have to understand when and why discrimination is wrong in the first place.

Consider, for example, discrimination based on race or sex that isn't arbitrary or irrational, but rather is grounded in observable patterns and conducted with care and apparent respect. This is often called "statistical" discrimination. Is such differential treatment morally suspect? If so, is it problematic for the same reasons that "classic" race or sex discrimination is objectionable, or for different reasons? And what are these different families of reasons? How do the material effects of discrimination, the attitudes or judgments to which it gives effect, and the social context in which it takes place combine to determine its moral status?

"Statistical" discrimination poses a hard case because it incorporates some features we ordinarily associate with wrongful discrimination but eschews others. There are many other hybrid categories of this kind. Take, as another example, discrimination on the basis of traits that are not relevant to a person's suitability for some benefit or position, but that also are not sites of widespread subordination or disadvantage. What should we make, for instance, of the British law that bars employment discrimination based on "philosophical beliefs"—including, according to some courts, a person's views about climate change or animal cruelty?[1] How does so-called lookism—targeted in some American jurisdictions by bans on "personal appearance discrimination"—compare to racism or sexism?[2] More broadly, how can we tell when claims of wrongful discrimination have tapped the moral root of our convictions about racism, sexism, and the like, and when they have misappropriated this normative heritage for fundamentally different ends?

We could ask similar questions about unwitting discrimination that gives effect to implicit biases, or about apparently neutral practices that give rise to disparate effects. Because the morality of discrimination is rarely thought through from first principles, the debates over all of these non-paradigm cases tend to devolve into contests among unmotivated analogies to (and distinctions from) what are, by acclamation, focal cases. To resolve these various predicaments, however, we need a *general* theory of discrimination—one that captures our convictions about paradigm cases, explains the normative grounds on which they rest, and thereby guides us in determining how far those grounds extend.

Laying such a foundation represents the most concrete "payoff" of this book. But the more fundamental goal of the book is not simply to offer practical prescriptions about some particular kinds of discrimination, but to help fill the underlying lacuna in our sense of our own ethical commitments. The fact is that many people who are certain that discrimination is a serious moral concern remain, if we're honest with ourselves, unsure just *what* we are concerned about. We know, of course, that it has to do with principles of equality, fairness, and justice. And, more specifically, we suspect it has to do with the fact that certain traits are beyond people's control, irrelevant to the decisions that are being made about them, or associated with pervasive, structural disadvantage. We think the concept of wrongful discrimination might also be connected to the principle that people should be treated as individuals, rather than subjected to group stereotypes. And we recognize that charges of discrimination sometimes target malignant attitudes or intentions, while other times they express concern about particular patterns of outcomes. But, still, we have little sense of what these different considerations have to do with one another or how (and if) they combine to form a coherent whole. This book is an effort to make some philosophical progress from that basic starting point, and, although it leaves much unresolved, I hope it will be helpful to others who find themselves starting from a similar position.

* * *

Questions about the morality of discrimination have gone oddly neglected by moral philosophers thus far. Since the idea of wrongful discrimination is expected to do so much normative work in our social and political lives, it is something of a philosophical embarrassment that so little has been done to explore or account for it.

There is, of course, a vast literature on the value of equality, particularly as it concerns distributive justice. One might root a theory of wrongful discrimination in one of the more general views defended there. But that transplant is not straightforward, and it may not be adequate. It is far from clear, after all, that discrimination is wrong principally (let alone only) because of its distributive consequences. Much the same could be said of the literatures on values such as fairness and respect. Put another way, the central moral question about discrimination is precisely how and where these more basic moral considerations figure in. It is striking, therefore, that relatively little work, much of it quite recent, has tackled the conceptual and moral significance of discrimination as such.[3]

By contrast, foundational questions about discrimination are much more familiar to legal scholars. Indeed, there has been a renaissance of interest in philosophical questions about antidiscrimination law in the past few years.[4] This book aims to contribute to that conversation, but it attacks the problems from a different direction than legal theorists commonly do—from the bottom up, we might say, rather than the top down. My central question, in other words, is not when discrimination should be prohibited, but why it is sometimes morally wrong to begin with.

There is reason to doubt how far theories pitched at explaining or justifying institutional rules *about* discrimination can carry us in this more basic inquiry. Because laws shape behavior as well as judge it, the reasons for having certain laws are often rooted in the collective effects of compliance throughout a society. There is, for example, a popular and intuitive view that racial discrimination in employment ought to be prohibited because this prohibition contributes to equalizing opportunity and breaking down a persistent caste-like social system.[5] It does not follow, however, that individual acts of employment discrimination must themselves be wrong, when they are, for the same reason.

Suppose, for instance, that a racist employer privately discriminates against a black candidate whom he knows will get a better job someplace else. Then, by hypothesis, the employer doesn't significantly constrict the candidate's opportunities, let alone entrench the second-class status of a whole group of people. If the act is wrong, as it certainly appears to be, it is for some other reason. More broadly, whereas antidiscrimination law has the power to open many opportunities to a person, and indeed to many people, individuals often confront the distinct choice whether to open or close one. Because those choice situations are so different, they will almost inevitably turn on different—although hardly unrelated—moral considerations. This disjuncture will be even more fundamental in domains of social life where antidiscrimination law is reluctant to tread at all.

While legal understandings of discrimination serve as a central foil throughout the book, therefore, I mean to leave the vital questions of what discriminatory conduct should be prohibited, and why, for another day. This distinction is all the more important because the law has a tendency to occupy a field of normative discourse and claim relevant concepts as its own, tacitly equating lawfulness with moral permissibility. When the legal construction of a concept—discrimination, causation, promissory obligation, or whatever—is shaped by concerns specific to the project of systematic and coercive enforcement, we have to guard against the risk that these considerations will come to distort our thinking about the underlying moral concepts as well.[6]

* * *

My effort to address the central philosophical questions about discrimination can be broken down into three parts—one devoted to conceptual analysis, one to moral theory, and one to an extended case study in applied ethics. At the risk of spoiling any surprise, it may help to summarize the central arguments of each component in advance.

Part I of the book clears the ground and delimits the subject by developing a formal analysis of the concept of discrimination, understood in non-evaluative terms. In particular, Chapter 1 argues that discrimination can be understood as a form of action that is, in itself, morally neutral, and which carries no particular connection to socially salient groups. What distinguishes discrimination from mere differential treatment, I suggest, is its special explanatory connection to some differential ascription of a property to the discriminatees. I explore how this explanatory connection should be understood, and I offer an interpretation of practices that discriminate between people without discriminating *against* any of them.

Because of the rhetorical power of "discrimination," there have been many efforts to extend the concept to embrace practices that seem on their face quite distinct from the core activity identified in Chapter 1. Hence the proliferation of prefixed notions of discrimination—*structural* discrimination, *institutional* discrimination, and so forth. Chapter 2 grapples with the most important of these proposed extensions, which is known in Europe as *indirect* discrimination and in the United States as discrimination based on "disparate impact." What is the relationship between this activity and the central concept of discrimination elaborated in Chapter 1?

I argue that the connection is in fact a distant one, and that unifying these two phenomena therefore should not be a desideratum for a theory of discrimination (or of what makes it wrongful). Many cases of indirect discrimination are, upon inspection, simply ordinary, direct discrimination of a certain characteristic kind, and are best understood as such. Others are not reducible in this way, but these may not be best thought of as *discrimination* at all. Rather, prohibiting "indirect discrimination" in such cases may be a roundabout means of equalizing opportunity for members of disadvantaged social classes. Conceiving of failure to go along with this program as itself a kind of discrimination—albeit an "indirect" kind—does not bring out underlying similarities between the phenomena as much as it invites equivocation between them. Chapter 2 concludes by applying the conceptual apparatus of the first two chapters to show why the conflict that some have posited between prohibitions on direct and indirect discrimination is illusory.

With this conceptual groundwork in place, the remainder of the book turns squarely to the morality of discrimination. Part II argues that the normative root of our convictions about core cases of wrongful discrimination is the recognition that these acts manifest disrespect for the discriminatees as persons. This general idea—that wrongful discrimination is connected to moral disrespect—is a very familiar one. Indeed, drawing on Kant, Martin Luther King, Jr, wrote half a century ago that segregation "debases personality," threatening to "depersonalize the potential person and desecrate what he is."[7] A disrespect-based account of wrongful discrimination thus begins from a potent moral intuition. The core task of the book is to develop that intuition into a theory—to explore how the general obligation to recognize certain features of other persons *qua* persons, such as the intrinsic value of their well-being or the character of their individual autonomy, can be employed both to explain and to critically assess our judgments about familiar and unfamiliar variants of discrimination. The first step in this project is to get clear on the *kind* of disrespect to which we should be appealing. So, in Chapter 3, I elaborate a working account of respect and disrespect for persons as these notions bear on the morality of discrimination. On this view, the relevant sort of respect—recognition respect for someone's standing as a person—imposes an affirmative obligation that one take to heart the various normative upshots of her being a person and regulate one's action accordingly. What is of fundamental importance to determining whether an action is disrespectful, then, is the set of reasons for which an agent acts, rather than the effects or social meaning of her action. But her deliberation is marred not simply by the presence of some form of animus or a defamatory belief, as some have suggested, but by the *absence* of appropriate responsiveness to someone's standing as a person, whether that absence comes about willfully or by neglect.

How then do we explain the important role of social conventions in fixing what is disrespectful? The answer lies in a distinction, also developed in Chapter 3, between *basic* and *conventional* disrespect. An act is basically disrespectful of X as a Y when it manifests a certain kind of deliberative failure—a failure to give appropriate weight to X's standing as a Y in deciding how to act. An act is conventionally disrespectful, by contrast, when it is *understood* to be basically disrespectful by the lights of prevailing social meanings.

What is of basic moral importance, I argue, is basic disrespect. But social conventions matter a great deal because it is usually *basically* disrespectful to ignore them in view of the psychological and material harms that come with being *conventionally* disrespected. By taking this approach, I argue, we can reconcile three commitments: the "expressivist" insight that the moral status of an act, including an act of discrimination, often turns on its social meaning; the conviction that the wrongness of discrimination does not rest on its contingent effects alone; and the commonsense view that social conventions do not have the power to determine directly what is right and wrong.

Once we have settled on a view of the general conceptual structure of respect for persons, we have to ask just *what* we are obligated to recognize about other persons, and how this obligation casts light on the various forms of wrongful discrimination. Different sorts of wrongful discrimination, I suggest, manifest a failure of recognition with respect to different attributes of personhood. Whereas discrimination on the basis of differential concern often fails to respect some people as beings of equal intrinsic value, discrimination on the basis of statistical generalizations often fails to respect them as autonomous individuals. The intuitive unity of our thought about these disparate cases—reflected, for instance, in the inclination to call each of these different sorts of discrimination at least potentially "racist" or "sexist"—is rooted in the unity of the personhood that, in different ways, the different practices demean or deny.

Each of these moral requirements must be specified carefully. In Chapter 4, I consider discrimination that manifests a failure of recognition for the equal *value* or *worth* of persons as such. I suggest that respect for a person's equal value is best understood as grounding a defeasible presumption of equal consideration—akin to the Principle of Insufficient Reason, which purports to govern probability judgments in the absence of relevant evidence. This presumption can be overridden, without disrespect, by genuinely relevant differences between persons' claims to one's consideration. But it is respect for people's equal value that sets a baseline of equal concern and requires a special reason for weighing some people's needs more heavily than others'. One paradigmatic form of wrongful discrimination stems from a failure to respect this presumption of equal regard. Chapter 4 also introduces an important distinction between ordinary disrespect and *contempt*, understood as willful defiance of normative authority; this distinction helps to explain what is and is not morally similar about classic bigotry and implicit bias. Finally, having analyzed the demands of respect for people's equal value in this way, Chapter 4 concludes by considering some forms of partiality that the requirement of recognition for a person's equality may *not* reach— including discrimination based on preferences that govern the way one "spends" the weight properly afforded to one's own interests, rather than how one weighs the interests of others.

Chapter 5 considers the complementary idea that people have a moral claim to be treated as individuals out of respect for their autonomy. That notion is often criticized as incompatible with the widespread and mundane use of statistical evidence in a host of contexts. But in fact, I suggest, respecting people as individuals is not a matter of forswearing the use of any sort of evidence about them. What respect for a person's individuality requires is not that we *exclude* informative patterns about those who share some of her traits, but rather that we at least *include* certain kinds of information where it is reasonably available—information that manifests her own efforts, as an autonomous agent, to give shape to her life. In this and in other particulars, the disrespect theory connects our understanding of wrongful discrimination to our grasp of moral personhood more broadly—to the question what constraints a person's standing as a person imposes on the way we should relate to her.

The disrespect-based theory of Part II aspires to explain what is characteristically and intrinsically wrong about core cases of wrongful discrimination. But one of the significant features of the account is that it does not condemn all of the discrimination that typically elicits moral concern. In Part III, I consider at some length one example of the kind of discrimination that is not necessarily ruled out by the moral demands of respect for persons: racial profiling in law enforcement. Such profiling, I suggest, exemplifies the challenges that arise in assessing discrimination that exploits statistical relationships among socially salient characteristics in pursuit of valuable social ends. I argue that this practice, and others like it, may be troubling on grounds that are fundamentally contingent and hence very different in character. What makes racial profiling morally wrong may not be that it is distinctly unfair or that it is necessarily racist, but rather that it contributes to a set of *conventional* social understandings that do unjustified harm.

Despite its title, therefore, the book ultimately offers a pluralist view of what makes discrimination wrong. On the one hand, the moral core of wrongful discrimination—what earns it its apparent place among the cardinal sins of modern social life—is the failure of recognition that it characteristically shows for the equal personhood of the discriminatees. This core is made up of the practices rightly described as *racist, sexist,* and the like. Different cases merit inclusion in this class for different reasons, reflecting the different morally significant facets of persons. On the other hand, discriminatory practices that do not manifest an attitude of disrespect for persons are not thereby excused from moral assessment. Many such practices are bad simply because the harm they do—including through the disrespect that they may foster or be felt to evince—is unjustified. I take racial profiling, under certain conditions, to pose an important and misunderstood paradigm of this sort of case.

PART I

Clearing the Ground

1

The Concept of Discrimination

What is discrimination? Relatively little philosophical attention has been devoted to the questions when and why discrimination is wrong. But philosophers have taken even less interest in this more basic question: what *is* it?

Perhaps this question has attracted little discussion because the answer simply seems obvious. We are all familiar with many cases of discrimination—in employment, in public accommodations, in private relationships—and the interesting question about these seems to be what makes at least some of them morally objectionable.

To a certain extent that is true: the main reason to be interested in the concept of discrimination, I think, is that discrimination is sometimes a serious moral wrong. Discrimination is probably not an especially important concept from the detached standpoint of philosophy of action, in other words. But that does not mean that we can or should skip right to the moral question. Rather, our interest in the morality of discrimination gives us a reason to get clear on what discrimination is in the first place—which may not itself be primarily a moral question.

It is also not as straightforward an inquiry as it may appear. To discriminate is a verb, something one *does*; but it involves a complex constellation of relations to one or more other individuals or groups, as well as to some manner of treatment and some dimension of difference. Each of these relations can be characterized in different ways. In this stage-setting chapter, I offer a working account of key aspects of this conceptual structure, with eyes to both ordinary usage and theoretical utility.

Of course, in everyday conversation, arguments about what constitutes discrimination are often normatively charged. As David Wasserman says, "to call discrimination 'wrongful' is merely to add emphasis to a morally-laden term."[1] One possibility, then, is that the question what discrimination is and the question what is wrong with it are really one and the same, for "discrimination" simply names a certain kind of wrong.[2]

I think we should resist that approach and instead take discrimination as a phenomenon with no built-in moral status. This too is consistent with important facets of ordinary usage. Many who support efforts at "positive discrimination," for instance, call them by this name. More broadly, it seems to be widely accepted that one can intelligibly ask whether or not discrimination of a certain kind is wrong, which suggests that it is not always so by nature. (One cannot do the same with a moralized concept such as murder.) But the most important reason for proceeding this way is not that it better reflects ordinary usage—which is undeniably inconsistent on this point—but that it structures our inquiry in a more fruitful way.

Here is what I mean. There is plainly something common to (1) wrongful discrimination (whether we understand this phrase as redundant or not) and (2) what *would* be wrongful discrimination if only it were wrongful—that is, conduct that is just like wrongful discrimination, except that it lacks the former's wrong-making features. Whichever construal of "discrimination" you favor, you cannot adequately understand the essential characteristics of discrimination without an account of the features that characterize (1) and (2) alike. For even if you think discrimination is necessarily wrong, you will want to know what properties it distinctively has besides those that make it wrong. Similarly, an account of murder presupposes an account of killing. So we need an analysis of the category that subsumes both and only the phenomena enumerated as (1) and (2). And easily the most natural name for that category, it seems, is "discrimination," since we can simply add the modifier "wrongful" to refer to (1) in particular.

Perhaps another contender for this role is the more general notion of "differential treatment." But that is not a viable alternative if there are significant features that are common to the two classes I've described that also are *not* common to all cases of differential treatment. I think there are indeed such features, and by offering a conceptual analysis of discrimination—understood without a necessary moral status—I mean in part to detail what they are.

So understood, the concept of discrimination can be decomposed into two fundamental parts. First, to discriminate against someone, one must treat him differently in some dimension than others, and this differential treatment must be comparatively disadvantageous to him in some respect. To be sure, this schematic formulation leaves various issues unsettled. It says nothing about what interests a person has or what constitutes a form of treatment, for instance, although both of these will necessarily contribute to determining whether something constitutes discrimination according to this definition.

Without denying that there are interesting issues here, I want to leave this first component of the concept—the part to do with disadvantageous differential treatment—largely unanalyzed for now. It suffices to say that discriminating against (or in favor of) someone requires treating her worse (or better) than others in some respect. At the end of the chapter, I will consider certain aspects of this condition more closely.

My primary focus, however, will be on a second aspect of the concept. What is distinctive of discrimination, as compared to differential treatment generally, is that it is necessarily responsive to a difference among people along some dimension. Even the broad dictionary definition of discrimination as a "process by which two stimuli differing in some aspect are responded to differently" builds in this feature: one discriminates by *responding* differently to some difference in the features *of the stimuli*.[3] For this reason, one can discriminate on the basis of religion, or on the basis of eye color, and so on, but one cannot discriminate on no basis at all. To discriminate on no basis is simply to not discriminate. An analysis of discrimination must specify, then, what has to be true of the disadvantageous differential treatment described above in order for it to constitute discrimination on the basis of a given trait (and hence also for it to constitute discrimination at all).

I proceed as follows. In §1.1, I offer a general definition of discrimination on the basis of some trait, and I highlight some of the consequences of this analysis. In §1.2, I consider and reject a proposal to limit the ambit of discrimination to differentiation on the basis of socially salient traits. Finally, in §1.3, I consider what is required for differential treatment with the appropriate etiology to qualify as discrimination *against* or *in favor of* someone, and what we should make of discrimination between people that is not discrimination against or in favor of anyone. With these conceptual clarifications behind us, we will be equipped to turn to the perplexing notion of "indirect" discrimination in the next chapter, and then to the morality of discrimination generally.

1.1 A Definition

If you treat various people differently out of pure whimsicality, you engage in differential treatment but not discrimination. This is why "discriminating" taste is a virtue: it suggests not just that a person responds differently to some objects than to others, but that her variable responses are sensitive to differences in the objects.

The sense of "discrimination" that concerns us does differ from this older sense of the word in two respects, however. First, to say that someone has discriminating taste is normally also to say that she is sensitive to *relevant* differences in the objects, an implication that is not shared by the use of "discrimination" that we are interested in. (Hence Christopher Hitchens' remark, exploiting the gap between these two meanings, that "the racist precisely shows himself incapable of discrimination.")[4] The laudatory use of "discriminating" only makes sense, however, because of the more basic feature—responsiveness to qualities of the objects—that the two conceptions share, and which distinguishes them both from mere differential treatment.

Second, to say that a person discriminates in the sense that concerns us is not necessarily to say that the differences he perceives in the discriminatees are genuine. Consider, for instance, the research showing that American employers often consider identical résumés less favorably when they carry stereotypically African-American names (e.g., Jamal, Lakisha).[5] If the mechanism of this differential treatment is that the employer ascribes different racial classifications to such candidates, and is less disposed to interview those she takes to be African-American, then I think it would be accurate, by the lights of prevailing usage, to describe this as a case of discrimination on the basis of race (or "racial discrimination" for short). In characterizing the case this way, we do not appeal to the fact (if it is a fact) that an applicant named Jamal, who is disfavored in this way, is *actually* African-American. We do not even presuppose a view of what "actually" being a member of a particular racial group involves. Thus to discriminate on a given basis is to respond differentially to what one *takes* to be a difference between the discriminatees in respect of that trait.

With these considerations in mind, I will adopt the following working definition of discrimination:

X (directly) discriminates against Y in dimension W on the basis of P if and only if:

(*Differential Treatment Condition*) X treats Y less favorably in respect of W than X treats some actual or counterfactual other, Z, in respect of W; and

(*Explanatory Condition*) a difference in how X regards Y P-wise and how X regards or would regard Z P-wise figures in the explanation of this differential treatment.[6]

Before turning to these conditions individually, let me make some initial points about the formula generally.

First, I mean for the variable "X" to range over agents only—be they people, corporations, institutions, or groups of these. So when we say that some act or enactment discriminates in such-and-such a way, as *is each instance of discrim by an enact attaching to agent, or only the initial enact? prob 1st be changing condits*

we often do, I take us to mean that it is an *instance of* discrimination, by some unspecified or implied agent—not that the enactment can itself be substituted for "X" in the definition and satisfy it.[7] *why not*

Second, "Y" and "Z" also range over individuals (be they persons or institutions) or groups of individuals. But it is important in this context that a group of individuals be understood as just that: a set of particulars. The problem is that often we specify the set of people that is discriminated against in a given case by reference to some trait that they share. This invites us to confuse whom X discriminates against with the basis on which X does so. If some act discriminates "against immigrants," for instance, Y is made up of people who are immigrants. But sometimes we read "against immigrants" with an implicit "as such" attached, allowing this one phrase to fix both who is discriminated against *and* on what basis (in this case, on the basis of being an immigrant). These are very different issues, however. Many immigrants are discriminated against on the basis of race, for example; and in some contexts it is important both that it is immigrants who are discriminated against and that it is on the basis of race that they are discriminated against. So the Differential Treatment Condition should be read without any implicit "as such" following "Y". Even if Y is a set specified by reference to a trait shared by its members, we should not infer anything about the *kind* of discrimination X commits.

Third, "W" ranges over dimensions of treatment. A dimension of treatment is a set of exclusive options regarding how one treats someone. You engage in differential treatment in the dimension of hiring when you hire some people and not others, for instance. The exclusivity that defines this dimension of treatment is not across individuals, however, but within them. That is, what makes "hiring" a dimension of treatment is not that you cannot hire both Y and Z, but that for each of Y and Z, you cannot both hire and not hire them.

this would seem to exclude favorable discrim, which is including by some excludes others

Finally, I have cast the definition as an account of "(direct) discrimination." I put it that way because, if we are pressed to distinguish between "direct" and "indirect" forms of discrimination, mine is a definition of what is generally described as the "direct" variety. In fact, however, I think "indirect" discrimination is not usefully thought of as a distinct form of discrimination at all, except as a piece of legal jargon—a position I will defend in the next chapter. So, relative to my preferred typology, the definition above is also a definition of discrimination generally.

With these clarifications behind us, let us consider the Explanatory Condition more closely. It seems obvious that one person's less favorable treatment of another must have some explanatory connection to the latter's possession of a given trait to qualify as discrimination on the basis of that trait. But not just any explanatory connection is sufficient. If it were, you would always discriminate on the basis of any traits that explain a discriminatee's possession of a trait on the basis of which you discriminate, which is not true.

Suppose, for instance, that the operator of a roller coaster turns away Sally, a seven-year-old girl, because he measures her height and determines that she is less than four feet tall. In so doing, he discriminates against her on the basis of height.[8] Plausibly, however, Sally's being less than four feet tall is explained by her age. If her age partially explains her height, and her height partially explains her being turned away, then her age partially explains her being turned away. But the operator obviously does not discriminate against Sally on the basis of age, at least not directly.[9]

The Explanatory Condition supports and explains this judgment by identifying a discriminator's *perception* of a trait, rather than the trait itself, as essential to discrimination on that basis. Sally's age may explain her height, but it is the operator's perception of her height—or, as I put it in formulating the Explanatory Condition, how he regards her height-wise—rather than his perception of her age that explains the way he treats her. So she is discriminated against on the basis of height, not age. Metaphorically, we might say that the grounds on which a person discriminates are marked by the links on a chain of explanation that go through her mind. The connection between Sally's age and her height simply precedes that point on the explanatory chain.[10]

By contrast, suppose that rather than measuring Sally's height, the operator explicitly or tacitly estimates her age, infers from this

estimate that she is probably less than four feet tall, and then excludes
her for this reason. In this case the Explanatory Condition implies
that he discriminates *both* on the basis of age and on the basis of
height. For how he regards her in each of these respects figures in the
explanation of the fact that he turns her away (when he would not
turn away others). A parallel analysis could be given in the case of
employers who disfavor applicants whose résumés bear stereotypically African-American names: they discriminate both on the basis of
name and on the basis of race, since they perceive one by way of the
other, and a difference in respect of either perception could therefore
have resulted in different treatment.[11] These cases make clear that
what matters for the purposes of the Explanatory Condition is not the
rationale for X's action, or the explanation X would adduce, but
rather which of his perceptions actually contribute to explaining the
way he acts.[12]

The possibility that a single instance of differential treatment may
constitute discrimination on multiple bases in the manner just
described is sometimes overlooked, so it is worth considering it
more closely. Of course, we are familiar with the notion that a person
can be disfavored on two grounds simultaneously—race and sex, for
instance. Such "intersectional" discrimination is one kind of discrimination on multiple bases.[13] The Explanatory Condition recognizes
this, but it also allows for multiple-basis discrimination of another
kind. To take another example, suppose that the director of an
adoption agency disfavors single applicants because, having reviewed
the empirical evidence, she concludes that single people prove less
effective on average than two-parent couples as adoptive parents.
Suppose that the director is then accused of discriminating on the
basis of relationship status. She might concede that she does this, but
deny that discrimination of this kind is wrong. Alternatively, however, she might respond that if she discriminates, it is simply on the
basis of *likely effectiveness*. That merely has an adverse effect on single
people—a fact that is traceable to the state of the evidence about
effectiveness, not discrimination on the basis of relationship status on
her part.

The Explanatory Condition disallows this second sort of argument. To be sure, the director *does* discriminate on the basis of likely effectiveness. Suppose that Mary is a single applicant and John and Michelle are a couple. Part of the explanation of the director's differential treatment of Mary relative to John and Michelle is that (i) the director regards Mary as less likely to be effective, and (ii) the director is more disposed to grant applications from people she regards as more likely to be effective. But it is no less true that she discriminates against Mary on the basis of being a single applicant. For the fact invoked in clause (i) is itself explained in part by the fact that she regards Mary as a single applicant, whereas she takes John and Michelle to be a couple. That means that the latter fact is part of the explanation of the differential treatment as well—which therefore satisfies the Explanatory Condition for discrimination on the basis of relationship status.

Put another way, the Explanatory Condition takes no notice of whether the explanatory force of X's P-perceptions, with respect to X's differential treatment of Y and Z, is due to their relevance to an operative premise or an auxiliary premise of X's reasoning.[14] In this case, relationship status figures only in an auxiliary premise of the adoption director's reasoning—her operative aim being simply to distribute children to promising parents—but that makes no difference, according to my account, to whether she discriminates on the basis of relationship status.

Indeed, by posing a question of explanation rather than rationale, this account allows that one may discriminate on the basis of a trait without really *reasoning* about it at all. The Explanatory Condition is satisfied whenever differential treatment is explained by "how X *regards* or would regard Y P-wise." All of the cases we have considered thus far involve simple *beliefs* that a person falls under one or another description—belief being the simplest form of regarding someone a certain way with respect to a certain dimension of difference. Suppose, though, that a driver stuck in traffic feels an impulse to lock his doors whenever a black pedestrian enters his visual field, but not when other people do. The driver may not even

but does this necessarily

be consciously aware of the approaching person or of perceiving *affect* anything about him; he may only be aware of feeling vaguely unsafe, and moved to lock the doors as a result. In such a case, it seems a stretch to say that the driver has any beliefs about the race of the approaching man. But it still seems possible that the driver discriminates—unbeknownst to himself, or even despite himself—on the basis of race.

The right way to characterize the mental state out of which this driver acts—a state that seems to fall, as Tamar Gendler says, "between reason and reflex"[15]—touches on subtle and actively debated issues in philosophy of mind. Without getting bogged down in the details, it seems that in the case I described, certain representational content is essential to accounting for the driver's action, but this content is "processed in a relatively shallow way," triggering certain affective responses that in turn conduce to a behavioral reaction.[16] When that content can be understood to represent a person as falling under a description—here, it seems that it must represent the man as black—the agent *regards* the person as being that way in the sense that I intend.*

The Explanatory Condition also implies, a fortiori, that even if one does consciously perceive differences in respect of some trait P, one need not be aware of the role of one's P-perceptions in explaining one's differential treatment (much less intend that they play this role) for one to directly discriminate on the basis of P. Instead, as we have seen, the definition rests weight only on whether these perceptions contribute to *explaining* one's differential treatment. It thus resembles Linda Hamilton Krieger's revisionist understanding of "disparate treatment" liability under U.S. employment discrimination law, according to which "[t]he critical inquiry would be whether . . . group status 'made a difference' in the employer's action, not whether the decisionmaker intended that it make a difference."[17]

---

* The "regarded as" language itself is borrowed from the Americans with Disabilities Act of 1990, which extends protection to those "regarded as" disabled. See 42 U.S.C. § 12102(1)(C).

but he's not saying all direct must be intentional, he's saying all intentional is direct

These views put me at odds with some others. Andrew Altman, for instance, contends that "direct discrimination *is* intentional discrimination."[18] But I think this proposed equivalence can't be true. We can begin from the observation that the act-type delimited by the definition of discrimination I have given, whatever we call that type, is such that acts of this type could be committed either intentionally or unintentionally. I think that much is unarguable. In choosing among raised hands, for instance, a teacher may call on male students more frequently than female students.[19] Suppose that this discrepancy is not a simple statistical accident or a consequence of some correlation between sex and other features, but rather explained by a conjunction of the sex-perceptions of the teacher and certain sex-sensitive dispositions of his. Holding this much constant, it is clearly possible that the teacher does not *intend* to treat male and female students differently. Alternatively, the teacher could intend to act this way—perhaps because he thinks male students are more likely to make comments that advance the class discussion.

Now there is some common thing that the teacher is doing in each of those two variants of the example, unintentionally in one case and intentionally in the other. I think we ought to call that thing discrimination on the basis of sex—and "direct" discrimination if pressed to distinguish it from what is called "indirect" discrimination. Altman would apparently say that there is direct discrimination only in the intentional case. But then what is there in the unintentional case?

no, he says unconscious can be direct

It seems absurd to say that there is no sex discrimination at all, so this must be a case of "indirect" discrimination. Without getting too far ahead of ourselves, Altman defines "indirect" discrimination in the typical way, as encompassing acts or policies with disproportionate negative effects on members of some group that fail some special standard of justification. But assimilating the teacher's unintentional differential treatment of men and women to that category would elide something essential about it. The teacher does not merely do something that is disproportionately to the disadvantage of women (and do so without sufficiently good reason)—as he might if he were simply more disposed to call on taller students, whatever their sex, and this led to his calling on women less often than men. Rather, he is less likely to call on women precisely because of the impression that their being women makes on him. There is nothing "indirect" about that; it is simply unintended. What he does should be counted as direct sex discrimination, therefore, and we should consequently decline to equate direct discrimination with intentional discrimination.

In an instructive article, Patrick Shin argues that dominant legal regimes for policing discrimination assume a "justificatory," rather than "causal," conception of discrimination.[20] The justificatory view understands the question whether a person discriminates on a given ground as fundamentally concerned with certain features of the agent's reasons for action or "putative justificatory rationale." As Shin notes, a turn toward causal explanation raises important issues concerning the nature of moral responsibility for wrongful discrimination (and related questions concerning legal liability), which we will consider in somewhat greater depth later on. But these questions are separable from questions about what constitutes discrimination in the first place. Even if we took the extreme view that a person should *never* be morally or legally liable for discrimination that is unconscious or unintentional, it would still be appropriate to describe him as engaged in unwitting or unintended discrimination on the basis of the relevant trait.

1.1.1 Structural discrimination

To conclude our discussion of the Explanatory Condition, consider Sally and the roller coaster once again. In the original version of that case, we concluded that Sally is discriminated against only on the basis of her height, and not on the basis of her age, because age is not what the operator is responding to—even if her height, to which he is responding, is itself largely explained by her age. There is nevertheless an important pattern of relations that obtains in this case between (a) the operator, (b) Sally's exclusion, and (c) Sally's age. It will help to have a name for this pattern of connections.

In fact, I think it is appropriate to think of this as a case of *structural* discrimination. On this understanding, an act or policy is structural discrimination on the basis of P if it is comparatively disadvantageous to one group defined in terms of P relative to another one, and its being so is partly explained by their difference in respect of P. The essential difference between ordinary and structural discrimination, according to this account, is that in the latter case the explanatory connection between the comparative disadvantage and the trait in question need not be mediated by anything to do with how the (structural) discriminator perceives or reacts to the trait.

This yields the result that Sally's height-based exclusion from the roller coaster is an instance of structural age discrimination against her committed by the operator.[21] Similarly, awarding scholarships to children on the basis of academic achievement may amount to structural discrimination on the basis of family wealth, if family wealth partly explains which students achieve highly. So too if banks grant loans to black applicants less often than whites, and this is because blacks have genuinely worse credit history than whites on average, but that fact is itself traceable to their being black—for instance, because blacks are targeted for predatory loans that damage their credit. (Here we have an instance of another common pattern, where the standing of one practice as structural discrimination on the basis of some trait is traceable to a distinct instance of ordinary discrimination on the basis of that trait in a different dimension of treatment.)

Acts that are structural discrimination on some basis need not be, or be connected to, an instance of ordinary discrimination on the same or another basis. If an agency offers a vaccine which, unbeknownst to it, only works for men, it may not engage in any ordinary discrimination at all. But this act arguably constitutes structural sex discrimination against women: it is comparatively disadvantageous to them, and its being so is traceable to their being women.

As I hope these examples demonstrate, my definition of structural discrimination captures the diffuse sense that this concept concerns the imposition of burdens on certain classes of people through formally neutral procedures—procedures that adversely affect these classes only because of underlying physical or social dynamics (or "structures") which, for instance, connect age with height, or race with credit history. At the same time, my proposal preserves a distinction between structural discrimination and situations in which burdens fall disproportionately on members of a given group but not in any way *because* they are members of that group.[22]

Still, because the scholarly and popular usage of "structural discrimination" is inconsistent, I hesitate to cast my definition as more than stipulative.[23] On some interpretations, moreover, the very point of recognizing "structural" discrimination as a distinct phenomenon is that it is not a discrete act committed by an agent; for better or worse, my definition does not allow the concept to serve that function.[24] And, importantly, by describing this category as structural discrimination, I don't mean to imply that it really is a kind of *discrimination*. Prefixed concepts are often ambiguous in this way: they can either mark out a subspecies of a phenomenon, or they can qualify the claim that the thing in question falls under the concept at all. Given my definition of discrimination, my definition of structural discrimination is of the latter kind.

We can set this category aside for now. In the next chapter, I will appeal to it in the course of considering possible interpretations of the idea of indirect discrimination.

1.2 Discrimination and Social Salience

We now have the fundamentals of a conceptual analysis of discrimination on the table. As it stands, the definition imposes no limits on the bases on which people can and do discriminate—that is, on the kinds of traits that can be substituted for P and satisfy the definition. We can discriminate on the basis of race or sex, but we can equally discriminate on the basis of handedness, position in a queue, trustworthiness, and indefinitely many other qualities.

Some have urged that the concept of discrimination relevant to moral analysis be hemmed in. Kasper Lippert-Rasmussen, for instance, says that to be discriminatory, differential treatment of Y and Z must be "suitably explained by Y's and Z's being (or [being] believed by X to be) distinguishable

(members of) different, socially salient groups."[25] He further specifies that "a group is socially salient if perceived membership of it is important to the structure of social interactions across a wide range of social contexts."[26] Lippert-Rasmussen acknowledges that this leaves it "somewhat unclear when a group is socially salient," but suggests, reasonably enough, that this "simply reflects the fact that the contours of our concept of discrimination are somewhat fuzzy." I will now argue that this conceptual constraint, which we can call the Social Salience Requirement, should be rejected.

In fact, the Social Salience Requirement is ambiguous between two significantly different positions. First, we might require that X's differential treatment of Y and Z be suitably explained by Y and Z's belonging to different groups, one or each of which has the feature of being socially salient. Second, we might require that X's differential treatment of Y and Z be suitably explained by Y and Z's *belonging to different socially salient groups*—that is, with the social salience of the groups itself contributing to the explanation of the differential treatment.

This ambiguity is not unique to Lippert-Rasmussen's explanation of the Social Salience Requirement. Altman, for instance, writes: "The wrongfulness of ... discrimination is tied to the fact that the discriminatory act is based on the victim's membership in a salient social group."[27] Again, either reading seems to fit this sentence equally well: what distinguishes wrongful discrimination could be (1) that (a) the act is "based on" the victim's membership in a group and (b) this group has the feature of being socially salient, or it could be (2) that the act is "based on" the victim's membership in a salient social group in such a way that, if the group were not socially salient, the act's basis would be removed.

Either interpretation of the Social Salience Requirement yields some unattractive results. On the first reading, whether a person discriminates turns on whether the basis on which he differentiates is in fact a socially salient cleavage, even if that social significance has no connection whatsoever to his action. As a thought experiment, then, suppose that an odd individual is born with an innate tendency to favor one kind of person over another: men over women, dark-skinned people over light-skinned people, left-handed people over right-handed people, or something like this. It would be very strange, I think, to say that whether *he* discriminates hinges on whether his idiosyncratic partiality happens to align with a distinction that is socially salient in his society at the time, although for reasons wholly unrelated to him or his partiality. That will bear on the consequences of his action in many cases, of course, in ways that are potentially important to its moral status. But the idea that it determines whether he discriminates conflicts with what seems to me a basic "internalist" intuition about the concept. If we know everything about how X treats Y and Z and why he treats them each as he does, we should know whether he is discriminating on any given basis in so doing.

So perhaps the second reading is better: whether a person discriminates depends on whether the social salience of the groups he differentiates between is *itself* part of the explanation for his differential treatment. Certainly this is closer to the intuitive idea reflected in paradigm cases of wrongful discrimination, in which a person discriminates on the basis of race or sex in part because of the social meanings of these categories. But this reading makes the Social Salience Requirement implausibly strong. Suppose, for instance, that the manager of a factory prefers to hire men rather than women because of a non-spurious generalization that men possess greater upper-body strength on average. Regardless of whether this policy is objectionable, it is obviously an instance of sex discrimination. But just as clearly, the manager's preferential treatment of men need not be *explained by* the social salience or significance of sex. Rather, it is explained by the manager's generalization about upper-body strength, which he could just as well have derived from a biology textbook as from his social milieu. Then the differential treatment would not be recognized as discrimination by the definition we are considering.

So I think the Social Salience Requirement is unsustainable, on either reading. The best way to reconcile our intuitions about the two cases I've described is simply to disconnect social salience from whether an act constitutes discrimination, and hence to recognize

[handwritten annotation at top: does setting rid of Social Science req: open door to morality totally random selection under discrim? The basis of discrim being the − or + perception of X?]

both of them as discriminatory. This seems to yield the right results in other cases as well. If a firm were to give a preference in hiring to blond-haired applicants, for instance, it would be perfectly sensible to say that it is discriminating on the basis of hair color, even if hair color bears little significance in social life writ large.

Lippert-Rasmussen suggests that restricting the concept of discrimination to socially salient groups has the virtue of "explain[ing] why we do not talk about discrimination against non-family-members, unqualified applicants or the undeserving."[28] A more straightforward explanation of this fact seems more plausible, however. Adverse treatment of non-family-members, unqualified applicants, and the undeserving is normally accepted as morally unproblematic, and as I observed at the outset, people often use "discrimination" in a moralized sense. If we simply shifted to a context where disfavoring non-family-members *would* normally be considered objectionable (such as in hiring for public offices), I suspect many people would be prepared to speak of a preference for one's own children as discriminatory.

In other words, if there is a theme to ordinary usage of "discrimination," it is not that the targeted groups are socially salient, but that the differential treatment is taken to be at least potentially objectionable. Witness, for instance, the popular idea that insurers should not "discriminate" against people with pre-existing medical conditions in the United States,[29] or the legal protections against discrimination on the basis of trade union membership or "philosophical belief" in the United Kingdom.[30] Similarly, the *New York Times* recently printed four critical letters to the editor regarding its reporting on hospitals that refuse to hire smokers; three of the letters described the practice as "discrimination."[31] Surely what is meant by invoking discrimination in these contexts is not that the policies in question injure people on account of their membership in groups that are important to the structure of social relations. Rather, it is that they objectionably employ these differences between people as grounds for adverse treatment.[32] *[handwritten annotation: why]*

There is certainly a mismatch between my account and ordinary usage here, since wrongfulness is no part of my proposed concept of discrimination. But both Lippert-Rasmussen and I have already bitten that bullet by defining discrimination as, in his phrase, "not necessarily morally objectionable."[33] What explains the intuitive appeal of the Social Salience Requirement, I think, is that it partially and indirectly patches this failure of extensional fit, by introducing a feature that is intuitively related to the wrongfulness we have decided to forgo including in the concept. But I have argued that there are good reasons for defining discrimination in non-evaluative terms, and regardless, splitting the difference in this way only invites confusion.

It should be clear, then, that by rejecting the Social Salience Requirement I do not mean to deny that discrimination on the basis of socially salient traits may be a morally significant category. If it is, however, this should emerge organically from comparing different kinds of discrimination, rather than by way of a flat stipulation that only one of them is discrimination in the first place. Indeed, this is the source of the most powerful reason for rejecting the Social Salience Requirement: it obscures what perhaps ought to be the default position about the moral significance of paradigm cases of discrimination, which do involve socially salient groups. It could be that rejecting a job applicant because of race or sex is bad in just the same way that rejecting her because of her eye or hair color would be, and that the former kinds of discrimination only command more of our attention because they are more widespread (which of course is itself largely due to the fact that these distinctions are socially salient).[34] Part of the job description for a moral analysis of discrimination is to determine whether there is more to the story than that—and, if so, what. But this fundamental question is necessarily marginalized when we build social salience into the relevant concept of discrimination.[35]

1.3 Discrimination Against, In Favor Of, and Among

Thus far we have focused on how differential treatment must be explained in order to constitute discrimination on a particular basis, and on which potential bases count as possible grounds of discrimination. But what makes a given instance of discrimination qualify as discrimination *against* or *in favor of* someone? This is a complicated issue, and it has received little direct discussion in the philosophical literature.[36]

Plainly enough, to say that X discriminates against Y is to say that X treats Y not only differently but *worse* than X treats (or would treat) Z. The Differential Treatment Condition thus specifies that X must treat Y *less favorably*, in respect of the dimension W, than Z. To say that X discriminates against Y is therefore necessarily an evaluative statement—evaluative not of the morality of what X does, but of the comparative value of the two treatments in question. Importantly, however, these judgments of comparative value are sometimes made in terms of overall value, and sometimes in respect of the satisfaction of some specific interests, which often go unidentified.

Suppose, for example, that the admissions committee at The Girls School automatically rejects all male applicants. Moreover, the committee does this in the correct belief that any male student would be disserved by attending The Girls School rather than some other school. It follows that the school's policy is not comparatively disadvantageous to male applicants in terms of their overall well-being; by hypothesis, they are better off having their applications handled this way than having them assessed in the way that female applicants' applications are. Nor does the committee value the well-being of male applicants any less than that of female applicants, or believe that male applicants would make worse students or contribute less to the school than female applicants. Indeed, we can imagine that the committee would count male students as a greater asset to the school, and would *prefer* to admit them, but excludes them out of an overriding paternalistic concern for the applicants' own well-being.

Despite all of this, it would be typical to describe the school as discriminating against male applicants, on the basis of sex, in admissions. After all, it denies their applications for admission, and it does so simply because they are male. (Discriminating in this way in this situation may or may not be *wrong*, of course, but that is a separate question.) The best way to make sense of this fact about our use of the *[handwritten annotations at top of page]: bad example that allows a too broad a stroke, then ... allowing a/shorter person on a taller coaster/RC of height is also discrim.*

concept, I think, is to say that being discriminated against must be comparatively disadvantageous to a person in some specific respect, but being comparatively disadvantaged in that respect need not be globally comparatively disadvantageous to him (and may even be globally comparatively advantageous to him). Here the specific interest at issue is in being admitted to the school.[37]

Unfortunately, I do not have a general theory about the specific interests people possess in the sense relevant here. But it seems that when people supplicate for some opportunity—whether by applying for a job or admission to a school, or by raising their hands in a class, or whatever—they thereby come to possess a specific interest in being granted it, whether or not they had such an interest prior to applying, and whether or not having the opportunity in question will make their lives go better overall. Many paradigm cases of discrimination involve differential satisfaction of such an interest in being granted an opportunity one has sought.

Besides specific interests in being granted the various things we have asked for, I think we also have specific interests in being dealt with in certain ways. I take for granted that people have an interest in being treated with respect, for example. James Woodward suggests a useful example: the racially discriminatory denial of an airline ticket to Smith harms Smith, even if the plane goes on to crash, because "the action violates a certain highly specific interest of Smith's in avoiding racial stigmatization and unfair or inequitable treatment."[38] Applying the framework developed thus far, we could describe this case as follows. If the denial of the ticket is motivated by racism, then Smith is treated comparatively worse, relative to those who are given tickets, in respect of two different interests of his: in getting a ticket (even if he would be better off without one), and also in being treated with respect. Either of these alone would suffice to make the denial of the ticket, on the grounds that it was in fact denied to him, an instance of discrimination against him.[39]

Consider, then, a rather different case. Many serial killers have some kind of preferred victim-type. Suppose that a particular killer targets white women. He discriminates against white women, then, insofar as he treats them comparatively worse than men and non-white women. But there also seems to be an intuitive sense in which his selection procedure could be described as disfavoring men and non-white women, although this is surely to their benefit.

When The Girls School disfavors male applicants, we say that this is discrimination against them, even though it is to their benefit. Should we similarly say that the serial killer discriminates against men and non-white women, then, by not targeting them for killing, even though this is to their benefit? I think we should not. According to my theory, that is explained by the fact that people do not have a specific interest in being targeted for killing. Fittingly, if a non-white woman did come to the killer requesting to be killed, and he rejected her because she was not white, I think we *would* be inclined to say that he discriminated against her on the basis of race, although we might still maintain that this was to her comparative benefit overall. That is because she would have created (or revealed) a specific interest in being killed by him.*

The example of the serial killer raises another important point. It seems odd, in a way, to say that the killer discriminates *against* white women. After all, he prefers them, seeks them out, and so on. But this appearance is due to the fact that what he does falls under what we might call the *non-interest-regarding* concept of discrimination, as well as the *interest-regarding* concept with which we are centrally concerned. To say that a person discriminates "in favor of" or "against" some class of objects, in the non-interest-regarding sense, is simply to say that he prefers or disprefers it. People discriminate among wines in this way, for instance. The killer does approach the field of possible targets in a manner akin to a selection among wines, and so in the non-interest-regarding sense, it would be wrong to say

---

* Suppose that he avoids killing non-white women out of a kind of racial contempt for them. Then *perhaps* he treats them worse than white women in terms of their specific interest in being respected. If so, it would not be entirely wrong to say he discriminates against non-white women even if none request to be killed. But the non-white women are clearly also treated better in terms of their interest in not being killed. I discuss cases of conflict among interests of this kind below.

that he discriminates against the targets he prefers. Whether he discriminates against them in the interest-regarding sense is a separate matter, however. In particular, whether something constitutes discrimination "against" or "in favor of" someone in this sense has to do with the interests of the discriminatees in being treated one way or another—interests that wines do not have. We should simply do our best to tune out the verbal influence of the non-interest-regarding concept on our judgments about what constitutes discrimination in the sense with which we are concerned.

As it turns out, then, the Differential Treatment Condition actually has two dimensional aspects. First, the differential treatment is itself understood by reference to a dimension of treatment—a set of exclusive options regarding how one treats someone. If X's discrimination against Y consists in hiring Z and not hiring Y, for instance, X discriminates in the dimension of hiring. Second, as we have seen, the comparative disadvantage to Y is *itself* found in a dimension or a respect—the specific interest of Y's at issue.

These two dimensional aspects of the concept are easily run together. To say that The Girls School discriminates against boys "in admissions," for instance, could mean either that admissions decisions form the dimension of treatment in which the school discriminates against boys, or that it is in respect of their interest in being admitted that the boys are treated comparatively worse. In this case, it likely means both. But although these features often converge, they are not the same.

This rather technical point is potentially important to understanding the moral structure of some discrimination. Suppose, for example, that an author accidentally submits a paper to the *British Journal of Political Science*, when she meant to submit it to the *British Journal for the Philosophy of Science*. I don't think she has an interest in having the paper accepted for publication by the political science journal, assuming she would not want that to occur. Nonetheless, if the journal's editors reject her paper out of sexism, they discriminate against her on the basis of sex. What's more, they discriminate against her in the dimension of paper acceptance. The interest of hers that *makes* their action in that dimension discrimination against her, however, is not an interest in having the paper accepted. It is rather an interest in being treated with respect.[40]

Two final notes about usage are in order. First, to say that X discriminates against Y in some dimension, without separately specifying an affected specific interest, can be to say *either* that the way Y is treated in that dimension is comparatively disadvantageous to Y in respect of *at least one* specific interest, or that it is comparatively disadvantageous to Y *overall*. This ambiguity is another recurring source of confusion. Consider, for example, the exclusion of African Americans from jury service in the United States. This exclusion constituted discrimination against African Americans in respect of various specific interests of theirs—in social recognition and prestige, in decision-making power, in protection from biased verdicts, and so on—but also discriminated in favor of African Americans in respect of a far less important, but nonetheless genuine, interest. Insofar as jury service is involuntary and burdensome, people are benefited, in one respect, by being exempted from it. So were African Americans discriminated against or in favor of in the dimension of social decisions about whom to include in jury service? It is not wrong to say *both*, since each is true in a respect. But it is also not wrong—and in this case it is pragmatically more appropriate—to say that they were discriminated against *rather than* in favor of, because they were so clearly comparatively disadvantaged overall.

Second, we might wonder how the Differential Treatment Condition handles cases of intentional but inefficacious discrimination. Sometimes, that is, the appropriateness of calling something discrimination seems to be settled simply by the intentions of the agent— independent of any actual effects on anyone's actual interests. I think such cases are handled well by the account we have developed. Some of them actually invoke the non-interest-regarding concept of discrimination: we simply mean that the agent prefers people of one description or another, not that she *treats* them better or worse.

In other cases we do mean that she treats some better than others, but we are supposing that is true simply by virtue of her differential aims: we are supposing that they have interests in her pursuing certain aims with respect to them. That possibility can be accommodated by the skeletal account of specific interests we have developed. Moreover, as I will suggest in the next chapter, recognizing this point is important to understanding the structure of some cases of "indirect" discrimination.

1.3.1 Discrimination among and "separate but equal" treatment

Our very general conceptual discussion to this point has particularly significant implications for how we should think about one distinctive class of cases. Specifically, it bears on cases in which differential treatment is explained in the way that discrimination must be, yet does not treat one party comparatively worse than another. Some "separate but equal" arrangements seem to have this character. What should we make of them?

Based on the foregoing analysis, we should distinguish between instances of differential treatment in which neither party is treated less favorably in respect of *any* interest, and those in which each party is treated less favorably in respect of a *different* interest, where these disadvantages have equal net effects on overall well-being. In a moment I will suggest that most schemes that promote or enforce "separate but equal" roles for different types of people can only claim, at best, to fall in the latter category. But the former category is not empty. It is populated by acts and policies that do not treat people more or less favorably in respect of any of their interests—and hence are not instances of discrimination in the interest-regarding sense— but which can nevertheless be described as discriminating among people, in the non-interest-regarding sense. Suppose, for instance, that I invite Alfred but not Betty to an event that I know neither of them has any interest in being invited to. And suppose that I treat them differently in this way simply because Alfred's name comes first alphabetically. I discriminate on the basis of name, then, but only in the non-interest-regarding sense.[41]

Attention to the role of specific interests in the concept of discrimination should lead us to sharply distinguish this kind of case from acts or policies that assign distinct but equally valuable opportunities to different classes of people. These *do* affect their various specific interests differentially; the discriminator may simply manage to do this in a manner that keeps the effects on the overall well-being of the parties in equipoise (though that would seem a remarkable feat in most cases).

For example, some claim that traditional religious doctrines prescribing distinct social and familial roles for men and women do not amount to sex discrimination, because the roles are of equal value and founded on a principle on mutual complementarity.[42] Of course, if what is meant by this claim is that the prescriptions do not call for *wrongful* or *unjust* discrimination, the conceptual analysis I have offered does not speak to that question.[43] But one might think that, insofar as nobody is treated worse than anybody else, these practices do not constitute discrimination against or in favor of anyone at all—not even discrimination of the possibly permissible kind.

According to the view I have outlined, that is mistaken. If an institution makes it more difficult for men than women to be homemakers, and more difficult for women than men to be breadwinners, it very likely thereby discriminates against (and in favor of) both men and women on the basis of sex. For I take it that many men have an interest in the opportunity to be homemakers, and many women have an interest in the opportunity to be breadwinners, even if the roles are in some more global sense equally valuable. Indeed, perhaps everyone has an interest in at least having these two *opportunities*. Even if that were not so, however, it would mean only that the sex discrimination in question is discrimination against only some men, and only some women—in each case, those who want to occupy the role for which they are disfavored. That does not make the practice any less an instance of sex discrimination, because not all sex discrimination is discrimination in favor of or against *all* people of a given sex. This is one reason I suggested above that it is important to distinguish in the Differential Treatment Condition between the sets of people who compose Y and Z—sets which may be defined in part by their members' possession of some trait—and the trait P, on the basis of which they are discriminated against.

1.4 Conclusion

The conceptual analysis of discrimination I have offered aims to bring out the features that distinguish the way we use this idea from the way we use its conceptual neighbors, like differential treatment, while also maintaining a healthy skepticism about certain regularities in usage— such as the tendency to employ "discrimination" as an epithet—that seem to confuse more than they clarify. It gives us some rules for when to describe something as discriminating *against* someone, and explains how this can be squared with its making him better off. Perhaps most importantly, the account specifies how differential treatment must be explained in order to constitute discrimination on the basis of a particular trait P (and therefore to constitute discrimination at all). In particular, the differential treatment simply has to be due, in part, to the fact that the agent regards the discriminatees differently in respect of that trait—whether or not she intends to be sensitive to this apparent difference, and whether or not she is sensitive to it only as a proxy for some other trait with which she is concerned. So, going forward, when we say that something is or is not discriminatory—or is or is not race or sex discrimination, and so on— we will know what we mean.

One influential idea that I have discussed only obliquely, however, is that of "indirect" discrimination. I turn to how we should understand this concept, and its practical significance, in the next chapter.

2

The Puzzle of Indirect Discrimination

I have now introduced a general conceptual analysis of discrimination. That analysis designates no place for the idea of indirect discrimination, however, although this notion figures prominently in the law and, to a lesser extent, in non-legal discourse.

In this chapter, I set out to map the uses of this derivative concept, and I argue that we should take a somewhat skeptical view of it. Under American, British, and European law, indirect discrimination is essentially conduct that imposes disproportionate burdens on some class of people and fails some special standard of justification. This category, I will suggest, encompasses two very different kinds of acts. The first type of act is indeed discrimination, but is not in any irreducible sense indirect. Rather, it is accommodated by the account of ordinary discrimination that we developed in Chapter 1.

The second type of act, by contrast, is not merely a kind of ordinary or direct discrimination. But I will suggest that it is not best thought of as *discrimination* at all. Rather, prohibitions on such cases of "indirect discrimination" are best seen as redistributive programs to expand access to opportunity, akin in many respects to a moderate but compulsory practice of positive discrimination or affirmative action. Conceiving of failure to go along with this program as itself a kind of discrimination—albeit an "indirect" kind—may not bring out underlying similarities between the phenomena as much as it licenses equivocation between them.

If this analysis is correct, it has significant implications. The question whether or not to recognize a category of indirect discrimination is settled for lawyers simply by the overt presence of the notion in many laws.[1] But those of us interested in discrimination itself must decide, on the merits, whether embracing this concept facilitates or impedes clear understanding of the underlying phenomena. The first aim of the chapter, therefore, is simply to clarify our thinking about the concept of discrimination by identifying what it should not be stretched to reach. To say that "indirect discrimination" is not discrimination is not, of course, to say that it is not sometimes wrong, or that it should not be prohibited. To the contrary, such a conceptual divorce might liberate "indirect discrimination" regimes from certain encumbrances or limiting assumptions that attach to discrimination prohibitions as such. Recognizing the distinctness of the two forms of conduct might, for instance, allow us to ask what should be the forbidden *grounds* of "indirect discrimination" free of the assumption that they should mirror the canonical grounds of wrongful discrimination.

But the chapter also has a second aim. One current question in American law is when efforts to avoid indirect discrimination constitute direct discrimination in their own right. The conceptual account of discrimination developed in Chapter 1 has the potential to cast light on this issue. At the end of this chapter, therefore, I will consider a decision of the U.S. Supreme Court, *Ricci v. DeStefano* (2009), that squarely engaged this question. I suggest that there is less tension between prohibitions on direct and indirect discrimination than the Court has taken there to be, and indeed that avoiding such tension may be a central virtue of indirect discrimination law— accounting for features of the legal concept that would otherwise be puzzling.

2.1 Second-Order Discrimination

Suppose you want to exclude or disadvantage some set of people, but discrimination on the basis of the trait that distinguishes them is prohibited. You will be tempted to simply discriminate on the basis of some other category that picks out roughly (or even exactly) the same people. If you do that, have you acted consistently with the prohibition?

I think it is clear that you have not. And, crucially, it is not only that you have violated the *spirit* of the prohibition. Some "loopholes" permit one to act consistently with a prohibition while violating its spirit. For example, taxpayers sometimes hold assets in certain ways to avoid their being taxed at the rates that the legislature contemplated. That may be impermissible, but it doesn't violate the operative tax rule itself; by hypothesis, the taxpayer evaded that rule. In the case I described, by contrast, you violated the core prohibition on discrimination itself: you discriminated on the basis of the original disfavored trait. You simply discriminated on that basis in a different *dimension of treatment* than you might otherwise have done. You discriminated in how you went about choosing the criteria for making some decision, rather than in the latter decision itself.

This is a case of what I will call *second-order discrimination*. Formally, a person commits second-order discrimination on the basis of P when she discriminates on the basis of P in adopting a rule or decision to discriminate on the basis of Q in some other dimension of treatment. Second-order discrimination on the basis of P is thus a special case of ordinary discrimination on the basis of P; it is discrimination on the basis of P in a particular kind of dimension of treatment. In such situations, the resultant discrimination on the basis of Q is not itself discrimination on the basis of P, but it bears a special connection to it. Indeed, speaking loosely, we sometimes say that the resultant discrimination on the basis of Q is itself "indirect" discrimination on the basis of P. But, as we will see, "indirect" discrimination also bears a stipulated meaning that does not simply identify an act as stemming from second-order discrimination, and it is therefore important to avoid confusing the two.

Cases of second-order discrimination often involve some form of subterfuge or gamesmanship on the part of the discriminator, as in the example I gave a moment ago. But such efforts to circumvent a rule are not essential to the category. For example, in the late nine-teenth century, Anatole France satirized French pride in "the majestic equality of the laws, which forbid rich and poor alike to sleep under the bridges, to beg in the streets, and to steal their bread."[2] One target of this satire is the sheer maldistribution of wealth, which, France sarcastically suggests, is not compensated for or remedied by equal treatment under the law. But I take it that he was also making a second point about the character of that equal treatment itself, which in turn can be understood as a charge of second-order discrimination.

In particular, I think he meant something like this. It is true that the law against sleeping under a bridge does not discriminate on the basis of wealth, since it applies to "rich and poor alike." But the glaringly disproportionate burden that this law places on the poor is powerful evidence regarding how the law came about. It suggests discrimin-ation on the basis of wealth in the dimension of how different people's interests are *valued* in making the laws. On this interpretation, in other words, France's commentary alleges discrimination on the basis of wealth in the law's genesis—discrimination that is no more con-sistent with the ideological commitment to "equality of the laws" than wealth discrimination in the content or enforcement of the law would be. Thus, when the state applies the formally wealth-neutral law, it does not discriminate against the poor on the basis of wealth; it discriminates only on the basis of where one sleeps. Nonetheless, the state may be guilty of second-order discrimination on the basis of wealth.

It is important to get the category of second-order discrimination in view before considering the significance of indirect discrimination because while there is certainly something "indirect" about it, it does not require us to recognize any novel or fundamentally distinct kind of discrimination. As I have noted, second-order discrimination is counted as ordinary, direct discrimination by the definition we devel-oped in Chapter 1; it is simply discrimination in the dimension of how the rules for some further determination are set. In some cases the discrimination in that dimension consists in the fact that the rule-setting process is undertaken with the *aim* of disfavoring certain people. In other cases it consists in the fact that certain people are treated worse in the rule-setting process in some other way, such as that their interests are unwittingly afforded less weight. No doubt attention to second-order discrimination is important to any accounting of the ways in which people discriminate—particularly in contexts where overt discrimination on some basis is prohibited or stigmatized. But it does not require us to extend or modify the conceptual analysis of discrimination we have adopted.

Situations involving second-order discrimination do, however, introduce some further conceptual wrinkles. Consider, for example, a university that decides to disfavor applicants from a certain region with the goal of improving student performance. The university's administrators believe that this policy will serve that goal because they believe that (i) students of a certain minority race perform less well than other students who are otherwise comparable and (ii) this regional preference will result in the university's admitting fewer of the minority students.[3] Nonetheless, the university gives no weight to an individual applicant's race in assessing her application.

Suppose now that, as expected, many students of the disfavored race are rejected by the university because they live in the disfavored region. It is natural to say that they were discriminated against not only on the basis of their region, but also on the basis of their race. And that is true: they were treated comparatively worse on account of race *in the selection of the admissions criteria*, since the school sought criteria that would make their admission less likely. Trying to thwart some people's admission is a way of treating them comparatively worse than others; and these people were treated that way by virtue of the university's reaction to their race (albeit as otherwise-unknown members of an indefinite class, rather than individually). Yet, as this description suggests, the racial discrimination they suffered was complete at the time the criteria were chosen—and the rejected regional applicants were therefore discriminated against in this regard no more than any other applicant of the same race. Counterintuitively, that is, a minority applicant who lives in a favored region and is admitted to the university has an equal claim of racial discrimination, since racial discrimination was involved only in the school's way of choosing its admissions criteria, and its *way* of choosing those criteria equally disfavored her.

Is it wrong, then, to say that an individual minority student is discriminated against on the basis of her race, albeit somehow indirectly, when she is rejected because of her disfavored region? This question persists because, despite what I've said thus far, the two rounds of discrimination she suffers (racial and regional) do not seem wholly separable—even though the sets of people disfavored by each are obviously quite different. What accounts for this apparent connection, however, is not that a minority applicant from the disfavored region is discriminated against (at the second stage) on the basis of *her* race, but that she is discriminated against (at that stage) on the basis of the racial makeup of her region. This is a common, but not a necessary, feature of second-order discrimination: the trait that figures in the first instance of discrimination may provide the needed mapping from possible values of the trait in the second instance to the treatments that people receive.* Still, the ultimate admissions decisions involve "racial" discrimination only in the limited sense that racial judgments are necessary inputs to the property on the basis of which the university discriminates. Thus, as far as this latter instance of discrimination goes, students of *other* races who are rejected because they come from the same disfavored region—a region that is only disfavored because the school sought to minimize the admission of the targeted minority applicants—are equally subject to it.[4] In any event, despite these complications, such forms of second-order discrimination can be understood as special cases of ordinary discrimination as it was defined in Chapter 1.

---

* Suppose, by contrast, that the university decides to include an essay component because it wants to promote the admission of minority applicants and it has found that minority applicants tend to have a comparative advantage in that area. This is second-order discrimination but, unlike in the example above, the decision of *which* essays to prefer may itself have nothing to do with how a person's essay compares to those written by minority students.

2.2 Indirect Discrimination in the Legal Sense

Under American, British, and European law, indirect discrimination has a meaning that cannot so easily be analyzed in terms of ordinary, direct discrimination. Roughly, an act constitutes indirect discrimination in this sense if it disproportionately burdens members of one group—paradigmatically, a group defined by race or sex—and fails to satisfy a special standard of justification. The details of how this idea is formulated differ across jurisdictions, but the following definition in the European Union's Racial Equality Directive is typical:

> Indirect discrimination shall be taken to occur where an apparently neutral provision, criterion or practice would put persons of a racial or ethnic origin at a particular disadvantage compared with other persons, unless that provision, criterion or practice is objectively justified by a legitimate aim and the means of achieving that aim are appropriate and necessary.[5]

To be indirect discrimination in this sense is not simply to be direct discrimination in a certain dimension of treatment, or to be connected to such direct discrimination in a certain way. So perhaps this is a distinct kind of discrimination, which we ought to incorporate both in our analysis of the concept and in a theory of when and why discrimination is wrong. Before drawing that conclusion, however, we need to consider why we would take this pattern of facts to constitute a kind of *discrimination*. For perhaps "indirect discrimination" in this sense is something else altogether, which has simply been given a misleading name in the law. There are two general answers to this question, which I will consider in turn.

2.2.1 Indirect discrimination as a presumed offense

One reason we might care about the class of conduct marked out by this provision of the Racial Equality Directive is that it is a contingent signal of covert or second-order racial discrimination. If an employer adopts a policy that disproportionately burdens members of a certain racial group, and if the (non-racial) reasons presented in favor of this policy are not very compelling, then we might have good reason to suspect that the employer discriminated on the basis of race in the *adoption* of the particular dividing line in question. According to this interpretation, then, the legal notion of indirect discrimination is not the name of a *kind* of discrimination, but rather a convenient legal fiction that empowers us to hold defendants liable for what is, in the end, ordinary (but second-order) discrimination.

As Christopher McCrudden notes, however, the supposed purpose of holding employers liable for concealed direct discrimination does not enjoy particularly good fit with the substance of indirect discrimination law.[6] The actual laws in question do not create a rebuttable presumption of directly discriminatory intent, but rather "say that a specific discriminatory intention is irrelevant."*

This lack of fit is not necessarily a decisive criticism. As Frederick Schauer has argued, the law often recognizes what Bentham called "presumed offenses."[7] To describe this category, Bentham gave the example of an English law that punished, as murder, "the concealment by the mother of the birth of an illegitimate child."[8] The reason, he explained, was that "such conduct is regarded as a sure proof of infanticide." Here the underlying activity to be identified and punished was infanticide, not concealing an illegitimate birth; but the correlative act of concealing the birth was made into an offense as well because the two were linked and the concealment was easier to prove. Schauer notes that modern examples of this kind abound: the United States criminalizes entering or leaving the country with *unreported* cash in excess of $10,000, for instance, not because this is wrong or socially disadvantageous in itself, but only because it is taken as an indication of covert money laundering, dealing in contraband, or the like.

It is an open possibility, then, that indirect discrimination law is best understood as creating a presumed offense in Bentham's sense, with the aim of sanctioning covert second-order discrimination

---

* Talk of "intention" here may be overly narrow, given my analysis of direct discrimination, but the point is the same: in determining the existence of indirect discrimination, it is irrelevant whether an explanation of the sort I specified in the Explanatory Condition is available.

that would otherwise go unaddressed. This possible rationale is attractive, moreover, because the underlying offense—second-order discrimination in the formulation of rules or decisions—will often be very difficult to prove in its own right. That theory draws further support from the evidence that many people, at least in the United States, are unwilling to attribute an action to discrimination in circumstances that are remotely ambiguous.[9] Bentham's original explanation of the need for presumed offenses, in fact, was that "[t]he English legislature fear[ed] that juries, too prone to lenity, would not see in these presumptions a certain proof of guilt," requiring the legislature to "erect the [a]ct which furnishes the presumption into a second offence."[10]

Even by the standards of presumed offenses, however, the fit between cases in which a person commits indirect discrimination under the law and cases in which she is engaged in direct discrimination seems markedly poor. It is no doubt common for employers to adopt standards that disproportionately exclude members of particular racial or sexual groups, and to do so without especially good reason, but in many such cases they do not do so *because* they mean to exclude these people, or because they are less sensitive to their interests than to those of others. They may do so, for example, simply by relying upon indicators—education, credit history, criminal history, or the like—that appear convenient and probative, but which are themselves skewed by long histories of systematic discrimination.

The wisdom of establishing a presumed offense seems to rest principally on the two factors I have just mentioned: the difficulty of proving the underlying offense, and the strength of the correlation between the underlying offense and the would-be presumed offense. When these factors point in opposite directions, the question whether to establish the presumed offense requires a judgment about the relative costs of prohibiting innocent conduct and permitting the underlying offense to go unaddressed. That in turn will require a sense of the importance of stamping out the underlying offense, on the one hand, and the value of the innocent conduct that might nonetheless satisfy the elements of the presumed offense, on the other. For our purposes, it is enough to say that if all indirect discrimination is to be prohibited, but in many cases the prohibition must be counted simply as a cost of an imperfect generalization, there might well be grounds for doubting the reasonableness of laws against indirect discrimination—particularly if we could simply replace them with rebuttable presumptions of the kind McCrudden describes. As far as unearthing the justification for the legal concept of indirect discrimination goes, then, construing indirect discrimination as merely a presumed offense should perhaps be an option of last resort.

In any case, if this explanation did exhaust the function of indirect discrimination in the law, it would probably be better to call the relevant category simply indirectly *proved* discrimination. The indirectness in such cases is really a feature of the scheme through which we hold a discriminator liable for discrimination; the discrimination itself is, relative to the dimension in which it occurs, direct. Even with this conceptual realignment, of course, it would remain open to those disadvantaged by some act or policy to prove that they were victims of direct discrimination indirectly, i.e., by reference to the disproportionate burden imposed by the act and the absence of a compelling rationale for it. The point is simply that, if indirect discrimination is a presumed offense, it should not be regarded as an irreducible kind of discrimination in its own right.

2.2.2 Indirect discrimination law as a redistributive program

Indirect discrimination might not be recognized solely or even primarily for epistemic or procedural purposes, however. Rather, we might think that instances of the pattern of facts laid out in the Racial Equality Directive are of independent significance. John Gardner, for instance, insists that "disproportionate group impact is not mere evidence... of indirect discrimination," but is rather "a constituent part of the wrongdoing that is indirect discrimination."[11]

What then, if anything, is significant about cases of indirect discrimination in the legal sense even when they do *not* indicate direct discrimination? As a characteristic example, consider a firm that discriminates against pregnant people in hiring.[12] Suppose that the managers adopt this policy because they are solely concerned with profits, and they accurately estimate that the risk of employees taking maternity leave soon after they are hired will reduce profit more than the exclusion of pregnant people from the applicant pool will. What is the purpose of condemning such a policy as indirect sex discrimination when, as in this case, it has an etiology free of direct sex discrimination by the firm?

Surely the salient fact about this policy with respect to sex, which could justify such a response, is that it disadvantages women in the labor market relative to men. Since a woman may be pregnant at the time the firm is hiring, but a man cannot be, the policy makes it more likely, *ceteris paribus*, that the firm will hire a man rather than a woman. That retards the progress of efforts to equalize professional opportunity for men and women, especially if other firms adopt similar policies. One way of addressing this obstacle is to recognize or impose a general obligation on employers not to adopt employment standards that have a differential negative effect on women, or at least not to do so without an especially compelling reason. The point would not be to hedge against pretext or bias, but rather to improve women's standing relative to what simple (but true) even-handedness with respect to sex in the firm's hiring would bring about.

Perhaps making such an intervention in the market is the central function of the legal category of indirect discrimination. McCrudden endorses a version of this view, arguing that the justification for the law is "forward looking and frankly redistributive, *i.e.* it is justified insofar as it increases the welfare of racial minority groups and women, expecting and intending that this increase will be at the expense of other groups."[13] Even if it is agreed that the aim of laws against indirect discrimination is redistributive, however, we can see them as furthering that aim in different ways. Cast in a weak form, this account collapses back into the concern over second-order discrimination that we considered above. Recall that second-order discrimination is not limited to intentional but covert discrimination. Rather, as in the case of the French law, a procedure can be discriminatory—e.g., if it does not weigh people's interests in the outcome equally, and this differential treatment is traceable to some perceived difference among the stakeholders—even if there was no intention to discriminate in this manner. One way of understanding the *mechanism* of the redistributive project McCrudden describes, then, is that prohibitions on indirect discrimination discourage this kind of second-order discrimination.

Both McCrudden and Jeremy Waldron sometimes write as if this is what they have in mind. McCrudden suggests that the law against indirect discrimination aims to "see to it that the welfare of women and minorities is increased... by having their interests and needs taken into account in circumstances where otherwise they are likely to be ignored."[14] Similarly, Waldron characterizes the law as ensuring that "employers... scrutinize the basis on which jobs and opportunities are offered to check that the interests of women and members of racial minorities are not, in fact, being prejudiced."[15]

Read one way, these formulations suggest a rather unobtrusive role for the law against indirect discrimination. The law compels an employer to take account of the disparate impact of a policy, which he or she might otherwise overlook or ignore, and to weigh its necessity appropriately in the light of this information. In so doing, the law serves as a check on the possibility of not only covert but also unintentional discrimination in respect of how the rules are (or would otherwise be) made.

In my example of the firm that discriminates on the basis of pregnancy, however, what is asked of the employer is more substantial. After all, presumably the firm's managers could insist that they had taken account of the needs and interests of female applicants, but nevertheless intended to maximize profits for shareholders—a goal that, by hypothesis, pregnant applicants are simply less able than others to further. Similarly, they might say, the fact that they had not hired the many candidates who were less qualified than the competition does not mean that they had failed to take account of the interests of those candidates, or that the firm had "prejudiced" their interests by passing them over. Nonetheless, this firm presumably *would* be counted as indirectly discriminating against women.

What is required of an employer, then, is not simply a kind of due diligence in avoiding second-order discrimination, but rather that he or she absorb a certain margin of lost productivity for the sake of equalizing opportunity for members of different groups. To be sure, even if it is cast in this stronger form, the law could still be characterized as requiring that the interests of certain groups be (as McCrudden puts it) "adequately considered."[16] But for the firm to adequately consider the interests of female applicants, on this account, is at least sometimes to put their interests *ahead* of its own.

How much loss the firm must absorb in this way is set by the various standards of "justifiability," "business necessity," and the like that operate in different jurisdictions and legal contexts. Thus under British law, for instance, justification of a rule with disparate impact has been taken to require "an objective balance between the discriminatory effect of the condition and the reasonable needs of the party who applies the condition."[17] Seen this way, indirect discrimination is, as Gardner puts it, "a doubly distributive idea": the law calls upon employers to distribute opportunities among job seekers in a way that promotes distributive justice, and also imposes certain burdens on employers for the sake of equalizing opportunity, the imposition of these burdens itself constituting a matter of distributive justice.[18]

I believe the redistributive account of the rationale for indirect discrimination law, in this stronger form, is fundamentally sound. If so, however, it may also vindicate the skepticism from which we began. Our goal, after all, is to develop a conceptual account of discrimination for the purposes of moral analysis. But if we understand the function of prohibitions on indirect discrimination along the lines just sketched, perhaps we should not view the prohibited conduct as a kind of discrimination at all.

2.3 Is "Indirect Discrimination" Discrimination?

Why conceive of acts of indirect discrimination, in the sense of unjustifiable disparate impact, as acts of discrimination? One answer would be that the acts in question are very much like ordinary, direct discrimination in character, except that they are somehow done indirectly. But since we have set aside the intuitive association between "indirect" discrimination and second-order discrimination, it should be clear that this is not so.

A second possibility is that the categories are alike in respect of what makes them *wrong*, when they are. We now have on the table a view of the normative rationale for prohibitions on indirect discrimination, which we can use to evaluate this possibility. Before doing that, however, it bears noting that classifying "indirect discrimination" as discrimination for this reason would have an odd consequence regardless. After all, we have supposed that direct discrimination is not necessarily wrong. It would be strange, then, if some other category of conduct qualified as a form of discrimination because what is characteristically wrong with it, when it is wrong, is the same as what is characteristically wrong with direct discrimination, when it is wrong. Could we conceive of indirect discrimination (like direct discrimination) as something that may or may not have anything wrong with it, if its standing *as* a kind of discrimination were due only to what it is like when it *is* wrong?

More fundamentally, perhaps, classifying indirect discrimination as discrimination because the two sometimes share common normative features seems to misapprehend "discrimination" as the name of a moral fault, rather than of an act-type. Even if one supposes, as I do not, that the act-type of discrimination is necessarily wrong, it would still be a misnomer to call something discrimination if it is not, in other respects, an act of the relevant type. Moral similarity *alone* should not suffice for something to constitute a species of discrimination, that is, because discrimination is at least not *only* a moral category.

Nonetheless, some do ground the unity of direct and indirect discrimination in a putative commonality among their wrongful variants. Indeed, Sophia Moreau has argued that it is a desideratum for a theory of wrongful discrimination that it not require us "to give up what I take to be a very fundamental intuition, which is that both [direct and indirect] forms of discrimination are forms of the same thing, the same kind of injustice."[19] Specifically, Moreau suggests that prohibitions on direct and indirect discrimination are unified by the common aim of protecting "the freedom to make decisions about how to live in a manner that is insulated from the effects of certain [normatively] extraneous traits."[20] With respect to indirect discrimination in particular, she writes: "Prohibitions on disparate impact ensure that we will not be disadvantaged *even indirectly* because we possess these traits, by rules that are not designed to exclude us but nevertheless tend to exclude people with this characteristic more than others."[21] An important threshold question is whether Moreau's proposed principle really fits the concept of indirect discrimination as unjustifiable disparate impact.[22] Suppose, for example, that a firm prefers children of long-standing employees in hiring. As it happens, fewer Muslims than others have parents who are long-standing employees, so this policy disproportionately excludes Muslims. Unless the preference for children of long-standing employees meets a special standard of justification, then, it seems to constitute indirect discrimination on the basis of religion. Nonetheless, it may well not be the case that Muslims disproportionately lack parents who have worked for the company for many years *because* they are Muslims. Perhaps Muslims are simply more likely to be recent immigrants, and this—not their being Muslims—explains their disproportionate lack of parents who have spent many years with the company.* If so, a rule against indirect discrimination is not insulating Muslim applicants from any *effects* of their religious identity, though it is apparently prepared to regard them as victims of indirect religious discrimination.

Or is it? Indirect discrimination law is a moving target, and Moreau's comparatively narrow view of it is not without some support. In deciding whether an age-discrimination law encompassed

---

* We can also assume that they are not disproportionately recent immigrants *because* they are Muslims (e.g., it was not their faith that deterred their parents from immigrating earlier).

indirect discrimination, for instance, the U.S. Supreme Court divided over how to interpret the law's reference to employment actions that adversely affect a person "because of such individual's age."[23] Some Justices took this "because" clause to refer to the reason for an employer's action, which would limit the law to direct discrimination. The plurality, however, took the "because" clause to refer to the reason why the employer's action, however motivated, had an adverse effect on older employees.[24] This latter view, they thought, warranted recognizing a cause of action for indirect discrimination (known as "disparate impact") under the statute. But a claim rooted in this statutory text *would* seem to require, at some level, a causal connection between the protected trait and the adverse effect—which is not a necessary element of indirect discrimination as we have so far understood it. Indeed, stressing the "such individual's age" provision, the plurality seemed to imagine that *token* and not merely type causation was essential to indirect discrimination.[25] Such a requirement seems inconsistent with the standard notion that indirect discrimination refers to practices "that in fact fall more harshly on one group than another and cannot be justified by business necessity,"[26] and with the standard practice of proving such claims through statistical evidence of disparities in outcomes.[27]

There is some uncertainty, then, about whether the legal concept of indirect discrimination on the basis of P is a subset of what I earlier described as *structural* discrimination on the basis of P—which covers cases where a person is disfavored because of some trait he is taken to possess, and he possesses that trait (or is taken to possess it) *because* of what he is like in respect of P. If indirect discrimination is more embracing than that, as I have supposed, Moreau's account offers at most a partial justification of it, even assuming that protecting people from the effects of certain traits is a suitable goal.

But this point is not crucial for our purposes. Suppose that indirect discrimination requires only that the neutral practice adversely affect members of a protected group, and not that its adversely affecting them itself be an effect of their group membership. Then Moreau's argument that both putative forms of discrimination instantiate the same kind of wrong—because both infringe her proposed principle—could be amended by simply dropping the principle's references to the "effects" of extraneous traits and to disadvantages imposed "because" of them. My larger point is that, with or without this amendment, it is not satisfying to say that indirect discrimination is a genuine form of discrimination because all that wrongful discrimination is, in the end, is that which has the effect of bringing about unequal opportunities for groups of people who differ in some salient dimension—perhaps because of their difference in that dimension—and which does so without especially good reason.[28]

Such an understanding of wrongful discrimination seems both over- and under-inclusive. On the one hand, it is likely to cast many unjustified failures to adopt an ameliorative measure that would promote equality along the relevant dimensions as themselves instances of wrongful discrimination. For example, greater public investment in high-quality preschool could substantially expand the opportunities of children from disadvantaged backgrounds.[29] So the failure to make this investment likely contributes to racial inequality. Moreover, it is certainly plausible that this investment would be particularly beneficial to people who will face racial discrimination over the course of their lives. The failure to make the investment is therefore especially injurious to those people, and it is so in part because of their group membership. But I doubt we would say that the failure to make this general investment itself *is* racial discrimination, unless the failure is due to an indifference that is racially specific.[30] More broadly, as Iris Young has argued, equating group inequality with wrongful discrimination may distort our thinking about the distinct wrong of *oppression* by shoehorning it into the paradigm defined by characteristic cases of discrimination.[31]

On the other hand, this view is likely to unduly constrain our understanding of wrongful discrimination as well. If we conceive of wrongful discrimination as essentially a threat to equality of opportunity—in order to ensure that direct and indirect discrimination involve "the same kind of injustice"—that will have the effect of casting what would otherwise seem to be paradigm cases of wrongful discrimination as peripheral cases at best. When, for instance, an individual anti-Semite or homophobe discriminates against a Jewish or gay person, in a context where these traits are no longer widely disfavored, that will not be a central case of wrongful discrimination. From the perspective of the purposes that motivate concern over *indirect* discrimination, as we have analyzed them, that may well be appropriate. But although I have not yet given an account of what makes for wrongful direct discrimination, I think it ought to extend to what this person does—and indeed ought to regard his act as a central case. If that is right, it is just not true that direct discrimination and indirect discrimination are always wrong, when they are, for the same reasons. Imposing continuity on them will therefore involve significant distortion, and our thinking about both would be better served by giving each the compass appropriate to its distinct character and rationale.

For these reasons, I think the appeal to count "indirect discrimination" as discrimination by virtue of its normative features is not persuasive. Perhaps the strongest reason *against* so counting it is simply that this fosters obfuscation, whether strategic or inadvertent. Precisely because the connotation of "discrimination" as an act of a certain kind—in which an agent is sensitive to some feature of the discriminatees, and engages in some manner of differential treatment in response—is inescapable, describing indirect discrimination as discrimination is a serious obstacle to clear communication in this fraught domain.

By way of example, consider a recent headline in the *Los Angeles Times*: "Kaplan Higher Education sued for race discrimination."[32] Turning to the article itself, one learns that the company is being sued for screening job applicants on the basis of credit history, which, it is alleged, unnecessarily and disproportionately excludes people of some racial backgrounds. Since nobody has even suggested that Kaplan employs credit history as a proxy for race, however, this makes the headline seem rather unfair in retrospect. The company might well be wrongfully shirking its duty, as an agent with social and economic power, to contribute to equalizing opportunity and correcting social dislocations rooted in racism. But charging it with racial discrimination both fails to convey that message and risks provoking unnecessary defensiveness and mistrust by conveying a very different one.[33]

The room for insinuation or miscommunication of this kind is even greater outside legal contexts, where the meaning of indirect discrimination is less likely to be given by stipulation. In describing education reform in post-apartheid South Africa, for example, Fiske and Ladd write:

[T]he authority granted to local school governing bodies by the South Africa Schools Act has allowed many of the formerly white schools to maintain disproportionately white student bodies by pursuing admissions and related strategies that in effect limit black enrollments.... Since apartheid ensured that race and class would be highly correlated, any admissions policy that favors students with middle-class values indirectly discriminates against most black students from the townships and homelands.[34]

Similarly, Geoffrey Walford, reporting on developments in British education, says:

[W]here curriculum specialisms are being introduced by schools, they are acting as selection mechanisms for high academic ability and middle class children. In particular, the development of specialisms such as dance or music indirectly discriminates against working class families, and allows schools a greater chance to select 'appropriate' children.[35]

In both of these cases, I find it impossible to tell whether the schools are being accused of second-order discrimination or of indirect discrimination in the sense of disparate-impact-plus-unjustifiability.

It seems to me this is of the nature of the term. The notion of "indirect discrimination" surely reflects an effort at "persuasive definition," seeking to "increase the scope of what may be prohibited while, at the same time, trading on the emotive appeal of the traditional usage of the term."[36] One worry about such efforts is that they will backfire: as Waldron observes, "an attempt to extend the meaning of 'discrimination' may have the effect of weakening or diluting the current level of feeling opposed to racial prejudice."[37] The use of "race discrimination" to describe the Kaplan hiring policy seems a potent example of this danger. But there is a second risk that is perhaps more straightforward. In the course of transferring the normative charge of one category of conduct to another, we are very likely to blur the underlying conceptual differences between them as well. That seems to be the state of play with the notion of indirect discrimination at present.

Fortunately, we don't have to firmly resolve here whether the law is right to conceive of indirect discrimination as a form of discrimination, as opposed to a distinct offense of some other kind. I have suggested some grounds for skepticism, but I mean to allow that there may be institutional or political reasons why the status quo represents the better course on balance. Perhaps, for instance, persuasive definition is essential to sustaining the limited political will for prohibiting what is known as indirect discrimination. And perhaps the reasons for making direct and indirect discrimination *unlawful* have more in common than the reasons for considering them wrong.[38] Our central question, however, is whether we should recognize an act-type of indirect discrimination, on the model of the legal category, as a distinct kind of discrimination more generally. In light of the divergent conceptual structures of the two phenomena, and the distinctive moral logic of indirect discrimination rules, I conclude that we should not.

2.4 Symmetry and Indirect Discrimination

Let us now set aside the question whether indirect discrimination should be thought of as discrimination. Another striking feature of legal prohibitions on indirect discrimination, if they are understood in distributive terms, is that they are formally symmetrical, concerned with policies that disproportionately exclude privileged and disadvantaged groups alike. Title VII of the Civil Rights Act, for instance, rests indirect discrimination claims on whether an "employment practice...causes a disparate impact on the basis of race," no matter whom that impact may harm or benefit.[39]

This is puzzling. It is easy enough to see why it might be regarded as morally important that employers absorb a measure of loss in order to counteract the chronic exclusion of disadvantaged groups from important opportunities. But it is difficult to see why they should be required to do that simply so that traits like race and sex are probabilistically independent of obtaining a given position. If black women perform disproportionately well on a promotional examination in a municipal police department, for instance, what is problematic about that result? Suppose that the exam could have been calibrated differently so as to undo this disproportionality at only a small loss to the department. What of it? There seems to be nothing regrettable about the results as they stand—assuming that they reflect the effects of no direct discrimination against other candidates, and that men and non-blacks are not chronically excluded from opportunity, either in general or in policing.[40]

To be sure, even if the rule against indirect discrimination were not neutral between advantaged and disadvantaged groups, we might still want to tailor the specification of the groups it should protect to more local pockets of disadvantage than simply the labor market at large. In certain sectors, perhaps we would want the prohibition on indirect discrimination to deviate from neutrality on behalf of men, whereas in many other cases we would want it to deviate from neutrality on behalf of women. In effect, then, a pervasively symmetric indirect discrimination law may represent a rough-and-ready alternative to that kind of carefully calibrated approach, since the groups we would be inclined to protect in a given context are presumably more likely to find themselves on the losing side of a disparate impact in that domain.

A second possibility is that the symmetry of indirect discrimination rules is a further unfortunate consequence of the taxonomical premise we considered above—that indirect discrimination is itself a kind of discrimination. Many believe that directly discriminating against people on the basis of race or sex in employment is at least presumptively wrong no matter their race or sex. Perhaps casting the redistributive obligation at issue—the obligation to choose selection criteria so as to expand, rather than contract, opportunities for members of groups that might otherwise continue to face systemic exclusion—as itself a prohibition on a *kind* of discrimination has created the false impression of a comparable symmetry, which is precisely at odds with the normative foundation of the rule. One consequence of recognizing the conceptual distinctness of direct and indirect discrimination, then, might be to suggest that the symmetry of indirect discrimination rules should be revisited.

Understood simply as a legal implement, however, the curious conceit that it is deviations from racial and sexual proportionality *as such* that stand in need of special justification might offer a tactical advantage to those who hope to equalize opportunities for members of excluded and disadvantaged groups. I conclude this chapter by considering one way in which this gap between the principled rationale for a redistributive law of indirect discrimination and the substantive symmetry of the law may contribute to shaping actual controversies over direct and indirect discrimination.

2.5 The Interplay of Direct and Indirect Discrimination: An Example

In 2003, the City of New Haven, Connecticut administered written and oral tests to determine who in its Fire Department would be considered for promotion over the next two years. The test results revealed a striking racial imbalance. Of the 118 candidates, sixty-eight were white, and fifty were black or Hispanic. Of the nineteen candidates whose scores entitled them to immediate promotion, however, all but two were white.

In light of this distribution, and after holding several public meetings, the City decided to set aside the test results altogether and allocate promotions another way. According to some, the City government was simply caving to pressure from a key black activist and political supporter of the mayor. For their part, however, City officials claimed that using the test results would have constituted indirect discrimination against blacks and Hispanics, leaving them little choice but to invalidate the test.

A group of eighteen firefighters who had performed well on the test—seventeen white and one Hispanic—then sued the City, alleging that by discarding the results, New Haven had engaged in *direct* racial discrimination against them. Frank Ricci, the lead plaintiff, recounted the immense investment he had made in preparing for the test, only to see the fruits of his labor invalidated after the fact because of the racial distribution of the results. In a landmark decision, the U.S. Supreme Court sided with Ricci by a vote of 5–4. Whatever the City's motives, the Court majority concluded, it had discriminated against the plaintiffs on the basis of race.[41]

It is instructive, I think, to examine how this case might be parsed by the account of discrimination we have developed thus far. The first point of interest is that if the letter of indirect discrimination law were faithful to its most plausible spirit—ordering a measure of redistribution of opportunities to members of excluded and disadvantaged groups—this controversy would take on the familiar character of debates over affirmative action. In purely theoretical terms, that seems to be the debate that should be had. Proceeding on the basis of the initial exam results is troubling precisely because (and if) it would unnecessarily perpetuate the exclusion of blacks and Hispanics from important opportunities.

It is surely relevant in this regard that New Haven has a long history of racial inequality in the staffing of its Fire Department and other municipal services,[42] and that racial minorities remain conspicuously under-represented in fire departments throughout the United States. Less than six percent of supervisors in American fire departments are black, for instance, although blacks make up nearly thirteen percent of the general population.[43] In the early 1970s, when the main U.S. discrimination statute was made applicable to state and local government employers, the U.S. Commission on Civil Rights noted that public services at the municipal level had been slower to integrate than much of the private sector, in part because they long relied on political patronage and nepotism in filling positions.[44] These dynamics might suggest an especially strong case for proactive intervention.

If New Haven acted to address these concerns openly, either by considering race in its promotion decisions explicitly or by deliberately devising a test more favorable to blacks and Hispanics, that would plainly be a form of positive discrimination on their behalf— and hence, by the same token, racial discrimination against Ricci. (One consequence of the definition adopted in Chapter 1, though we did not dwell on it there, is that discrimination in favor of Y is always discrimination against Z.) The arguments for and against the practice would proceed from this conceptual starting point, with the central question being whether direct racial discrimination is permissible under these circumstances and for the sake of these ends.

Interestingly, Justice Ginsburg noted in her dissent that the Court majority's robust enforcement of the rule against direct discrimination on behalf of the aggrieved firefighters was apparently in tension with the Court's past embrace of some affirmative action plans. The Court had previously held, for instance, that preferring female applicants for a job category traditionally regarded as "male" could be consistent with Title VII.[45] Under the case law, the legality of such affirmative action plans turns on some of the considerations generally thought relevant to the justification of positive discrimination, such as the existence of a "conspicuous imbalance in traditionally segregated job categories." Justice Ginsburg argued that although the New Haven case "does not involve affirmative action," this precedent at least implied that some race-conscious differential treatment could be upheld as permissible. Perhaps in principle the New Haven case *should* be seen as involving something close to affirmative action, rendering this analogy even more relevant than Ginsburg took it to be.

Because indirect discrimination law is officially concerned with disproportionality as such, however, this natural debate is pushed to the sidelines. The reason that most plausibly justifies setting aside the test results in this case—that promotions should be made so as to reduce, rather than amplify, racial inequalities in opportunity and social status where possible—is not given legal force, but rather treated as formally irrelevant. This artificially weakens the case for siding with the minority firefighters in one respect, but it also reorients the debate in a way that ought to favor them. For if New Haven's action is not understood as an act of positive discrimination on behalf of the minority firefighters—with the potential to be justified in the way such acts sometimes are—then Ricci cannot be a victim of such discrimination either.

Unfortunately, this point is lost in the Court's analysis to an apparent conflation of measures that are "race-conscious" or "race-based" with those that are racially discriminatory. Rejecting New Haven's argument that it had merely endeavored to comply with indirect discrimination law, Justice Kennedy wrote:

> Whatever the City's ultimate aim—however well intentioned or benevolent it might have seemed—the City made its employment decision because of race. The City rejected the test results solely because the higher scoring candidates were white. The question is not whether that conduct was discriminatory but whether the City had a lawful justification for its race-based action.[46]

On the understanding of direct discrimination we have developed, the inference at the heart of this passage—from the fact that the racial distribution of the results explained the City's action, to the judgment that the City obviously engaged in racial discrimination—is unwarranted. While it is true that an aim of avoiding indirect discrimination is not *incompatible* with employing direct discrimination as a means to that end, it is not true that one employs direct racial discrimination as a means simply by making an "employment decision because of race" (as one presumably does whenever one acts so as to avoid indirect *racial* discrimination).

Recall that direct racial discrimination, as I have proposed to define it, involves differential treatment in some dimension that is explained in part by how the discriminatees are regarded or classified racially. This definition serves to exclude cases in which a person is disfavored, and this treatment is traceable to some property she possesses, but only by way of the bearing of that property on some other property, to which the discriminator is responding—as when Sally is excluded from the roller coaster because of her height, but not, in the relevant sense, because of her age. In much the same way, it is possible for the City to make a decision "because of race," or to "reject[] the test results solely because the higher scoring candidates were white," in a way that fails to satisfy the conditions for direct racial discrimination against those candidates.

Suppose, for instance, that before City officials viewed the racial distribution of the test results, they computed a measure of the mutual information of two variables: applicant race and score attained.* Imagine they found that this value was quite large, meaning that an applicant's race was significantly predictive of how she scored on the test. The officials did not know, however, which racial groups performed relatively well or poorly. On the basis of the mutual information finding alone, they decided to discard the test results and start over, because—given that promotions could reasonably have been determined in various other ways—using these results would constitute indirect racial discrimination against some applicants (though they do not know whom).

Now clearly this would be an employment decision made "because of race." Moreover, if the underlying racial distribution of results was like the one in the actual case, we might even say that the City had "rejected the test results solely because the higher scoring candidates were white." Had more of those applicants instead been of other races, the mutual information would have been less, and the results would not have been discarded. But nonetheless it seems obvious that nobody was directly discriminated against on the basis of his or her race in this case. That is confirmed by the Explanatory Condition: the racial identities of the applicants collectively contribute to explaining

---

* Mutual information is a dimensionless "measure of the amount of information that one random variable contains about another random variable. It is the reduction in the uncertainty of one random variable due to knowledge of the other" (Cover & Thomas 1991, 18). I suggest this rather than a traditional correlation because it conveys nothing about *which* racial groups performed better or worse relative to one another.

the City's action, but only by way of their bearing on something else—the degree of racial proportionality in the test results—to which the City is sensitive. Indeed, the Differential Treatment Condition does not seem to be satisfied either, since discarding all of the test results does not amount to treating different applicants differently.

Of course, sometimes an effort to achieve a particular distribution involves discrimination on a given basis even if the desired distribution is more proportional in that dimension to the pool of candidates. In the early twentieth century, for instance, some American universities sought to increase geographic diversity in order to reduce the statistical over-representation of Jews.[47] But such cases are plainly unlike the hypothetical case that I have just described. If geographic diversity is adopted as an admissions objective in order to exclude Jews, that is a straightforward case of second-order discrimination. The same could be said of New Haven's conduct, then, if it aimed at racial proportionality *in order to* advantage one or another racial group, or out of greater concern for them. But that need not be so: the City may seek racial balance as an end in its own right or, most notably, as a means to avoid legal liability for indirect discrimination. In this way indirect discrimination law, precisely by departing from its principled justification, sets employers a task that need not constitute discrimination against the people who bear its costs.

Whether New Haven committed direct racial discrimination under the actual facts of the case, then, is not clear. The bare fact of discarding the test results does not settle the question, even if (unlike in my hypothetical) the officials knew that the results were racially imbalanced because black and Hispanic applicants had underperformed relative to white applicants. On the one hand, discarding the imbalanced test results because of their imbalance does not treat people of different races differently; rather, the one way in which all candidates are treated merely has a disproportionate adverse effect on white candidates. On the other hand, even if the City's aim is simply to achieve racial proportionality, it certainly *could* employ direct racial discrimination as a means to achieving this end. The City would be doing that if it adopted measures to increase or reduce the scores of one racial group relative to another, rather than directly to reduce the bearing of race on performance. Such a procedure treats the racial groups differently, even if the rules adopted through the procedure do not.

Suppose, for instance, that after discarding the initial test results, the City analyzes them, identifies a section of the test on which black and Hispanic candidates performed especially well, and proceeds to order a new test with a higher concentration of questions of this kind. Or suppose that rather than discarding the test results altogether, the City identifies the questions on which blacks and Hispanics most underperformed whites, and discards only those items. Plainly enough, these would constitute efforts to improve the results of black and Hispanic candidates. That is direct, positive discrimination on behalf of the groups in question, even if it is intended as a means to reduce the mutual information of race and test score, or to thereby avoid indirect discrimination.

By contrast, the City might collect data on the results of past tests in other jurisdictions, and compute the mutual information of race and test score for each. If it then replaces the test it initially performed with a test chosen in part because of its low mutual information score in past use, that would constitute a non-discriminatory means of avoiding indirect discrimination. So would discarding the individual test questions that proved most strongly related to race, on the basis of mutual information alone.[48]

Richard Primus has described the Supreme Court's *Ricci* decision as inaugurating "the idea that disparate impact [i.e., indirect discrimination] remedies are as a conceptual matter disparate treatment [i.e., direct discrimination] problems."[49] The upshot of my discussion is that, in principle if not under legal precedent, this idea is false: simultaneous prohibitions on direct and indirect discrimination are not in any kind of conceptual conflict, and need not place an employer in a dilemma. A prohibition on all *race-conscious* decision-making would obviously conflict with a prohibition on indirect racial discrimination, since compliance with the latter often requires one to attend to the racial distribution of candidates selected by one's policies. As we have seen, however, not all race-conscious decisions are racially discriminatory, let alone wrongfully so.

To be sure, my characterization of the law of indirect discrimination casts it as a rather strange thing. The best moral account of why the class of conduct that it prohibits ought to be outlawed, I have suggested, rests on the harm done when members of disadvantaged and systematically excluded groups are disfavored—including when they are disfavored on grounds having nothing to do with their membership in these groups. That concern enjoys a highly imperfect fit with the substance of the law, however, since the law prohibits unnecessary disproportionality as such. At the same time, it is precisely by virtue of its deviation from the redistributive principle that indirect discrimination law might hold the promise of bypassing the familiar affirmative action debate—and thereby offer a mechanism for bettering the situation of the disadvantaged that cannot be undercut as mandating "reverse discrimination" by employers. Of course, some people are still made worse off by the prohibition embodied in indirect discrimination law, and they may reasonably object to it. But they are not, or at least they need not be, victims of direct discrimination at the hands of an employer who endeavors to comply with the law.

2.6 Conclusion

I have argued that, in constructing a general conceptual account of discrimination, we should not seek to incorporate indirect discrimination as a distinct form of the phenomenon in question. When we attend to the essentially dimensional character of ordinary, direct discrimination, it becomes clear that much of what we might be inclined to call "indirect" discrimination is simply second-order discrimination—that is, direct discrimination in respect of the criteria by which possible grounds for selecting among individuals are assessed.

There are many other cases of "indirect" discrimination that lack this structure, however, at least as the notion is construed in Anglo-American and European law. In these cases, one or another class of people is comparatively disadvantaged by rules or criteria that may have nothing to do with their membership in that class, and which fail some special standard of justification. I have argued that laws prohibiting this sort of conduct can best be understood as redistributive programs that commandeer employers (or others) as partners in an effort to equalize opportunity for members of systemically disadvantaged groups. Far from a basic concept to be accommodated in a general account of the ethics of discrimination, then, indirect discrimination is in effect a construct for improving the status and welfare of disadvantaged groups indirectly by improving the representativeness of workforces in general. This program might have succeeded in the New Haven case, but for the Supreme Court's treatment of an employer's "race-based" actions as discriminatory even when they do not involve treating individuals differently—in any dimension—on account of the racial groups into which they are classified. In any event, we can set aside the distinctive issues raised by this device in considering when and why discrimination, in its core sense, is wrong.

PART II

Intrinsically Wrongful Discrimination

3

The Role of Disrespect in Wrongful Discrimination

Nearly everyone agrees that discrimination is sometimes morally wrong. It would be outrageous for a bank official to refuse a loan to a black candidate out of racial contempt, for instance. But despite the breadth of consensus on this point, there is remarkably little agreement about what, precisely, makes such paradigm cases of discrimination wrong. For this one act can be viewed, and objected to, under many different descriptions. Here are a handful of possibilities:

- The official invokes an irrelevant consideration in making a choice with significant consequences for another person; consequently, he may deny a valuable good to a deserving claimant.
- He holds and acts on an attitude of contempt or disrespect for another person (and in particular an attitude held on account of the person's race).
- He engages with the candidate as simply an instance of a social kind, rather than treating her as an individual.
- He contributes to sustaining social patterns of entrenched disadvantage and inequality of opportunity.

So the question arises: when we condemn the official's action as wrongful discrimination, which of these concerns are we expressing?

Of course, we should not assume that only one of these objections is sound. Each has intuitive merit—though some certainly stand in need of more elaboration than others—and they are not mutually exclusive. Even so, it matters how we mete out the credit for our convictions about core cases of wrongful discrimination, for this in turn will determine which other practices we view as fundamentally continuous with the core. In this way foundational uncertainty about clear cases of wrongful discrimination contributes to an array of persistent disputes about more controversial forms of discrimination—including positive discrimination, statistical discrimination, indirect discrimination, and the application of the antidiscrimination norm to groups or individuals beyond its historical paradigm cases.

Although the wrongness of certain core cases of discrimination is not itself in question, then, it is still important to examine which principles do the lion's share of the work in explaining and justifying these judgments. Here is one obvious starting point: discrimination is normally harmful to the people who are discriminated against. The simplest explanation of the badness of some discrimination, then, is what Kasper Lippert-Rasmussen calls the *harm-based account*:

An instance of discrimination is pro tanto bad, when it is, because it makes the discriminatees worse off.[1]

As Lippert-Rasmussen says, this view implies that discrimination is "contingently bad."[2] In fact, the harm-based account can be seen as one member of a larger conceptual family that shares this characteristic. That is, it is one of several possible theories that locate the badness of discrimination entirely in the badness of its contingent effects. Those effects include not only harm, or a reduction in someone's well-being, but also the bearing this may have on the extent to which she gets what she deserves, as well as on the overall degree of injustice in the social distribution of resources and opportunities.

I think it is fair to say that the conventional wisdom falls outside this family, for it holds that some paradigm cases of discrimination are not only contingently but also intrinsically condemnable.[3] We can bring out this point by noting the stark disconnect between the badness of a discriminatory action's effects and the moral concern it occasions. For example, as I suggested in the introduction, many would consider it wrong to reject a job applicant out of racial animus even if the employer knows that the applicant will soon find an equally appealing job elsewhere (so this action would not make her significantly worse off).[4] Or consider the research suggesting that American drivers are less likely to stop at a crosswalk to let a black person cross, contributing to longer wait times for black pedestrians compared to white ones.[5] The foreseeable effects of this discrimination—a few extra seconds on the sidewalk—are surely de minimis.[6] But the moral unease we feel about the drivers' behavior, or that the pedestrian would feel if she knew *why* she was waiting those extra seconds, is not similarly trivial. Likewise, discrimination on the basis of a crude generalization about a social group sometimes seems morally egregious even if it leads a discriminator to benefit members of the class about which he generalizes—that is, even if its contingent effects are *good* for them. All of this suggests a fundamental disjuncture between our moral convictions about discrimination and our assessment of its contingent effects.

In this chapter and the next two, I will offer an account that elaborates and endeavors to vindicate these intuitions. According to this theory, acts of discrimination are intrinsically wrong when and because they manifest a failure to show the discriminatees the respect that is due to them as persons. Thus discrimination is sometimes morally objectionable not because of anything that it causes, but because of what it itself manifests by virtue of how it comes about.

I will argue that this principle does the best job of capturing the tenor of our condemnation of wrongful discrimination in its core cases, and of explaining the variety of forms those core cases can apparently take. But I do not mean to advance a grand theory of *the* factor that makes discrimination immoral whenever it is. Indeed, the account of the nature of discrimination that we developed in Part I casts doubt on the prospects for any such endeavor. According to the view I have suggested, discrimination is best seen as a very general kind of act—one that is only sometimes wrong. Acts fitting within that type may be wrong in different cases for different reasons. In Part III, for instance, I will take racial profiling in law enforcement as an exemplar of the sort of discrimination that may sometimes be bad only by virtue of its harmful consequences.

What can be said for the disrespect-based theory, then, is mainly that it identifies and develops the concern that underwrites appropriate outrage over wrongful discrimination in its intuitive paradigm cases, and thereby clarifies how far that special form of censure ought to extend. Yet the disrespect account also has the potential to explain how and why, notwithstanding the argument of Part I, we sometimes use "discrimination" as itself the name of a moral wrong. The most central cases of wrongful discrimination, I will argue, are distinguished by the fact that they not only manifest a lack of respect for a person, but manifest a lack of respect *that is itself discriminatory*. The best account of discrimination as a kind of moral wrong, in other words, identifies discrimination in this narrow, moralized sense with discrimination, in the wide sense, in the specific dimension of respect for persons.

Of course, the thought that wrongful discrimination is connected to disrespect is not a new one.[7] I have two main objectives relative to the existing literature that shares this basic orientation. First, I offer an account of the sort of disrespect relevant to the wrongness of discrimination that aims to navigate between two apparent difficulties. On the one hand, some understand disrespect as necessarily involving an attitude of hostility or contempt, or a belief that some people are of inferior worth.[8] But this fails to explain what is wrong with discrimination that occurs in the absence of these positive factors—including much discrimination that is unconscious or based on sincere statistical beliefs—independent of its contingent effects. On the other hand, some understand disrespect in terms of the objective conventional meaning or expressive content of an act. This strategy avoids resting the wrongfulness of discrimination on what may or may not be going on in the mind of the discriminator. But it makes it implausible that disrespectful discrimination should be intrinsically and not merely contingently bad, since the conventional meaning of an act, in itself, does not seem to be of any intrinsic moral significance.

I will reject accounts of both of these kinds. I propose instead that the relevant sort of respect—recognition respect for someone's standing as a person—imposes an affirmative obligation that one take to heart the various normative upshots of her being a person and regulate one's action accordingly. On this view, what matters is how an agent deliberates, rather than the social meaning of her act. But her deliberation is rendered morally defective not simply by the presence of some positive factor of animus or a defamatory belief, but by the *absence* of appropriate recognition of someone's personhood, whether that absence comes about willfully or by neglect.

Second, and relatedly, I mean to propose a *unified* account of why discrimination is sometimes intrinsically wrong. Here we should pause to observe that people discriminate against (and in favor of) one another for many different reasons. You might discriminate against someone because you value her interests at a discounted weight relative to somebody else's. Or you might discriminate against her because the choice you make will affect *you* in some way, and (for instance) you prefer contact with one kind of person rather than another. In yet other cases you might discriminate against a person on the basis of a judgment about what he is like that you form by appeal to your beliefs about a wider class of people. Despite their structural differences, we nevertheless perceive a common potential moral violation in these cases—a perception reflected in the inclination to describe each as at least potentially racist, sexist, or the like.

Disrespect, I will argue, is the common thread. These various forms of discrimination each sometimes fail to respect someone as a person, though under different aspects. In addition to offering an analysis of the connection between respect and wrongful discrimination generally, therefore, I also set out to trace in a systematic fashion when and how particular kinds of discrimination show disrespect for particular facets of our standing as persons. Together, this account suggests a deep connection between wrongful discrimination and literally dehumanizing a person—engaging her in a way that strips her of the moral incidents of personhood. This is a fundamental moral wrong. But it is one that comes in degrees of severity and intentionality, and it appears in different guises in different settings.

This chapter introduces a working conception of respect for persons, develops its normative foundations, and contrasts it with other views on offer. Chapters 4 and 5 will then elaborate the moral content of the disrespect-based account of wrongful discrimination, considering in turn the demands of respect for a person's equality and for her autonomy.

3.1 Respect for Persons

There are different kinds of respect, and hence of disrespect. The kind that concerns us here, I will argue, is what Stephen Darwall has influentially labeled "recognition respect," that is, "a disposition to weigh appropriately in one's deliberations some feature of the thing in question and to act accordingly."[9] The object to which this attitude is the appropriate or fitting response is a form of "dignity or authority."[10] In considering the morality of discrimination, I will try to show, we should be centrally concerned with recognition respect for persons, as persons. As Darwall explains, this form of respect requires that in dealing with people one "take seriously and weigh appropriately the fact that they are persons in deliberating about what to do."*

I will argue that this is what people characteristically fail to do in paradigm cases of wrongful discrimination, and what makes those acts intrinsically objectionable. As such, the moral theory I advance here is centrally concerned neither with weighing up the good and

---

* In his later work, Darwall identifies this earlier formulation as having "missed" "respect's second-personal character" insofar as it suggests that "one need only adequately register a fact about or feature of someone," which one can accomplish "outside of a second-personal relation" (2006, 130–1). And he argues, relatedly, that the "dignity of persons is second-personal" in such a way that "it cannot be wholly summed into (non-second-personal) values or norms, say, into a set of requirements on conduct that are rooted in our common nature as persons or even into certain ways that persons must and must not be treated" (2006, 121). Such an accounting of dignity's significance would be incomplete unless it "also involves an equal authority as persons to claim or demand compliance with such requirements." In embracing the idea of recognition respect as a schema for understanding wrongful discrimination, I don't mean to take a position on the deeper question whether moral reasons derive ultimately from a kind of second-personal authority.

bad consequences of an act, nor with whether the act, thinly described, falls under a prohibited type (such as killing or stealing). The basic theoretical premise, rather, is that sometimes an agent's commission of an act is morally condemnable because it involves and gives effect to a failure of recognition—a *deliberative* failure of a certain kind.

This theoretical approach has a firm foothold in ordinary moral thought. In assessing the way an agent acts, we often care about the attitudes to which his action gives effect. If you vote for a referendum to ban same-sex marriage, for instance, I will want to know whether you acted out of contempt for gay people, or a good-faith belief about the connection between the recognition of same-sex marriages and the psychological well-being of children. Moreover, this difference seems relevant not only to my moral appraisal of you or your character, but also to my assessment of *what you did*. If you voted for the referendum out of contempt, you acted wrongly. If you voted out of good-faith concern for the welfare of children, then there is a real sense in which you did not, or at least in which your wrongdoing is much less severe.

Some will insist that these moral judgments attach not to what you *did*, but to your character or motives. But it is more accurate to think of these judgments as attaching to the complex of the act *and* its motives, or, as Richard Arneson puts it, to the act "thickly described."[11] What is singularly bad in the referendum example, I am suggesting, is "voting for the ban out of contempt for gay people." This is a perfectly acceptable characterization of what you may have done, for one way of describing an act is by reference to how it is arrived at by an agent. Similarly, many have thought that it is wrong to bomb a town in war in order to kill enemy civilians, but potentially permissible to bomb the town in order to destroy a munitions factory there, even if the consequences will be the same in either case.[12]

Elizabeth Anderson and Richard Pildes offer another helpful example of normative judgments that center on thickly described actions in this way.[13] They suggest that it may be (a) wrong to avoid visiting my mother in the hospital in order to spare myself discomfort, but (b) right to avoid visiting my mother in the hospital in order to avoid transmitting a contagious disease to her, and (c) right to avoid watching television in order to spare myself discomfort. It follows from this triad of plausible judgments that the condemnation in (a) must somehow attach to the connection between avoiding visiting my mother in the hospital and sparing myself discomfort. It cannot target simply the motive (sparing myself discomfort) or the act-type thinly described (avoiding visiting my mother in the hospital), since each of these is deemed permissible, or even required, by one of the other judgments.

Specifically, Anderson and Pildes propose that what is wrong in this case is taking sparing myself discomfort as sufficient reason to forgo visiting my mother in the hospital, and acting accordingly. As they put it: "[A]voiding her for this reason is wrong because taking this as one's reason for acting is callous, and it is wrong to express such an uncaring attitude toward one's mother."[14] More generally, "[a]n attitude toward a person is a complex set of dispositions to perceive, have emotions, deliberate, and act in ways oriented toward that person," and "[t]o express an attitude through action is to act on the reasons that attitude gives us."[15]

Recognition respect for a person can be understood as an attitude in this sense: like love or antipathy, it gives us reasons to deliberate and act in certain ways where she is involved. One acts disrespectfully, then, by failing to act on the reasons that would be given by recognition respect.[16] If we are going to speak of respect and disrespect as *attitudes*, however, it is important to eschew one misleading connotation of that idea. For sometimes to act on or out of an attitude is simply to have a certain psychological motive, which can be described without appeal to any normative principles. I might steal something out of envy, for example. Presumably we could figure out whether that is so in a particular case by peering into my mind and determining whether a mental state of a certain kind explained my stealing—an investigation that itself involves no normative inquiry. Put another way, the only moral questions about acting out of this attitude directly concern the morality of so acting—i.e., whether it is wrong to steal out of envy, whether it is worse than stealing out of other motives, and so on.

By contrast, because respect is a matter of integrating some feature of an object into one's deliberation appropriately, the content of the attitude is itself only discernible by appeal to a theory about the normative significance that feature has. So in this case, unlike in the last one, there are two normative issues in play. First, there is the question whether it is wrong to act out of disrespect for someone's personhood; I assume that it is. Second, however, the question what that attitude consists in is also itself a moral question, not a psychological one. So we should not be misled, by conceiving of respect for persons as an attitude, into thinking of it as a mental state on a par with admiration, love, or envy. Schematically, respect and disrespect for persons are states of mind that consist in taking (or failing to take) certain considerations as reasons for or against certain actions; but which considerations these are depends on a theory of the moral significance of being a person.[17]

Developing or defending such a theory is obviously a very large project, and I will not presume to do either in fully systematic terms. Rather, I will simply invoke as needed two notions that are, I hope, reasonably uncontroversial attributes of persons. First, persons are of value in themselves, and equally so. There are many things that are good or bad about particular persons, of course, and these are found in different degrees in each of us. But there is a further value that we have simply *qua* persons, and which we therefore necessarily have equally.[18] Second, persons are autonomous: they possess a faculty of self-control through which they can make their lives, in significant part, their own.

I will have a good deal more to say about each of these attributes as we proceed. But the upshot for now is that, in the overall picture I am suggesting, one disrespects someone as a person if one fails to recognize and afford the appropriate deliberative weight to either of these features. To respect persons as persons, in other words, one must treat them as autonomous beings that are of value and that are, in one fundamental respect, of equal value as one another. My thesis is that core cares of wrongful discrimination manifest a failure to abide by one or another facet of this requirement.

3.2 Permissibility and Meaning

According to my account, an act is disrespectful because of its roots in a certain kind of deliberative failing, and wrong because it is disrespectful. As such, my theory presupposes the intelligibility and propriety of making moral judgments about what, following Arneson, I have been calling thickly described act-types.

I cannot mount a full defense of that premise here. There is one particular challenge to this view, however, that I think we ought to explore in a bit more depth—both because it has been invoked in the recent literature on discrimination,[19] and because it potentially bears on the way that a disrespect-based account of wrongful discrimination should be understood.

In particular, T.M. Scanlon has suggested that we should distinguish between an act's permissibility and its meaning.[20] Moral principles speak to both questions, he says, but in different guises. To employ a principle in its *deliberative* use is to invoke it in determining whether an act is permissible. To employ a principle in its *critical* use, by contrast, is to use it "as the basis for assessing the way in which an agent went about deciding what to do," which bears on what the action, as done by that agent, means.[21] Blame, he then argues, is more closely connected to the meaning of an act—to "the reasons for which a person acted and the conditions under which he or she did so"— than to the act's permissibility.[22]

Scanlon leverages this distinction to argue that an agent's reasons for action are not normally of fundamental relevance to an act's permissibility. Thus if I stab a voodoo doll in the belief that this will kill someone I dislike, I have not done anything morally impermissible. He explains: "There does seem to be *something* wrong with the action.... What is wrong with it, however, is not that it is impermissible but rather that the agent should (given his beliefs) *see it as* impermissible."[23] That bears on the *meaning* of the agent's doing the act, and thereby on his blameworthiness, but does not make the act itself wrong.

This theory is sometimes appealed to in support of the claim that the wrongness of discrimination is not fundamentally a matter of an agent's intentions, reasons, or attitudes. Interestingly, however, that is not Scanlon's own view of the matter. Rather, he presents discrimination as an example of an *exception* to the general rule that an act's meaning does not bear on its permissibility. In particular, he says that individual acts of discrimination, when done in a certain social context, are

> wrong because of their consequences—the exclusion of some people from important opportunities—and because of their meaning—the judgment of inferiority that they express and thereby help to maintain. The latter objection, because it depends on the meaning of an action, depends on the agent's reasons. But the former does not.[24]

Scanlon's view sounds much like the one I will develop here. Discrimination may be objectionable intrinsically, on account of an agent's reasons for acting as she does; and also contingently, on account of the act's consequences in a given social context. But I am not sufficiently certain what Scanlon has in mind to firmly claim him as an ally. In particular, I am not sure how the second objection he describes—the one that is dependent on an agent's reasons—could have to do with the act's "help[ing] to maintain" a social judgment of inferiority. The act's *conventional* meaning will bear on that prospect, but that kind of meaning does not depend on an agent's *actual* reasons for action.[25] I return to this point about basic and conventional forms of disrespect in the next section.

Of course, the fact that Scanlon takes discrimination to be a special case where permissibility depends in part on an agent's reasons for action does not settle the question whether that is so. There are also reasonable grounds to doubt the broader claim that an agent's reasons generally bear only on meaning, however. Consider again the claim that what is wrong with stabbing the voodoo doll "is not that it is impermissible but rather that the agent should (given his beliefs) *see it as* impermissible."[26] One natural response to this is that a person should not do things that, given his beliefs, he should see as impermissible. In other words, Scanlon's claim that the action in this case is not itself impermissible depends on our describing that action thinly. If we view the agent as "stabbing the voodoo doll with the aim of killing one's enemy," then it seems perfectly natural to say that what he does is wrong. That is consistent with the possibility that stabbing the doll *as such* is morally insignificant.

Scanlon's argument for focusing on thinly described act-types when we assess permissibility turns out to rest on the view that, at least in many cases, we cannot *choose* among thickly described acts.[27] Rather than pursuing this issue further, however, let me simply suggest that Scanlon's distinction makes less of a difference for our purposes than it may seem. It would be a mistake, for instance, to take Scanlon's view to imply that an agent's reasons, intentions, and attitudes are relevant only to the assessment of the *agent*. For what we assess when we use a principle in its "critical" mode is "not the agent's overall character but rather the quality of the particular piece of decision making that led to the action in question."[28]

With that in mind, I think we can proceed open to the intriguing possibility of distinguishing between a thickly described action's being morally impermissible and its being morally defective in some other way. In other words, an interesting and important question about acts of discrimination is when (and why) they are morally defective, and as gravely so as they intuitively seem to be. What, exactly, is so wrong with them? If this constitutes an inquiry into what makes these actions bad or reprehensible and not what makes them impermissible, that is not, so far as I can tell, a significant problem for the project.[29]

It *would* be a problem, in my view, if we were confined to talking about defects in the characters of discriminators as such; for I mean to propose, as an answer to my question, that acts of discrimination themselves are morally condemnable when they are disrespectful of the personhood of the discriminatees, that is, because they manifest certain deliberative failings that are at odds with this status. But I don't see Scanlon's theory as threatening that suggestion. It could well be that discrimination is sometimes bad, independent of its consequences, by virtue of what Scanlon calls its meaning and not by virtue of its deontic status.

Strict neutrality on this question would require us to forswear the unmodified use of "wrong" or "wrongful" in describing the class of discrimination that we are interested in, limiting ourselves instead to "bad," "condemnable," "objectionable," and the like. But I won't do that, because I don't mean to assume the truth of Scanlon's view. On the contrary, I think it remains plausible that thickly described actions very often have their own deontic statuses, and that the way an agent deliberates is often relevant to determining these.[30] As we have seen, Scanlon agrees that there is something bad about many thickly described actions, which badness is due to the agent's reasons for action; perhaps we should see this bad feature of the actions as grounding a moral reason not to do them, which implies that it bears on judgments of permissibility.

So I only mean to point out that if Scanlon's view is ultimately correct—and if, contrary to Scanlon's somewhat compressed suggestion, discrimination is not in fact an exception to it—that would bear on the interpretive cast that should be given to the disrespect account more than on its soundness. Throughout, the suggestion that discrimination of such-and-such a type is wrong could be replaced with the claim that it is *bad* in a wider sense of moral evaluation that is (by hypothesis) better suited to the assessment of thickly described actions.[31]

In broad terms, then, this part of the book will try to show that the point of kinetic contact between thought and action is where our moral convictions about paradigmatic cases of discrimination are properly anchored. Our moral sense about discrimination is best captured and articulated, that is, through norms about how people engage with one another—modes of moral relationship and misrelationship that are not reflected in time-slices of events that represent only "thin" descriptions of either actions or their consequences. The ideas of respect and disrespect offer the right normative vocabulary for this sort of moral thought, but whether those ideas should in turn be understood to bottom out in claims of deontic status, or something else, is a deep issue that need not control our inquiry here.

3.3 Basic and Conventional Disrespect

Before proceeding to develop the disrespect-based account of wrongful discrimination, there is another important conceptual issue about disrespect that needs to be addressed in some detail. To disrespect X as Y is, in its primary sense, to fail to give due regard to X's standing as Y in one's practical deliberation. Acts that manifest such a failure are disrespectful acts. Thus whether an act disrespects someone as a person is determined by whether it is traceable to a deliberative failing of the kind that is constitutive of such disrespect.

Such acts, I will say, are *basically* disrespectful. In determinations of basic disrespectfulness, no fundamental role is played by social conventions about respect. Moreover, thinly described acts or act-types cannot be basically disrespectful, for an act's standing as basically disrespect is a feature of how it is arrived at by an agent.

This is often obscured, however, by the fact that we also use "disrespect" in a purely conventional sense. In this sense, an act can be called "disrespectful" simply because it is such as to be *conventionally understood as evincing* basic disrespect.[32] Although this conventional sense of disrespect is rooted in the basic sense—basic disrespect, I have just suggested, figures in its definition—conventional disrespect thus takes on a semantic life of its own as well. A parent might tell a young child that it was disrespectful of her to make a certain gesture, even if the parent knows that the child did not realize the gesture's significance.[33] The parent means to say that the child acted in a way that, by the lights of the operative conventions, is a mark of basic disrespect, even though in this instance there may have been no basic disrespect to signal, because there was no deliberative failure of the kind that constitutes basic disrespect. Unlike basic disrespect, conventional disrespect can be predicated of thinly described acts or act-types.

Basic respect and conventional respect are, of course, closely related. Consider the moral permissibility of acting in a way that is conventionally disrespectful of someone: spitting on him, for instance.[34] Normally this is done in order to show contempt for a person, in which case it almost certainly manifests basic disrespect. Making one's disrespect for him manifest is, in fact, the point of the act.

In principle, however, the act of spitting on someone need not be done with that purpose. He might just be standing in the most convenient place to spit. Still, by virtue of its conventional meaning, spitting on him can be expected to cause him psychological or material harm, either directly or by influencing the way others treat him. And even if it causes no such harm, the action may prompt others to act towards him in ways that are basically disrespectful, by lowering his moral "stock." These possible bad effects of a conventionally disrespectful act normally ground a significant but contingent moral reason not to perform it, which applies even if one is not transgressing the convention *in order* to show disrespect.

By creating such contingent reasons, conventions about disrespect play an important role in determining what is basically disrespectful. Suppose that I am well aware of the social meaning of spitting on people, but I do it anyway—not to make use of the convention to express something, but in simple indifference to it. My failure to consider the offense someone may take at being spat on, and to count this as a reason against spitting on him, makes my act a manifestation of basic disrespect for him. For that way of deliberating and acting is inconsistent with the measure of concern for him mandated by basic respect. In order for a conventionally disrespectful act to be made basically disrespectful in this way, however, the moral reason against performing the act, grounded in its detrimental effects, must exist in the first place. Crucially, then, it is not the convention itself that determines that my act is basically disrespectful, but rather my disregard for the harm that my act may cause *in light of* the convention.[35]

This account of the connection between disrespect and convention differs significantly with a view that is articulated by Anderson and

Pildes in the context of their "expressivist" moral theory, and which is echoed in some recent writing about discrimination.[36] That contrast is instructive. In particular, Anderson and Pildes write:

> Expressive theories of action tell us to express certain attitudes adequately.... [T]he standard of adequacy is public, set by objective criteria for determining the meanings of action. What attitudes people intend to express or think they are expressing can deviate from the public meaning of their action ... [For instance,] people may act in ignorance of social conventions or norms that set public standards for expressing certain attitudes. Thus, a person from a different culture might not know he is expressing disrespect for another by failing to shake his hand.[37]

There is no need to take a view here on what constitutes *expressing* an attitude. But it is important to see that, on my view, this person's action may not be disrespectful—in the basic sense—at all. That is not because one only acts disrespectfully if one intends to do so, or because disrespect is always transparent to its subject. On the contrary, one can act disrespectfully by *unwittingly* failing to integrate someone's standing as a person appropriately in one's practical deliberation; and whether one has done that is a matter of "objective criteria," as opposed to a subject's own self-assessments. But one does not fail to satisfy the relevant criteria *simply* by acting in ways that are conventionally disrespectful, such as failing to shake someone's hand in a culture with which one may be unfamiliar. To disrespect someone is to fail to take account of the normative significance of some facet of her moral standing; and it is just not up to a culture to decide what constitutes such a failure.*

Nonetheless, some have proposed to analyze the morality of discrimination in terms of whether actions express disrespect, in

---

* Of course, there will normally be reasons of respect for acquainting oneself with the respect-conventions in a culture, since this knowledge is essential if one is to avoid offending people. But not all ignorance of these conventions reflects a failure to take account of and act on these reasons. Suppose that the protagonist in the example is stuck in a foreign country unexpectedly because of a delayed flight. That he acts disrespectfully, in the conventional sense, does not imply that his action manifests basic disrespect.

something close to Anderson and Pildes' sense. For example, Deborah Hellman has proposed a thoughtful account of wrongful discrimination according to which "it is morally wrong to draw distinctions among people and treat them differently as a result when doing so demeans any of those affected."[38] Hellman emphasizes that one "need not *feel* demeaned to have a moral claim," however.[39] She explains: "To demean is to treat another as not fully human or not of equal moral worth. To demean therefore is partly an expressive act. One's action expresses that the other is less worthy of concern or respect."[40] Now, if the notion of "one's action express[ing]" an attitude towards someone were understood in terms of its *effectuating* or *arising out of* that attitude, this would be entirely consistent with the view I am suggesting. And we do sometimes speak of one thing as an "expression of" another in a way that could describe this relation. But, like Anderson and Pildes, Hellman affords social meaning a fundamental, constitutive role in determining whether an act expresses disrespect and therefore demeans.[41] She writes:

It is our common history and culture and its conventions and social understandings that determine which actions express a rejection of the equal humanity of others.... Demeaning is related to being disrespectful and to that extent depends on convention.[42]

As an example, Hellman says, ordering blacks to the back of a bus in the United States is "fixed by social convention as an instance of demeaning blacks."[43]

As will become clear, I think it is quite right to say that discrimination is wrong when it involves "treat[ing] another as ... not of equal moral worth." But I doubt that whether one has done that depends on convention in the fundamental way that Hellman suggests. As we saw above, the fact that an act-type is conventionally disrespectful does play a role, indirectly, in determining whether it is compatible with basic respect, since conventional disrespect is often materially or psychologically harmful, and basic respect normally requires us to count this risk of harm (like other risks of harm) against the act. Moreover, a long history of oppression of some groups has endowed us with an especially wide array of meanings and practices through which we can conventionally disrespect their members; and this special power, joined with the ordinary requirement of respect, grounds a duty to exercise special caution.

But Hellman is apparently suggesting that what is disrespectful in the morally relevant sense is fixed by respect-conventions themselves—independent, that is, of both the predictable harms of violating these conventions and the practical attitudes these violations sometimes signal.[44] True, the wrongness of infringing any particular respect convention is taken to derive from a general, non-contingent obligation to avoid showing conventional disrespect for a person's equal worth. So it is not as if the individual respect-conventions bootstrap *themselves* into full-blown moral requirements.[45] But, still, I find this a difficult view to motivate or accept. Why would it be wrong to act in ways that happen to show disrespect by the lights of the operative social norms (whatever these ways are), even if the act carried no possibility of material or psychological harm to anyone, reflected no failure to take account of such harms in regulating one's action, and manifested no failure to integrate anyone's standing appropriately in one's deliberation? Such acts would not *actually* manifest an *actual* lack of recognition respect: they would not reflect an agent's failure to deliberate and to act in the way that this attitude requires.*

This line of argument raises doubts about the plausibility of affording facts about conventional respect and disrespect an unmediated role in determining the moral reasons for and against actions, including acts of discrimination. But, while this question of moral foundations is not unimportant, Hellman's respect-centered view and mine

---

* I have argued here that conventional disrespect is not sufficient for a violation of the moral duty of respect. But my account also implies that it is not *necessary*, since one can fail to take someone's status as a person seriously without doing anything that, thinly described, would be taken as disrespectful. As Leslie Green writes, "it is open to doubt whether treatment (or omissions) of a certain kind generally satisfies our duty to respect persons. People are sensitive not only to the way they are treated but also to the spirit in which that treatment is afforded" (2010, 219).

may often converge in practice. This is particularly likely because Hellman argues that for an action to constitute wrongful discrimination, an actor must not only treat another as not of equal moral worth, but must also act with a measure of social power sufficient for her to put down or subordinate the other.[46] Actors with such social power are even more likely than others to have the responsibility to acquaint themselves with respect conventions, in order to avoid the predictable harms of violating them; and their failure to do so, barring special circumstances, will often involve basic, not merely conventional, disrespect. It might therefore be the case that those who commit wrongful discrimination in Hellman's sense—though not all who treat others disrespectfully in her sense—very often show basic disrespect as well, because they either embrace the predictable harms of violating respect conventions, or else shirk their obligation, by virtue of their power, to know enough about the conventions in order to avoid threatening these same harms through negligence.[47]

A similar concern might be raised about Patrick Shin's illuminating account of what he terms the "substantive principle of equal treatment." Specifically, Shin proposes that "[t]he treatment of an individual violates the requirement of equal treatment in the substantive sense when that treatment, in view of its rationale, expresses unequal respect for the moral status of that individual under some differentiating description."[48] The fact that this norm involves attention to an act's *rationale* suggests that it applies to thickly described acts, which I have argued is the right approach. In elaborating this requirement, however, Shin says that "we may be justified in regarding an action as expressive of an attitude of unequal moral respect even if the agent responsible for it does not actually act on any such attitude," because whether an act expresses an attitude is a matter of whether "it would be objectively reasonable for observers to attribute [it] to the agent."[49] Among other considerations, whether it is reasonable to attribute such an attitude "may be affected by ... symbolic connections between the action and historical examples of injustice."[50]

It might seem that this confuses epistemic and constitutive questions. After all, it is trivial that "we may be justified in regarding an action as expressive of an attitude...even if the agent...does not actually act on any such attitude," because we may be in justified error. But Shin is clear that he thinks whether the act *actually* expresses the attitude turns on whether attributing the attitude is reasonable. That may be right: the concept of expression, as we have seen, can be understood in terms of conventional meanings. But if, as Shin says, one can express attitudes one does not hold, then expressing disrespect in such cases must be bad because of its contingently harmful consequences—or because one's disregard for these consequences makes it the case, after all, that one's action *does* manifest a defective way of relating to another person. By contrast, Shin appears to suggest that certain acts can be objectionable simply because of their conventional meanings, even if they reflect no basic disrespect on the agent's part and involve no prospect of injury to anyone. There is no evidence that I can see for such a moral requirement; to acknowledge it would be to invest social norms with a freestanding moral force that is difficult to explain or understand.

Most fundamentally, then, my disagreement with Hellman and Shin turns on a question about what respect and disrespect *are* in the first place. Following Darwall, I've suggested that our basic concept of respect is of an attitude a person holds towards another. We use conventions to signal and to detect when actions manifest this attitude, and for this reason a thinly described act-type can itself be called "respectful" or "disrespectful." But this sense of respect is purely derivative. And so on this picture, it is simply a category mistake to invest "disrespect" of the conventional sort with the moral force that we naturally impute to the attitude it characteristically manifests.

3.4 Comparative and Non-Comparative Disrespect

According to the view I am proposing, acts of discrimination are often wrong because they disrespect someone's standing as a person.

You can disrespect someone in this way, however, without engaging in discrimination; your failure to respect him may not be attributable to how you perceive or regard him along some dimension of difference. So this objection to some discrimination does not justify regarding wrongful discrimination as a distinct or irreducible kind of wrong.

At the same time, wrongful discrimination, in its core cases, fails the general requirement of respect in a certain characteristic way. It distinctively involves *comparative* disrespect. That is, it involves failing to respect someone as a person when one does not (or would not) so fail in the case of an actual (or counterfactual) comparator. Given the account of discrimination we adopted in Chapter 1, we can also put that point this way: Paradigm acts of intrinsically wrongful discrimination are, in addition to being discrimination in whatever material dimension—employment, friend-selection, and so on—also instances of discrimination *in the dimension of respect for personhood.*[51] They are cases in which classifying individuals differently on the basis of some trait leads one to fail to show some of them the respect due to them as persons.

Importantly, not all acts that are disrespectful and discriminatory are wrongful discrimination in this central sense connected to comparative disrespect. For example, on the view I will defend, if an assessor decides how to treat someone exclusively on the basis of her racial background—ignoring readily available evidence of her particular character—he disrespects her as a person. He also discriminates on the basis of race, since his differential treatment of different candidates is traceable to how he views them racially. But if he *consistently* focuses exclusively on race, in assessing members of all racial groups, he may not do anything that is comparatively disrespectful, or racially discriminatory in the dimension of respect for personhood. Rather, he may disrespect them all alike—treating each as less than an autonomous individual, but to an equal degree.[52]

It's not clear that there is any fundamental significance to whether an instance of disrespect for persons is comparative, or even to whether it is connected to an act of discrimination. People are owed respect as persons non-comparatively: if one has failed to show a person due respect, after all, it is no defense to say one has similarly mistreated others. Nonetheless, for whatever reason, we often go about disrespecting people in the distinctively comparative way. And it seems we have a specific vocabulary for describing such comparative disrespect: the notions of racism, sexism, and the like.

As I suggested above, the apparent applicability of these terms is a common thread that connects our reactions to many different forms of discrimination—preference-based, generalization-based, and so on. In my view, that is because these different forms of discrimination often evince the same failing, to wit, comparative disrespect for personhood. We can therefore use these notions to distinguish between acts that are merely both discriminatory and disrespectful, on the one hand, and those that are comparatively disrespectful, or discriminatory in the dimension of respect, on the other.

Joshua Glasgow has persuasively argued that something is racist if and only if it is "racially disrespectful."[53] Let us suppose that is right, but tweak the definition to require that racist acts be racially disrespectful of someone *as a person*.[54] And let us say that an act is *racially* disrespectful—in the basic, non-conventional sense of disrespect—if it is disrespectful of someone and its being so is traceable to how the agent perceives or regards him racially. This interpretation of "racially disrespectful" is not the same as the gloss Glasgow suggests in his more formal statement of his analysis: "ϕ is racist if and only if ϕ is disrespectful toward members of racialized group R as Rs."[55] But, as we have seen, disrespect for X *as* a Y is naturally understood as involving a failure to abide by the reasons or requirements given by X's standing as a Y. A student may show disrespect for Mr. Smith as a teacher, for instance, by ignoring his directions in class. In this sense, racism is typically not disrespect for a member of a racialized group *as* a member of the targeted racialized group, but rather disrespect as something else—a teacher, an equal, a person—that is *due to* one's perception of or reaction to his race. Adopting these definitions and building on Glasgow's analysis of racism, we can then say that on my view something is intrinsically wrongful racial discrimination, in the central comparative sense, if and only if it is racist. More generally, we might say that something is intrinsically wrongful P-based discrimination, in the central comparative sense, just in case it is P-ist, where for something to be P-ist is for it to be disrespectful of someone as a person because of how he is regarded P-wise.[56]

The vocabulary of racism, sexism, and the like, I have suggested, seems naturally to capture the distinctively comparative form of disrespect. Although I have argued that we should understand discrimination as a very general form of action, we can nonetheless understand the word "discrimination," when used in a certain sense, in a way that is also closely connected to this form of disrespect. Notwithstanding the argument of Chapter 1, that is, there is undeniable force to the intuition that "discrimination," used in a certain way, denotes a specific kind of moral wrong or injustice. The central comparative form of intrinsically wrongful discrimination elaborated here can be understood to identify that wrong—and hence to cast light on the relationship between this understanding of discrimination and the broader one elaborated in Chapter 1. The concept of discrimination, on this view, has a distinctive nested character that may help to explain its elusiveness. To discriminate in the narrow sense *is* to discriminate in the wide sense, but in the specific dimension of respect for persons.

3.5 Conclusion

This chapter has introduced a basic normative point of view, centered on the demands of moral respect or recognition, that we will explore in greater depth, and with more specific application to wrongful discrimination, in the next two chapters. The most basic theoretical claim is that certain actions are morally defective not merely because of their contingent effects but because of something wrong with the agent's mode of engagement with the moral reasons she has for acting in one or another way. The idea of recognition respect for persons as such marks out a subset of objectionable failures to respond to reasons—those that amount to failing to fully take heed of the normative significance of the fact that the person one is dealing with is a person. The next question is how the various normative facets of personhood, and the various forms of failure duly to appreciate them, can help us to better understand our convictions about core cases of wrongful discrimination.

4

Respect for Equality

The previous chapter introduced and clarified the thesis that discrimination is intrinsically objectionable when it is basically disrespectful of the personhood of those who are discriminated against. The next two chapters are organized around two elemental facets of moral personhood—a person's moral worth and her autonomy—that are proper objects of recognition respect. These chapters aim to explain why and how some forms of discrimination manifest wrongful disregard for these normative characteristics.

This chapter concerns the foundational idea that people are owed a form of respect in virtue of their equal moral worth or value. First, in §§4.1–4.3, I describe how attention to disrespect fits and explains our ordinary moral judgments about cases of discrimination in which people's interests are valued at different weights without good reason. I argue that my account compares favorably in this regard with two alternatives, which emphasize a discriminator's beliefs or hostile motives, and that it suitably accommodates the notion of implicit bias. In §4.4, I then turn to discrimination motivated by preferences that are not necessarily reducible to differential concern for people's interests. I suggest that attention to disrespect helps to explain why some such discrimination, but only some, is wrong independent of its effects. To subdivide the analysis into manageable pieces, I will bracket discrimination that arises from reliance on generalizations or stereotypes, as far as possible, for the moment. I extend the disrespect-based account to such cases in the next chapter.

4.1 Differential Concern

Suppose that Adam is choosing whether to promote Fatima, who is of Arab descent, or Christopher, who is white. Adam considers the benefit to Christopher of getting the promotion, and gives this some weight in his decision. But because Fatima is of Arab descent, Adam gives the equal benefit to Fatima of getting the promotion less weight in his decision, no weight at all, or even negative weight. It is widely agreed, I take it, that this discrimination is morally wrong. I believe that is primarily because the way Adam makes his decision is disrespectful of Fatima. In other words, Adam fails to take appropriate account of something important about Fatima in making his decision.

What does he fail to recognize about her? In the most familiar cases of racial discrimination, the answer seems very straightforward. Suppose that Adam discounts Fatima's interests because he denies her equal value as a person—say, because he regards people of Arab descent as intrinsically less valuable than white people. Then his failure to respect Fatima as a person is direct and explicit: he flatly denies that she has the value that all persons have, and acts on this belief.

This is the kind of disrespect that finds its natural expression in dehumanizing images and metaphors: of Jews as parasites, or Tutsis as cockroaches, or aboriginal people as savages. It is not limited to such genocidal mindsets, however. You can view some people as being of lesser intrinsic value, that is, while not denying their value altogether. This is the ideology that structures openly caste-based social systems, or the caste-like attitudes of individual people.

Beliefs of this kind are clearly fundamental to the most extreme forms of bigotry. That recognition has led some to suggest that the sort of disrespect involved in intrinsically wrongful discrimination necessarily rests on such a judgment of differential moral worth or inferior status. I think that is a mistake, however. One can fail to accord someone the respect demanded by her status as a person without taking her to occupy a lower station on an explicit hierarchy of value.

I develop this concern about belief-centered views below. My point here is to suggest how Adam's reduced concern for Fatima, relative to

Christopher, may manifest disrespect for her equal value even if he makes no direct judgment about her value at all. The key claim in staking out this position is what I will call the *interest thesis*:

To respect a person's equal value relative to other persons one must value her interests equally with those of other persons, absent good reason for discounting them.

There is not much that I can say in defense of this thesis, beyond making it explicit. And it should be acknowledged that the thesis is not entirely trivial. There is a sense in which one can recognize the value of classical music without really *valuing* it oneself. By contrast, the interest thesis holds that one cannot appropriately recognize a *person's* value without actually valuing her, and by extension, her interests—for instance, by counting it against an action that it would be bad for her.[1]

The interest thesis plays an important if implicit role in popular discourse about discrimination. For example, after a series of incidents in which police officers and private citizens have been acquitted (or not indicted) for the killings of black men in the United States, many activists have embraced a unifying exhortation in their organizing and protest: "Black Lives Matter."[2] That message stresses that the fates of black people are too often treated as though they were of little normative significance. It suggests an understanding of respect for people's equal value that centers on the *weight afforded to their interests*—the extent to which they are taken to *matter*—rather than on, say, correct and incorrect beliefs about their moral worth.

If we accept the interest thesis, it follows that Adam's action fails to respect Fatima as a person even if he does not discount her interests because of some malignant belief about people of Arab descent. The reason is that the difference between Fatima and Christopher to which he is responding simply does not, in fact, override her presumptive entitlement to equal concern.

Some differences between people may well override that presumption. I take it that our attachments to particular people—to those we love, or to whom we bear special obligations, or whose projects we have adopted as our own—not only justify but sometimes demand partiality.[3] What is disrespectful of Fatima is not the bare fact of discounting her interests, then, but doing so for no good reason.

It is natural to object here that the conceptual machinery of respect turns out to do no work in our indictment of Adam's discrimination. And it is true that it does not do all the work. In particular, it does not satisfy our need for a theory of when and why personal attachments give rise to special permissions and obligations with genuine normative force, for a theory of desert, and so forth. But it does do *some* work. The requirement of respect for Fatima—and in particular for the claim to presumptively equal consideration that is rooted in her equal value—is what sets the baseline of impartiality from which various differences may or may not warrant deviation.

Put another way, we can think of the requirement of respect that is operative here as a moralized version of the Principle of Insufficient Reason. It dictates how we must weigh people's interests in the absence of reasons to weigh them in any way in particular. As Harry Frankfurt writes, "it is the moral importance of respect and hence of impartiality... that constrains us to treat people the same when we know nothing that provides us with a special reason for treating them differently."[4]

If I am begging a question, then, it is this: Why is race not itself relevant to determining how much concern Adam owes Fatima and Christopher respectively? But this is a question we should be content to beg. There is simply no reason to think that Fatima's race *does* warrant discounting her interests. The point of the respect requirement I have been describing is to insist on the need to justify partiality on any given basis. That is the upshot of saying that people have, as beings of equal value, a presumptive claim to equal consideration. And nobody has made any sign of meeting that burden in the context of race. As Paul Brest says:

The most pernicious feature of racial prejudice and discrimination is their underlying premise that members of some racial groups are less worthy than members of others. The antidiscrimination principle holds that this assumption is fallacious because race has no moral salience.[5]

The first thought—that the premise of core cases of wrongful discrimination is a judgment of differential worth—can be understood narrowly or broadly. I have just suggested that it should be understood broadly, as concerning the weight we afford to people's interests—our revealed preferences if you like—rather than simply an explicit judgment of comparative value. But the second point applies either way: race has no salience with respect to either a person's intrinsic worth or the correlative concern one presumptively owes her.

Before proceeding, it is important to distinguish the view I am suggesting here from another line of thought that might sound similar. In particular, one might explain the wrongness of core cases of wrongful discrimination by appealing *directly* to an agent's failure to act only on the basis of morally relevant differences between people—that is, without taking these differences as possible justifications for the differential concern that motivates some discrimination. This is what Patrick Shin calls the "*relevant-difference* view of the substantive requirement of equal treatment."[6]

In criticizing this view, Shin offers the example of "an employer [who] decides to hire Benson but not Johnson for a position as a tollbooth operator because Benson graduated first in his class from Harvard, whereas Johnson graduated second."[7] Shin notes that this does not seem to constitute a relevant difference between Benson and Johnson relative to the decision at hand, but that nonetheless Johnson seems to lack a moral claim of "unequal treatment" against the employer. Nor, in our terminology, does the act seem to manifest disrespect for Johnson as a person. But I think this example has little intuitive pull against the way we are appealing to the notion of relevant differences in analyzing respect for persons. For if the employer chose Benson over Johnson because she valued Benson's *welfare* more heavily than Johnson's, and she did that because of their relative standing at Harvard—which is plainly not relevant to the concern their interests are owed—this would indeed seem to be a wrong of the kind involved in many cases of wrongful discrimination.

It is also important to be clear about the ways in which the disrespect-based objection to discrimination from differential concern does and does not depend on the effects of the discrimination. Fundamentally, the objection does not depend on them. We can suppose that Adam would have chosen Christopher even if he weighed the interests of both candidates impartially. Nonetheless, Adam wrongs Fatima in making his decision as he does, because he treats her disrespectfully. As Frankfurt writes:

Failing to respect someone is a matter of ignoring the relevance of some aspect of his nature or his situation. The lack of respect consists in the circumstance that some important fact about the person is not properly attended to or is not taken appropriately into account. In other words, the person is dealt with as though he is not what he actually is.[8]

This captures an important aspect of what is objectionable about Adam's treatment of Fatima—she is treated as though she is of less value than Christopher—and it is an intrinsic feature of that treatment.

In what way *does* the objection rest on consequences, then? If Adam disrespects Fatima in making his decision, that is wrong irrespective of whether she is injured. But whether he commits that offense in the first place is itself determined in part by the predictable consequences of his decision for Fatima's interests: he disrespects her *by* giving less than equal weight to her interest in having one set of consequences obtain rather than another.

This raises the question what respect demands regarding how we *judge* people's interests in various states of affairs. Thus far, that is, I have been treating the discriminator's perceptions of the interests of each discriminatee as given. I stipulated, for instance, that Adam takes getting the job to be equally in Christopher's interest and in Fatima's interest. But what if Adam disfavors Fatima because he does not recognize *that* Fatima has as strong an interest in getting the job as Christopher does—and what if that in turn is traceable to the ethnic differences between them?

Choosing Christopher for this reason may not be disrespectful of Fatima, since it may be consistent with both recognizing her value and regarding the satisfaction of her interests (whatever they are) as just as important as the satisfaction of Christopher's. But there is a second-order issue here as well. Genuinely taking the fulfillment of Fatima's interests (as a class) as valuable will normally mandate a measure of effort to empathize with her as necessary in order to identify these interests, and their magnitudes, with reasonable accuracy. For one cannot bring about the satisfaction of someone's interests without knowing what they are, and valuing a person's interests (as a class) means taking their satisfaction as a goal, or a reason for action. Thus while it is not *necessarily* disrespectful to disfavor someone in the allocation of some scarce good because one takes his interest in it to be weaker than another person's—even if one is mistaken in this judgment, and even if this mistake is rooted in a failure to adequately empathize with people unlike oneself—one may act disrespectfully by failing to make a serious effort to ascertain a person's interests accurately, at least where one knows one's choice is liable to affect him.

4.2 Degrees of Recognition

We now have the basic structure of a disrespect-based theory of wrongful discrimination, as it applies to cases of differential concern, on the table. Much of what is important about it, however, comes out in comparisons with alternative possibilities. In this section and the next, I juxtapose my view with several others and introduce important refinements to the theory that flow from these comparisons.

First, and most simply, the emphasis I have placed on discounting a person's interests here recalls J.L.A. Garcia's theory of racism as "racially based disregard for the welfare of certain people."[9] Indeed, Garcia speaks of racism as "essentially a form of racially focused ill-will or disregard (including disrespect)."[10] My proposal reverses the conceptual priority of these two notions, however.[11] Discrimination is intrinsically wrong if it is disrespectful of the personhood of the discriminatees, and one central *form* of such disrespect—though not the only one—is unwarranted disregard for a person's interests or welfare. This reversal is key to developing a unified account of core cases of wrongful discrimination, for it is this shared foundation in disrespect that is common to discrimination arising from disregard for welfare and other paradigm cases, including those which rest on certain kinds of group generalizations.

Some understand the moral objection to discrimination from differential concern as rooted in disrespect, but understand the relevant kind of disrespect in turn as necessarily involving a defamatory belief about a person's equal value as a person. Larry Alexander thus suggests that:

When a person is judged incorrectly to be of lesser moral worth and is treated accordingly, that treatment is morally wrong regardless of the gravity of its effects. It represents a failure to show the moral respect due the recipient, a failure which is by itself sufficient to be judged immoral.... [B]iases premised on the belief that some types of people are morally worthier than others are intrinsically morally wrong because they reflect incorrect moral judgments.[12]

Matt Cavanagh likewise suggests, in somewhat different terms, that discrimination is wrongful when it "expresses unwarranted contempt," and that whether an instance of discrimination does that depends on whether it "is based on some theory about the 'moral worth' of" the discriminatees.[13]

As Kasper Lippert-Rasmussen has argued in criticizing disrespect-based accounts of wrongful discrimination, a belief-based view of this kind entails implausible judgments in certain cases.[14] Consider, for instance, painful and inessential experimentation on non-human animals for the benefit of humans. Specifically, Lippert-Rasmussen suggests, compare two cases:

(*Inegalitarian Belief*) a person engages in this practice believing that non-human animals are of lesser moral status than humans; and

(*Egalitarian Belief*) a person engages in this practice believing that non-human animals and humans are of equal status.

Suppose, moreover, that as a matter of fact non-human animals and humans are of equal status, and that the person in Inegalitarian Belief, though mistaken in this regard, comes by his belief honestly and reasonably, rather than on account of some defect of character or lack of epistemic virtue. Intuitively it seems that what the correctly informed person in Egalitarian Belief does is no better, morally speaking, than what the misinformed person in Inegalitarian Belief does. Thus, Lippert-Rasmussen argues,

> it follows that discrimination cannot be bad simply because it reflects an incorrect judgement of moral status. For if it were bad for this reason, the presence of the incorrect judgment [in Inegalitarian Belief] would make the act worse.[15]

This argument does appear to seriously undermine the view that it is only the possession of a certain belief about a person's moral worth or status that makes suitably related cases of discrimination intrinsically objectionable.

On my view, by contrast, discrimination is intrinsically wrong when and because it manifests a certain kind of failure of recognition. That failure to recognize someone as a person of equal value as others *may* be expressed in a belief or cognitive judgment that has a mis-estimate of her value as its content. Whatever you believe, however, the interest thesis implies that respecting someone as a being of equal value also entails *responding to* her status as a bearer of interests with presumptively equal normative weight. And to act consistently with what that presumption requires—to actually succeed in respecting it—it is not enough to reason in good faith. Your deliberation and action must actually track the relevant moral facts.

This requirement in turn yields a very different take on Lippert-Rasmussen's examples. For if non-human animals are of the same moral value as humans, there is grave disrespect in *giving* their interests much less weight in one's practical deliberation than the interests of humans—not simply in *believing*, as a matter of informal moral theory, that their interests deserve less weight. This moral fault in a person's process of decision, however, is apparently common to the agents in both variants of the animal experimentation case. We are told that the agent in Egalitarian Belief believes that humans and non-human animals possess equal value or moral standing, but we are not told that he actually gives their interests equal weight—and the fact that he goes ahead with the experiment presumably suggests that he does not. Put differently, Lippert-Rasmussen's attempt at a controlled comparison, isolating the moral significance of an incorrect judgment of moral worth, fails if the relevant judgment is understood as constituted by taking certain considerations as reasons for certain kinds of acts, rather than as simply a propositional attitude.*

This response is a good start, I think, but it is not entirely satisfying. Thanks to the interest thesis, my account explains what is disrespectful about the agent's action in Egalitarian Belief, even though he does not underestimate the value of the beings whose welfare he discounts. But it does not explain why what the agent does in Egalitarian Belief does not at least appear *better* than what the agent does in Inegalitarian Belief. For even if we accept the interest thesis, it still seems that discrimination rooted in an outright denial of people's value, of the sort involved in classic bigotry, shows more profound disrespect than the simple failure to satisfy someone's presumptive claim to equal consideration. If that is so, then we should apparently regard the action in Inegalitarian Belief as worse than the action in Egalitarian Belief; but I agree with Lippert-Rasmussen that this is at odds with the intuitive view of these cases. Can the theory we are developing cast light on this discrepancy?

The explanation, I think, requires us to distinguish among forms or degrees of misrecognition. Take the ideas of disrespect and contempt. Although these are sometimes treated as synonymous, that may be a

---

* The disrespect in this case cannot be disrespect for the animals' standing *as persons*, since they are not persons. It might simply be described as disrespect for their value. It is still evidently a case of wrongful discrimination: it is discrimination per the account in Chapter 1, and it is wrong, independent of its effects, in virtue of the disrespect for the animals' value. This means that disrespect for certain attributes other than personhood can suffice for intrinsically wrongful discrimination. Disrespect for persons may be only a special case, then, although it is the case with which we are primarily concerned. One reason for posing the theory in these narrower terms, despite the option to generalize it, is that not all of the failures of recognition that can constitute disrespect for persons could apply to non-persons, as I argue in Chapter 5.

mistake. One of the distinctive features of the notions of respect and disrespect is that they are jointly exhaustive, at least as applied to cases where you owe something respect. You disrespect something in such a case simply by not respecting it, so you cannot neither respect nor disrespect it. But while contempt is closely related to disrespect, it does not seem to share this feature. You do not show contempt for something whenever you fail to respect it as you should. Rather, contempt has a more positive aspect. In particular, contempt seems to involve a refusal to respect something—a kind of defiance of what you at some level realize its significance to be.

Whether an agent makes such a refusal depends on her mode of engagement with the reasons for respecting something. To show contempt for something is, roughly, to see these reasons and yet refuse to acknowledge their authority. Thus, in the law, criminal contempt of court ordinarily requires *willful* disobedience of a court order.[16] Many bigots act out of contempt in a similar way—spurning the normative authority of the claims to equal consideration made by the equal personhood of some persons. Indeed, contrary to some of our earlier discussion, it is too charitable to think of most textbook racists as simply holding false beliefs about the value or moral status of those whom they disfavor. Some cases may be like that: white people coming to the Americas for the first time could—perhaps— have simply failed to recognize the phenotypically novel human beings they encountered as persons of equal value. But it seems far more common that racists *repudiate* the equal personhood of those they disfavor than that they simply fail to grasp it. To take an extreme case, the genocidaires in Rwanda clearly did not *mistake* Tutsis for the evaluative equivalents of cockroaches, in anything like the normal sense of a mistake. Rather, they chose to treat them *as if* they were. Similarly, Jonathan Glover documents at length the strenuous efforts the Nazis undertook to "den[y] any moral standing to their victims" by "*convinc*[ing] themselves that there was no dignity there to respect."[17]

Such contempt is still a form of disrespect for the standing as persons of its victims—a failure of recognition, in the sense of a failure to pay appropriate heed. But it actually necessitates recognition in a thinner, more cognitive sense: you can only show contempt for something that you recognize, in a minimal way, to make a normative claim on you, which you then go on to willfully reject.

Consider, then, the puzzle left hanging above. It seems plausible that acting on the belief that some people are of lesser value as persons is morally worse than acting on a simple failure to respond to that value appropriately, but, in Lippert-Rasmussen's examples, what the agent does in Inegalitarian Belief does not seem worse than what the agent does in Egalitarian Belief. The answer, I think, is that the first thought is actually mistaken. When we endorse it, we are tacitly supposing that the judgment of inferior value involves contempt, whereas the failure to act in the manner that respect for a person's value requires involves only simple disrespect. It is this distinction, not the distinction between actions rooted in false beliefs about value and actions that simply do not respect it, that is fundamental.

In other words, it is especially bad to deny or refuse to recognize people's value as persons, as compared to simply *failing* to recognize it. But the recognition in question is not specially connected to beliefs one forms about a being's moral status. It is especially bad to contemptuously refuse to acknowledge a person's value in the abstract, as compared to simply failing to do so; and it is especially bad to contemptuously refuse to weigh her value appropriately in one's practical deliberation, as compared to simply failing to do so.

So my theory need not hold that, contrary to appearances, what the agent in Inegalitarian Belief does is worse than what the agent in Egalitarian Belief does. The agent in Inegalitarian Belief misestimates the value of non-human animals, but his judgment is rooted in a good-faith mistake concerning the value of a class of beings about which there at least remains debate. Unlike in many cases in which people take some persons to be of inferior value, there is no contemptuous denial of the animals' worth; and that is why his action is not worse than the action in Egalitarian Belief. Indeed, perhaps the agent's action in Egalitarian Belief is worse than the agent's action in Inegalitarian Belief. That could be because the action in Egalitarian

Belief, unlike the action in Inegalitarian Belief, *is* contemptuous: it involves a knowing refusal to take account of the moral standing of the animals, in the face of a minimal sort of recognition of it.

It may help to take a step back and summarize here. One difference between my theory and views like Alexander's is that, by virtue of the interest thesis, mine implies that the agent in Egalitarian Belief acts disrespectfully. However, it might seem that a disrespect-based theory should at least regard Inegalitarian Belief as *worse* than Egalitarian Belief, since Inegalitarian Belief involves an apparently more fundamental or direct denial of the animals' value or standing. I have argued that we should reject that imputed commitment. What is especially bad, rather, is contempt—which can inhere in judgments about a creature's value and in practical failures to value it alike, and which is not present in either form in Inegalitarian Belief.

Given the focus of this chapter, I have introduced the distinction between ordinary disrespect and contempt in the specific context of respect for a person's equal value (and the presumption of equal concern for her interests that this involves). But it is important to bear in mind that it marks a general cleavage in the modes of misrecognition or disrespect—cutting across the various possible objects of this attitude. In many cultures, gender-based disrespect, for instance, involves condescension that is better understood as showing disrespect for women's standing as independent reflective agents—that is, for their autonomy—than for the equal value of their well-being as such.[18] Such condescension, too, could be classified as contemptuous in some cases and not in others.[19] I will turn to exploring the requirements of respect for a person's autonomy in the next chapter.

4.3 Differential Concern, Implicit Bias, and Animus

The distinction between disrespect and contempt suggests another advantage of the present account over belief-centered views. There is a growing consensus that much discrimination against stigmatized groups in contemporary liberal societies now stems from implicit bias rather than from malice or conscious calculation.[20] Because it operates below the level of consciousness, such bias is widespread even among people who may honestly profess strong egalitarian commitments. Summarizing this diverse body of research as it bears on racial bias, Tamar Gendler concludes that "[e]ven among those who are explicitly and sincerely committed to anti-racism, the legacy of having lived in a society structured by hierarchical and hostile racial divisions retains its imprint."[21] Although the important question of how to understand and reckon with this cultural inheritance is not my main focus here, an account of the paradigm cases of wrongful discrimination ought to at least lay a foundation for the conceptual extensions that this body of research demands.

Suppose, then, that someone is less moved by the interests of one class of people, despite the absence of relevant differences between members of this group and others, and discriminates against them as a result. To take an everyday example, consider again the study finding that black pedestrians waiting to use a crosswalk in Portland, Oregon, were ignored by passing cars nearly twice as often as white pedestrians were.[22] To determine the intrinsic moral status of this kind of discrimination, a belief-based account requires us to inquire into whether the discriminators believe or judge that members of the disfavored group are of inferior moral worth and act on that belief.[23] Alexander thus concludes that, in part because "unconscious 'judgments' are judgments in only an extended metaphorical sense," he is "unable to reach any firm conclusion on the matter of . . . unconscious biases."[24]

Because my account does not locate the intrinsic wrongness of discrimination from differential concern exclusively in beliefs or cognitive judgments about a person's moral status, it does not face this difficulty in making sense of discrimination that is motivated by differential concern of which one is unaware. For whatever the discriminators in the case I just described believe or consciously judge, it remains the case that, in Frankfurt's phrase, "some important fact about the [disfavored] person is not properly attended to or is not taken appropriately into account."[25] What is not taken fully into account is just what *is* apparently taken into account in the case of a white pedestrian—the value of the pedestrian's interests, as reflected in the reason for stopping one's car that these interests spin off. Not to value his interests equally is, *ceteris paribus*, not to respect his equal value. In this way a moral requirement of respect, understood as I have proposed, imposes an affirmative duty of recognition—a duty one can fail to execute just as well by unconscious oversight as by conscious repudiation.

At the same time, it is true that unconscious bias of this kind will not involve *contempt*. This, I think, explains why it is likely to strike us as comparatively less objectionable. But it will still involve disrespect for persons. In other words, the agent is not responding aright to the moral reasons given by the equal personhood of the members of the disfavored class—but neither is he willfully repudiating or disobeying those claims. A virtue of the account is thus that it furnishes an explanation of both what is common to conscious and implicit biases and what is not.

Philosophical discussions of implicit bias have tended to approach these issues from a different direction—leaving the badness of the relevant sorts of discrimination assumed and unanalyzed, and focusing instead on questions of moral responsibility, blameworthiness, and character. To be responsible for one's biases, it seems, one must be aware of them (or else willfully blind to them), and one must be able to control them.[26] The proper specification of each of these conditions poses difficult issues, and the empirical research bearing on whether each condition might be satisfied by typical implicit biases is subtle and uncertain. Thus, for example, Alex Madva argues that people *are* often phenomenally conscious of even "implicit" biases, although these biases are not always reflectively accessible. That is, the biases "may often be *felt* without being *noticed*, just as a person can be in a grumpy or lighthearted mood without noticing as much."[27] Drawing on this analogy to moods, Madva argues that, in both cases, phenomenal awareness suffices to justify reactive attitudes of blame based on actions stemming from one's state. In parallel, Jules Holroyd and Daniel Kelly argue that implicit biases are subject to the requisite sort of *control* for responsibility as well, because "ecological control"—roughly, the ability to manipulate one's environment in ways that in turn shape one's thinking, such as through debiasing techniques—can suffice for the kind of control relevant to character judgments.[28]

My proposed distinction between disrespect and contempt is related to but distinct from these important lines of inquiry. What makes a discriminatory act wrong on non-instrumental grounds, I have suggested, is often that it effectuates a failure of recognition for the moral equality of the disfavored person. And action of this kind seems to be morally worse when it involves a kind of willful repudiation—what I have termed "contempt"—rather than disregard stemming from even culpable obliviousness or recklessness. Questions about conscious awareness and control are important to understanding this distinction, but the issue takes a different form here than in the context of questions about responsibility. Whereas the distinctive questions about responsibility and blame posed by implicit biases center on how one relates to one's own attitudes, the disrespect/ contempt distinction turns on how one relates to *the moral reasons one fails to heed*. Thus, as in the first of the animal-experimentation cases above, a person might be fully aware of her bias against some class, but guilty of only ordinary disrespect and not contempt because she does not recognize, in even a minimal way, their moral claim to equal consideration. On the other hand, because contempt involves willful disregard for certain reasons or claims, one cannot act out of contempt without both awareness that one is doing so and a kind of control over this refusal. Contempt, unlike ordinary disrespect, thus involves a form of self-awareness as well as an awareness of reasons. It follows that discrimination that manifests contempt, unlike that which manifests ordinary disrespect, may almost never be blameless.[29]

In this section and the last one, I have identified some advantages to a disrespect-based account of wrongful discrimination that understands disrespect as a feature of the agent's reasons for action rather than as a kind of cognitive judgment about another's moral worth. It is important to be clear about the costs that come with these apparent advantages as well. Indeed, there is a difficult theoretical trade-off here that confronts any account of wrongful discrimination grounded in the duty of respect for persons. After all, "cognitive" views like Alexander's can furnish a direct and compelling explanation for cases of benign differential concern. As Alexander says, my partiality toward my family does not rest on a judgment that those who are disfavored are of less intrinsic worth; they are simply worth less *to me*.[30] I cannot put this distinction to work in the same way, since disrespect for someone's value as a person, according to the interest thesis, is not limited to cases in which one explicitly takes a person to be of lesser intrinsic worth. On the contrary, treating some people's well-being as worth less *to me*—that is, as of less reason-giving force in my practical deliberation—is the precise lapse of recognition respect at issue.

It may be helpful to think of the difference here in the following way. Belief-centric views create a space for permissible partiality by effectively hemming in what respect demands, and in a categorical way. If you do not act on the judgment that someone is of inferior worth, there is no disrespect.[31] Special concern for our friends and families fits comfortably in the space that this move opens up, since these attachments do not involve judgments of relative intrinsic worth. But less benign forms of partiality will seize on that opening as well: unreflective biases in favor of people superficially like oneself, for instance, which also involve no judgment of differential intrinsic worth.

By contrast, my approach is not to hem in the moral requirement, but to emphasize its relative weakness or defeasibility across the board. The claim to equal consideration is taken to apply uniformly, that is, independent of an agent's beliefs about anybody's intrinsic worth. But we recognize the requirement as only a presumption, because there is more to morality than respecting people's equal value as persons. Genuine personal attachments, for instance, are of normative significance in their own right, and there is no disrespect in acting consistently with what they allow or demand.

This strikes me as a plausible resolution, but it gives my view an undeniable buck-passing aspect. We will not know whether a case of discrimination from differential concern manifests disrespect until we know whether it is responsive to attachments of bona fide normative significance, valid claims of desert, and so forth. As I suggested above, this cost is mitigated somewhat by the fact that the jury is not really out on all such possibilities. Paradigm cases of wrongful discrimination are ones in which the claim that one's relationship to a group grounds special duties or permissions to favor co-members— fellow white people, or straight people, and so forth—can be dismissed as frivolous.[32]

An alternative theory posited by Richard Arneson helps to fill out this contrast.[33] Crudely, the view that Arneson develops is similar to belief-based views in insisting upon a certain positive mental impetus, but it identifies this special factor as a kind of aversive attitude rather than a cognitive judgment of status. Setting aside discrimination arising from culpably defective generalizations, to be considered later, Arneson argues that discrimination is intrinsically wrongful only when it arises from unwarranted animus, which he understands as "hostility, or, more broadly, a negative attitude, an aversion."[34] This conception of animus is much narrower than my understanding of disrespect, so the theories yield different prescriptions. That is reflected in the fact that animus, as Arneson construes it, is fundamentally asymmetric or directional: partiality towards the interests of whites does not necessarily imply animus towards blacks, for instance.

Arneson's account is thus vulnerable to a version of the charge, also advanced by Lippert-Rasmussen against disrespect-based accounts, that it cannot explain the wrongness of discrimination that is undertaken out of special concern for a preferred group. The reason a disrespect-based account lacks the resources to condemn such discrimination, Lippert-Rasmussen says, is that "being excessively respectful of some people does not entail being disrespectful of others."[35] Similarly, in Arneson's case, being especially sensitive to the interests of some people does not imply animus or hostility towards others.

Arneson recognizes this implication, and simply accepts that there is often "no deontological case for holding racial partiality to be intrinsically morally wrong."[36] He casts this feature of his view as a virtue, because it explains the permissibility of certain cases of ostensibly benign group-based partiality. In particular, Arneson offers a kind of racial solidarity among African Americans as one possible example of discrimination that is intrinsically unobjectionable because it does not arise from animus against others.[37]

Perhaps certain forms of racial solidarity are indeed morally unobjectionable. This judgment can be accommodated without surrendering as much ground as Arneson does, however. First, many manifestations of solidarity that do not involve animus do not involve disrespect either, so they are consistent with my view as well as with Arneson's. African Americans can find distinctive comfort and community in associating with other African Americans, for instance, without treating the interests of others as less weighty, or otherwise failing to give due consideration to something important about the standing of others as persons.[38]

To the extent that solidarity among African Americans *does* involve true partiality or bias, it is significant, I think, that there is something closer to a genuine African-American community in the United States than there is to a white community. This is in part the natural consequence of minority status, and in part the result of group-oriented injustice, which tends to cement the significance of membership in the group for its members, encourages the group to develop internal institutions to which members can turn for support, and so on. It would take a good deal more argument to draw a firm conclusion about this case. But it is possible, at least, that attachments within such a community can justify partiality in the same way that attachments to one's family, neighbors, or co-nationals might do. By contrast, the notion of a white community in the United States seems to be a fiction invented precisely in order to justify racial partiality, rather than an extant network of special attachments that might, inter alia, justify differential concern for fellow members.[39]

In any case, an animus-based view like Arneson's is committed to accepting partiality in many cases where the rationales I have described are not available. If a white person is simply more sensitive to the needs and interests of white people, and acts accordingly, Arneson's account will often ground no objection to what she does (independent of the act's possible contingent effects). This constitutes a significant failure of fit in capturing the fixed points of pre-theoretical common sense. Moreover, in a recent theoretical review summarizing several bodies of psychological research, Anthony Greenwald and Thomas Pettigrew conclude that we should understand "ingroup favoritism as not just *a* cause but as the *prime* cause of American discrimination."[40] It is also noteworthy, therefore, that an animus-based view would imply that a very large share of the discrimination against disadvantaged groups in the United States today is at most contingently bad.

Unlike Arneson, however, I can simply reject Lippert-Rasmussen's claim that disrespect-based accounts of wrongful discrimination must recognize a moral asymmetry between bias against one group and bias in favor of another. In my earlier example, for instance, I take it that Adam's extra concern for Christopher and his interests, simply because of his race, is itself disrespectful of Fatima. Perhaps Lippert-Rasmussen would say that by favoring Christopher Adam only does something "in which disrespect is implicit," or that disrespect of Fatima is only a "logical implication[] of his judgment" about (or treatment of) Christopher—leaving a disrespect-based theory no basis for criticizing Adam.[41] But on the account of disrespect I have put forward, disrespect need not consist in a belief or an occurrent sentiment, and it is not necessarily transparent to its subject. Rather, at its core, the moral requirement of respect is a regulative principle mandating that certain considerations enter into one's practical deliberation in certain ways—a mandate that Adam does not obey, whether because he hates Fatima or because he simply can't be troubled to attend to her interests.

Thus far, my exposition of the disrespect account has focused on cases in which people or their interests are valued at different weights for reasons that do not track morally relevant differences. In the next section, I argue that disrespect also captures the central intrinsic moral concern about discrimination motivated by certain other kinds of preferences.

4.4 Preferences

Clearly not all discrimination is motivated by differential concern for the interests of different people. What if Adam decides to simply promote the applicant he would prefer to work with, and he prefers the prospect of working with Christopher because Christopher is white? Or what if Adam decides to promote whomever he predicts will do the best job, and his prediction is influenced by his general belief that white people work harder than others? An important virtue of a disrespect-based account of wrongful discrimination is that disrespect can be predicated of many sorts of things, including not only differential concern, but also other judgments and preferences.[42] But how do we determine when these constitute or manifest disrespect for someone as a person?

We should first distinguish between two different kinds of preferences that sometimes give rise to discrimination. Following Ronald Dworkin, we can call these "personal" and "external" preferences.[43] I might discriminate against immigrants in hiring because I will have to work with whomever I hire, and I'd rather not have to work with immigrants. Or I might discriminate against immigrants in hiring because I prefer, in the abstract, that immigrants not be hired for jobs also sought by others. The latter is an external preference—a preference with respect to how things stand with other people, independent of any direct bearing of those different possibilities on oneself.[44]

We can consider discrimination motivated by external preferences first. Conveniently, many such cases simply constitute discrimination from differential concern in a different guise. If I discriminate against immigrants in hiring because I prefer that the available jobs go to natives, for instance, this preference may simply be a consequence of my greater concern for the interests of natives. Then the relevant moral question about the discrimination is simply whether the underlying discrepancy in concern constitutes a failure to recognize the equal value as persons of immigrants, as discussed above. If the discrepancy does constitute such a failure, then the discrimination is disrespectful, and no novel issue is introduced by casting the discriminator's preference as its motivating reason.

On the other hand, my external preference that the jobs in question go to natives rather than immigrants might not reflect differential concern for their interests. I could prefer this state of affairs, for instance, because I worry about the political backlash that immigrants will face if natives come to feel that immigrants are responsible for their joblessness, as will happen if certain high-profile jobs go to immigrants rather than natives. In this case I discriminate against immigrants in hiring because of an external preference that does not reflect differential concern.

Such discrimination motivated by external preferences is often disrespectful in other ways. Preferences about who holds what roles in society, for instance, represent one important class of external preferences that need not reflect differential concern. At the extreme, some people think it is better that women not pursue careers.[45] That is compatible in principle with valuing their interests at equal weight relative to the interests of men: such a preference could reflect a particular view about what *is* in women's interests, or it could be rooted in what one takes to be a distinct moral imperative, independent of anybody's interests. Nevertheless, it certainly seems plausible that discrimination undertaken to satisfy such a preference manifests disrespect for women as persons. A business school would seem to show disrespect for the moral standing of women if it rejected their applications out of a preference that women not pursue careers in business, for example.

To press this example, let us suppose that it is presumptively morally permissible for a business school to pursue its own conception of the kind of graduate it wants to produce—including by admitting the students who best further that mission—even if its mission is ultimately misguided. What makes it specifically disrespectful for the school to exclude women, then? It is not the equal normative weight of their interests as such, for there may be no failure to grasp that equality here; indeed, there may be no weighing of the interests of the various candidates at all.

We cannot form a judgment about a case like this, I think, without investigating why the school's officials are committed to their ideology in the first place. In particular, if they view the gendered division of labor as proper because of certain demeaning or homogenizing beliefs about what women are like, their reliance on these beliefs may itself be disrespectful—an issue we will consider in the next chapter— and if so, that taint condemns the resultant discrimination as well. Many oppressive role ideologies will fall to some version of this objection to disrespectful generalizations about social groups.

In other cases, discrimination in the pursuit of role ideals disrespects a discriminatee's standing as a person more directly. Suppose, for instance, that someone interprets the biblical injunction of Ephesians 5:22—"Wives, be subject to your husbands, as to the Lord"—to mean that married women are not autonomous persons in their own right, but are rather fully bound by the moral authority of their husbands. If this person engages in discrimination against married women motivated by this belief, then that act, thickly described, obviously fails to recognize the equal standing of these women as persons. The motivating belief constitutes essentially a per se denial of that standing. The same would be true of a belief directly concerning women's value, rather than their autonomy. Simply put, then, discrimination undertaken in pursuit of role ideals is often disrespectful because, in one way or another, affirming the ideal itself manifests a failure to relate to some people in the manner required by respect.

There is an important second class of cases, however, in which disrespect may be found not in the preference itself, but in the pursuit of it. To take another example, suppose that someone prefers that only opposite-sex relationships be granted legal recognition. This may not be motivated by a desire on his part that people in such relationships be treated better than people in same-sex relationships, or a preference that one group have priority over the other in the division of some scarce good. Conceivably, his preference could also rest on no disrespectful generalizations about each class of relationships, or about the people who compose them. Perhaps tradition serves as a kind of exclusionary reason for this person: he thinks it better that same-sex relationships not be recognized simply because it has traditionally been thought better, not for the underlying reasons (presumably consisting of disrespectful judgments) for which it has traditionally been thought better.

That insulates discrimination he may commit against same-sex couples from the charge of disrespect on one front. It does not ensure that such discrimination is consistent with respect for people's equal value as persons, however. After all, having the preference is one thing. But *enforcing* the preference, despite the serious material and stigmatic harms it imposes on people in same-sex relationships, is itself disrespectful if, as seems likely, anyone who took such people's interests seriously would see the satisfaction of his own external preference as insufficient to justify that price.

I think this last objection has a good deal of explanatory power with respect to our intuitions about discrimination for the sake of furthering compliance with role ideals, although the case against such discrimination is more often made in terms of an attack on the ideals themselves. That latter approach can leave the proponent of discrimination an easy out, if not in public discourse then at least in private introspection. For a person can easily convince himself—without self-deception, even—that he affirms a role ideal because it is dictated by some tradition he takes as authoritative, and not on the grounds (which he can concede would be disrespectful) that critics assume.

For this reason it is worth seeing that, as I have just suggested, discrimination undertaken *in furtherance of* that ideal can itself show disrespect in a different way. At the extreme, traditionalists sometimes seem prepared to endorse discrimination that imposes serious harms on some in order to avoid states of affairs that strike them mainly as unseemly. As Alexander says, arguments for traditional gender roles, though put forward as moral ideals, "look suspiciously like aesthetic appeals."[46] Such efforts disrespect the value of those who are discriminated against because, either by design or by oversight, they do not treat the discriminatees' interests as being normatively significant.

A particularly extreme example of the dynamic I have in mind was offered a few years ago by Donald Trump, who was at the time a possible candidate for President of the United States. Trump described his opposition to legalizing same-sex marriage as follows:

It's like in golf... A lot of people — I don't want this to sound trivial — but a lot of people are switching to these really long putters, very unattractive.... It's weird. You see these great players with these really long putters, because they can't sink three-footers anymore. And, I hate it. I am a traditionalist. I have so many fabulous friends who happen to be gay, but I am a traditionalist.[47]

Trump's analysis is, of course, absurd, and I don't mean to disparage the arguments of others by equating them with his. Yet Trump's explanation does helpfully distill a certain defective way of thinking about discriminatory practices that is rarely articulated in so transparent a fashion. The problem with Trump's thinking is that—as he anticipates—his distaste for same-sex marriage *does* sound trivial. In other words, the manifest disrespect here lies in allowing the direction of one's practical influence on the lives of others to be settled directly by one's personal sensibilities, bypassing a serious weighing of the injury to those sensibilities against the expressed interests of others who are more gravely affected by the norm one seeks to enforce. Much discrimination in pursuit of role ideals shows disrespect for the equal value of others in this way—not because the ideal necessarily denies the equal value of some people, that is, but because action to effectuate the ideal, given the relative importance of the issue to different sets of people, is simply conceited or narcissistic.

Moreover, this objection will combine with the earlier one to put pressure on many external preferences from two sides. The less sheer or brute a preference about people's social roles is, the more likely it is to be discredited as disrespectful by virtue of its explanatory roots; but the shallower such a preference is, the more likely it is that a respectful agent could not regard its enforcement as sufficiently important to justify the imposition of significant costs on those whose opportunities would have to be restricted in its name. This dilemma will have less purchase, however, when the discriminator understands her preference as a weighty moral conviction: for then she could plausibly reason that enforcement of it is justified despite the injury done to some people, even when that injury is accorded full weight.

There is no tidy resolution to the analysis of discrimination motivated by external preferences or role ideals to be found here. I think we have to settle for a patchwork of partially overlapping objections that may prove relevant in different cases. But I hope to have shown that the disrespect-based account has the conceptual resources to bring out many of the morally salient features of such cases and the intuitive concerns they raise.

Setting aside both external preferences and simple cases of differential concern, then, we are left with two possible sites of disrespect that often figure in an act of discrimination: (1) *personal* preferences for or against some kinds of contact with some kinds of people, and (2) beliefs that an individual is more likely to possess some trait because of an (imputed) aggregate tendency of a set of which he is a member. Because these are interrelated, it will help to think of them in terms of a two-by-two matrix, as depicted in Table 4.1.

In the remainder of this chapter, I will focus narrowly on the question raised by the lower-left cell of this table: When does discrimination motivated by a personal preference for or aversion to having certain kinds of relations with certain types of people, which is not based on a generalization, manifest disrespect? Can it be disrespectful to discriminate against someone because one simply prefers having as one's doctor (or dating, playing football with, etc.) a person who does or does not hold a given trait?

Suppose, for instance, that Michelle prefers to see a female gynecologist. She holds this preference not because of a generalization about male gynecologists—e.g., that they are unable to examine her

Table 4.1. Forms of preference- and generalization-based discrimination

	Personal preference	No personal preference
Generalization	Jane promotes Sarah rather than Bill because she prefers the prospect of working with Sarah to the prospect of working with Bill. She has this preference because she believes Sarah will be more considerate than Bill, and she believes that in part because Sarah is female.	Margaret votes to impose the death penalty on Alfred because she believes he is beyond rehabilitation, and she believes that in part because Alfred is African-American.
No generalization	Michelle chooses to see Dr. F rather than Dr. M as her gynecologist because Dr. F is female and Dr. M is male, and Michelle feels uncomfortable being examined by a male doctor.	

with professional detachment—but rather simply because of her own discomfort or self-consciousness when being examined by a man.[48] (In a sense her preference necessarily rests on a generalization about male gynecologists—that she reacts in a certain way to being examined by them—but that is naturally seen as a bit of self-knowledge on Michelle's part, not a belief about what the men are like.) This leads her to discriminate against male gynecologists, and in favor of female ones, based on sex. Does she thereby fail to respect anyone as a person?

I think she does not. For what is at issue here is not the weight Michelle gives to the interests of other people, but how she "spends" the weight properly given to her own interests; and within that sphere she does not fail to recognize the equal value of others by giving effect to her genuine preferences, whatever their consequences for their objects, unless the preferences are themselves somehow rooted in a denial of the value of the others. Put another way, no part of being a person is being desirable as a gynecologist, so Michelle does not reveal a failure to recognize a male doctor's standing as a person *simply* by failing to desire him as a gynecologist, even if that is because of his sex.

What would it take, then, for discrimination on the basis of a personal preference to constitute such a failure of recognition? Recall Arneson's suggestion that—setting aside reliance on certain kinds of generalizations—discrimination is intrinsically wrong only when it arises out of unwarranted animus. Although I argued above that this quality is not *necessary* for discrimination to be intrinsically wrongful, I do think that, suitably described, it is sufficient. While the interest thesis holds that respect for persons as beings of equal value imposes requirements on how we take account of their interests, it is not supposed to supplant the more basic requirement that we recognize people's value directly. Some preference-based discrimination manifests a failure to do that.

Hardcore racists, for instance, do not recognize the objects of their racism as beings of equal fundamental value as others, or perhaps even as beings of value at all. This failure of recognition is at the heart of such racists' various preferences against having contact with the people in question, whether in intimate relationships or by using a common drinking fountain. As such, a racist's acting to satisfy these preferences is not on a par with Michelle's acting to satisfy her preference about the sex of her gynecologist. The former, but not the latter, manifests an important failure of recognition for persons as such.

Nonetheless, it is now clear that, according to my account, discrimination on the basis of group-based personal preferences is often not disrespectful. We have identified two classes of situations that override that presumption of innocence: those in which a preference rests on a generalization that is itself disrespectful, and those in which a preference rests on a tacit or explicit denial of the value of certain people. But many cases, like Michelle's, may fall into neither of these categories.

This conclusion helps to explain our intuitive judgments about a wide range of cases in which people are apparently allowed to be "selfish"—or, equivalently, in which overriding concern for self-interest is not regarded as "selfish" at all. The choice of a gynecologist is one example of such a case, but there are many others. Choosing whom to date or marry, for instance, is not normally seen as a matter in which one must give much weight to the competing interests, in being chosen, of the various candidates for one's affection or commitment. Fittingly, these are also contexts in which group-based differential treatment that might be seen as wrongfully discriminatory in other settings—with respect to sex, most obviously, but also with respect to body-type, religion, and even race—are often seen as comparatively unproblematic. This makes a good deal of sense on my account. The prior judgment that intimate choices are primarily to be dictated by self-interest effectively sidelines the interest thesis. It foregrounds a sphere of deliberation in which discriminating along the lines in question—lines which are unlikely to ground morally relevant differences in the consideration owed to people's interests—is less likely to disrespect them.

This is an important result, for it is sometimes thought that the moral issues raised by social or intimate discrimination and by discrimination with respect to formal opportunities cannot be understood by appeal to the same theory. Glenn Loury, for instance, distinguishes "discrimination in contract" and "discrimination in contact," and suggests that "one is unlikely to find a single moral principle upon which to ground all judgments about the propriety of these two kinds of discrimination."[49] While I would not say that the disrespect account grounds *all* judgments about either of these kinds of discrimination, it does suggest that a theoretical integration is possible. The fact that we regard these kinds of discrimination differently may suggest not that they are governed by different principles, but that they are governed by common principles that are abrogated more regularly by one than by the other.

To be clear, I am not suggesting that "discrimination in contact" is always morally benign. There is undeniably something troubling about a person who simply prefers contact with people of one ethnic background, for instance, or avoids people of another one. This is reflected in the fact that we would see Michelle's conduct quite differently if she not only chose female gynecologists over male ones, but also chose white female gynecologists over non-white female ones. I think a good part of our unease about such a case is explained by the suspicion that either (1) this particular preference is an application of a wider preference against contact with less worthy or valuable people, with non-white people being taken to have this quality (a per se case of disrespect); or (2) the preference rests on a racial generalization about the qualities of the people in question, which may itself manifest disrespect.

But if in a particular case neither of those conditions obtained, I think we would have to acknowledge that our unease was unwarranted, at least to this extent: there does not seem to be anything *intrinsically* objectionable about a person allowing his intimate or social life to be shaped by an ethnic preference. To flesh out the example in a way that avoids both conditions, suppose that Michelle is a committed anti-racist, and that, precisely because she is immersed in the literature on implicit bias, she is exceedingly anxious about her behavior around black people. She obsesses about saying the wrong thing, blinking too little or too much,[50] and even about manifesting her own interracial anxiety, which she fears will be misunderstood as racism rather than anxiety about racism. Caught in this spiral of self-consciousness, and predisposed to anxiety already, she finds herself seeking to limit her contact with black people in high-stress situations, such as doctor's appointments.

Michelle's situation is perverse and she undoubtedly has reasons, including reasons of integrity, to work on controlling her own mental habits. But I don't think her aversion to having a black doctor involves any failure of recognition for the doctor as a person, and the disrespect-based theory thus suggests that her acting on this preference is not racist or otherwise wrong in itself. Although Michelle's situation is, in some ways, particularly sympathetic, the broader point is that the bare fact of preferring some kind of contact with people of one type or another is not ipso facto disrespectful. Many such preferences will reflect not a failure of moral recognition but rather more mundane patterns in how we have been socialized.

Crucially, we can acknowledge this while also recognizing that the social forces that constitute and channel private preferences are important objects of moral concern. Writ large, private discrimination has tremendous consequences for social stratification and economic inequality, because social capital is closely connected to material advantage and opportunity. Even the most intimate discrimination has important social consequences, for as Elizabeth Emens notes, "the intimate sphere is literally where we make the next generation."[51] Thus if members of an economically disadvantaged group are also dispreferred by others in the market for reproduction, this inequality is much more likely to be reproduced across generations even as formal barriers to opportunity may be lifted.[52]

So although it would be wrong, in my view, to regard someone who is more attracted to whites than non-whites as necessarily engaged in disrespectful or racist discrimination, it may indeed be *regrettable* that he has this preference. And there may be powerful reasons for doing what we can to ensure that such preferences do not align to the systematic disadvantage of certain classes of people. If people are generally attracted to others who are similar in appearance to those they grew up around, for instance, or simply are likely to end up with those very people, this knowledge should add to the moral urgency of efforts to promote school integration.[53] Similarly, if mass media portrayals of certain types of people as desirable are important in shaping our own preferences, then recognition of the moral consequences of private discrimination implies that those portrayals ought to be more diverse than they often are today. A similar line of thought, emphasizing the negative instrumental consequences of certain patterns of preferences, might be raised in some versions of the original gynecologist case as well—if, for instance, gynecologists were hired on a freelance basis, concordant discrimination in favor of female gynecologists threatened to drive some physicians out of business, and we saw that prospect as a serious form of unfairness or injustice. My point here, however, is simply that we can acknowledge the moral significance of these issues while also recognizing a fundamental moral discontinuity between those who engage in one or another form of disrespectful discrimination, which is intrinsically wrong, and those whose pursuit of their social or intimate preferences contributes to bad aggregate social results but manifests no failure of recognition on their parts.

4.5 Conclusion

Where have we gotten to thus far? I have suggested that often discrimination is morally troubling not simply because it gives rise to harm or unfairness, but because it manifests a form of basic disregard for the standing as persons of those who are discriminated against. This failure of recognition is not exhibited only by those who embrace a hostile ideology about some people's moral worth, or by those who are motivated by animus towards members of a particular group. No doubt disrespect of the fundamental kind I have described very often underlies these phenomena, which are also among its most harmful manifestations. But disrespect itself is more basic, and more widespread. It consists in the failure (or refusal) to take account of another person's standing as a person—including his equal intrinsic value, and the presumptive claim to equal consideration that it implies—in regulating one's behavior. This imperative of recognition helps to explain why discrimination from differential concern is often intrinsically objectionable—and also why purely preference-based discrimination often is not.

The disrespect theory is fundamentally incomplete, however, without an account of whether and when discriminating by appeal to a group generalization or stereotype manifests disrespect. Whereas we have focused on appreciation for a person's value thus far, I will argue that we cannot make sense of the morality of such discrimination without also attending to a second imperative grounded in respect for a person's standing as an individual autonomous agent. How to make sense of this idea, and what it ultimately demands, is the subject of the next chapter.

5

Respect for Individuality

Let me begin by recapping the argument of the last chapter. The intrinsic wrongness of paradigm cases of wrongful discrimination, I have been suggesting, is rooted in their failure to respect the standing of the discriminatees as persons. That is the source of the fervor of our condemnation of wrongful discrimination, in its core cases, even when it makes little or no difference to anybody's material or psychological well-being. We rightly perceive the discriminator as failing to regard and treat his victims in the way that persons ought to be regarded and treated. The core images of wrongful discrimination as dehumanizing capture the essence of this type of misrelationship; but it is present, in a more dilute form, in many other situations as well.

As we have seen, one paradigm of wrongful discrimination, and perhaps the most familiar one, involves differential concern for people's welfare. In these cases, some people are wrongly taken to matter less than others. In other cases, however, people discriminate on the basis of preferences and aversions that may not rest on differential concern. I have argued that in cases of differential concern, as well as in some other preference-based cases, the intrinsic wrongness of discrimination can be understood in terms of disrespect for the discriminatees considered as persons of *equal value*.

Equal value in this sense is one attribute of personhood, so failure to recognize it is one way of failing to fully recognize someone as a person. But it is not the only such attribute of personhood, so failing to respect someone's equal value is not the only way to fail to respect her as a person. Persons are also, in a morally important sense, autonomous individuals. In this chapter, I will argue that some discrimination is disrespectful of the victim's standing as a person not because it fails to treat her as a being of equal value as other persons, but because it fails to treat her as an individual autonomous being. This is an essential and distinct ingredient in a satisfying account of the morality of discrimination—particularly of discrimination on the basis of generalizations about social groups—but one that has more often been overlooked.

Indeed, even those who support a disrespect-based account of wrongful discrimination in cases of differential concern have tended to reduce the moral concern about generalization to a contingent worry about unfairness or some kind of social harm. Thus Larry Alexander, for instance, concludes that "irrational proxy discrimination, based upon inaccurate stereotypes or generalizations, is morally troublesome because it imposes unnecessary social costs."[1] Discrimination on the basis of accurate generalizations may be objectionable as well, he says, but primarily because it "may cause resentment and may reinforce biases and other inaccurate stereotypes."[2] Alexander does make an exception for generalization-driven discrimination that is "intimately linked" with judgments of differential moral worth, which he considers "intrinsically immoral."[3] Except for this special case, however—and setting aside the contingent harms of reliance on certain generalizations—there is nothing wrong per se about discriminating by appeal to any kind of generalizations about people.

By contrast, Richard Arneson suggests that generalization-based discrimination is sometimes intrinsically wrong, even if the generalizations in question are not themselves rooted in judgments of differential worth. But Arneson grounds this conclusion in "[o]ne's culpability with respect to the epistemic quality of the process by which one forms beliefs about people with whom one might interact or whose lives one's behavior might affect."[4] Accordingly, he views the possibility of "morally inappropriate attitudes...concerning those people" as simply one among several possible reasons why one's belief-forming processes could be culpably defective in epistemic quality.

Of course, I do not deny that discrimination on the basis of group generalizations is often troubling because it is connected to inaccuracy, unfairness, and harm. Moreover, these concerns are not outside the bounds of a disrespect-based account, since respect for a person requires one to take risks of harm or unfairness to him seriously. In addition, in many cases a selective willingness to employ indiscriminate (and typically negative) generalizations about one group of people reveals an attitude towards those people that is incompatible with fully recognizing them as beings of equal value.

I will argue, however, that these do not exhaust the grounds for judging generalization-based discrimination intrinsically wrong in many cases. For even when discrimination involves no failure to value people or their interests appropriately, it can fail to recognize them as autonomous individuals. We cannot fully map the distinct ways in which discrimination can show disrespect for persons without attending to this concern. Recognizing this distinct form of disrespect for persons is also significant because it suggests that, although discrimination necessarily involves inequality in one sense, a disrespect-based account of wrongful discrimination should not be framed in terms of disrespect *for* the moral equality of persons alone.*

I proceed as follows. First, in §5.1, I consider the explanatory power of the two straightforward reasons why discriminating on the basis of a generalization is sometimes wrong, mentioned already: because the generalization is itself rooted in a failure to recognize some people's equal value as persons, and because reliance on the generalization, in context, constitutes a wrongfully cavalier approach to the question at hand. I argue that both of these concerns are well founded, but that each has rather limited scope. As such, even together they do not

---

* It is possible that autonomy, or its value, partly *constitutes* the value of persons. In that case respect for persons, for my purposes, just involves recognition of their value, including this particular part thereof. That would fit nicely with Joseph Raz's suggestion that respect is "a species of recognising and being disposed to respond to value, and thereby to reason" (2001, 160). I won't pursue this extra claim, however: it is enough for our purposes to say that autonomy is something about persons recognition of which is required as a matter of respect.

plausibly capture the full range of intuitive grounds for objecting to discrimination on the basis of generalizations.

In §§5.2–5.4, I develop the suggestion that this is because recognition of someone's standing as a person requires, in some sense, that we treat her as an individual. This demands more than that we be epistemically conscientious in making decisions about her claims, or that we not deal with her on the basis of beliefs rooted in a failure to recognize her value. Although the principle that we ought to treat people as individuals is intuitively resonant, however, it is not clear what it actually means or requires.

To tackle this problem I outline an account of what it is to *be* an individual in the relevant sense, rooted in the literature on autonomy. From this I endeavor to derive an account of when and how the way one treats a person, by discriminating against her on the basis of a generalization, manifests a failure of recognition for this feature of her standing as a person. In short, I conclude that respecting a person's standing as an individual requires both (i) taking evidence of her autonomous choices seriously in forming judgments about her and (ii) making judgments about her likely behavior in a way that respects her capacity, as an autonomous individual, to choose how to act for herself. Discrimination on the basis of group generalizations is sometimes intrinsically wrong because it infringes one or both of these requirements.

5.1 Familiar Objections to Generalization

When and why is discriminating on the basis of a generalization—a belief that falling in some class is predictive of holding some trait—intrinsically objectionable? Sometimes this is wrong because the generalization is itself grounded in disrespect for some people. Regarding some people as beings of lesser value can certainly make it natural to believe that they also have various other properties that might legitimately make them less deserving of concern. Discrimination on the basis of beliefs formed this way makes manifest the underlying failure of recognition that contributes to explaining and sustaining the beliefs.

In addition, sometimes relying on generalizations does constitute a failure to give adequate attention to the accuracy of one's judgments, as Arneson suggests. Often we are obligated to make decisions about the merits of people's claims in a reasonably accurate or reliable way, commensurate with the importance of the determination to be made. Being unduly cavalier in such cases is morally objectionable, independent of the correctness of the judgments one ultimately reaches, because it constitutes a failure to take seriously the interests of the people whose claims one must adjudicate. As Scanlon writes:

> [P]rocedurally as it were,... [discriminatory] action can be wrong because the agent has not taken the steps needed to find and attend to the information that is relevant to making a correct decision. This fault is like a kind of recklessness, a failure to take due care.[5]

Importantly, for a judgment-forming procedure to be morally defective in this way, it need not involve the explicit invocation of unscrupulous inductive generalizations. Consider a school orchestra director who is more likely to admit Asian students to the orchestra than other students of the same objective ability level.[6] Perhaps the audition performances of Asian students simply seem better to him than they really are, because he is socially primed to associate Asian candidates with good performances. He may not consciously believe that Asian students are better musicians on average; indeed, depending on the proper analysis of belief, he may not believe it at all. Still, there is a defect in his decision-making procedure that yields unfairness. The extent to which his conduct is open to the objection we are considering, then, depends on what is at stake and on his capacity to be more conscientious.

In this case, it seems the director could correct for any inadvertent ethnic bias easily enough by having students audition behind a screen.[7] More broadly, psychological evidence suggests that simple training tasks can often make a difference in the extent to which we unconscientiously bring social heuristics to bear on judgments about individual people. In one study, for instance, experimental subjects who practiced responding "NO" to pairings of social categories and traits that are stereotypically associated with one another, and "YES" to the opposite sort of pairings, showed reduced automatic stereotyping in subsequent testing.[8] Similarly, subjects in another study who spent a few minutes crafting a mental image of a counter-stereotypic "strong woman"—contemplating "what a strong woman is like, why she is considered strong, what she is capable of doing, and what kinds of hobbies and activities she enjoys"—showed significantly less automatic gender stereotyping in a subsequent test.[9]

To the extent that these or other exercises prove efficacious, it would plainly be good for more people to perform them more often. Moreover, if those in positions to make consequential decisions where particular unconscious associations pose grave threats of harm or unfairness—jurors, police officers, academic assessors, and so on—fail to make a serious effort to disable or at least temper their bad cognitive habits, that could well constitute a failure to respect those affected. For example, failing even to try to correct for the known "shooter bias"—the greater tendency to perceive black males holding an ambiguous object as armed, and therefore to shoot at them[10]—may be a form of culpable disregard for the normative weight of their interests. Importantly, however, the argument here is not that the stereotypic associations are themselves somehow disrespectful, or that reliance on these generalizations in assessing individuals is objectionable as such, but rather that it is wrong not to take reasonable steps to ensure that important decisions affecting people are made accurately.

As a consequence, this objection cannot capture the concern many feel about decisions that rely on certain kinds of generalizations independent of their reliability. For example, David Miller has argued that it would be wrong for an employer to disfavor female job applicants because available statistics suggest that they are more likely than male counterparts to take parental leave. He writes:

A particular woman is not made less deserving because she happens to fall into a category of which it is true, *ex hypothesi*, that members have such-and-such a probability of reduced performance in the future.... [W]e cannot say of any particular woman we are considering for a position that she is liable to perform at a lower level because of a decision to have children. To make that assumption is to fail to treat her respectfully as an individual, and potentially to commit an injustice.[11]

If the employer's decision-making in this case is objectionable, it is not simply because his method of predicting performance is insufficiently reliable. The generalization about women and parental leave is, of course, highly imperfect. But the employer could come to equally unreliable predictions of performance for other reasons that would not occasion the same sort of objection. Suppose, for instance, that he simply fails to reflect in a serious way about which skills the job in question will actually require. That too would render his predictions of performance unreliable, but we would not object that he had failed to treat the candidates as individuals in choosing on the basis of his defective predictions.

Aside from the concern that some generalizations are themselves rooted in disrespect for people's equal value as persons, then, and aside from the concern that relying on some generalizations can constitute a generic kind of epistemic negligence, there is a distinct concern about the morality of discriminating on the basis of generalizations—to wit, that this fails, in some sense, to treat the discriminatees as individuals. I turn now to considering how we might develop and articulate this concern.

5.2 Treating People as Individuals

The idea that people ought to be treated as individuals is familiar but opaque.[12] Often it is taken to mean that we should not decide how to treat people on the basis of "statistical evidence," by which we mean beliefs about general classes in which we take a person to fall. That seems to be the idea underwriting Miller's objection in the parental leave case: he writes that he is proposing to exclude not "all probabilistic information about individuals, but only information that relates to the whole group or class to which someone belongs."[13]

It is difficult to specify this distinction in a rigorous way, however. As a contrasting example, Miller offers a decision to bench an "injury-prone sportsman who, for reasons specific to him, has a 10 percent chance of not being able to complete the game or the series." But surely this just means that, of competitors with the particular orthopedic condition that this person has, one in ten are injured if subjected to the relevant sort of strain. In other words, he "fall[s] into a category of which it is true, *ex hypothesi*, that members have such-and-such a probability of reduced performance in the future." What makes probabilistic information "relate to the whole group or class" in the case of female job applicants, but "specific to him" in the case of the sportsman?

Some have proposed answers to this question in the context of the legal admissibility of certain kinds of statistical evidence, and we will return to consider one such answer below. But outside the legal context, the idea that people should be treated as individuals in this sense has won few advocates in the philosophical literature, notwithstanding its rhetorical currency in the wider culture. Indeed, most of the philosophers who write about this idea at all set out to debunk it as an account of wrongful discrimination. Lawrence Blum, for example, suggests that the idea of treating people as individuals represents an "oft-cited account of the wrong of discrimination," but one that is "either misleading or false."[14] These skeptics note that the use of formal and informal statistical reference classes is simply a pervasive feature of social life. It does not seem plausible that so many apparently mundane practices constitute wrongful discrimination.[15]

If we want to give the intuitive idea of a moral requirement to treat people as individuals a charitable hearing, then, we should see if it can be understood in some other way. Lippert-Rasmussen has recently offered one "revisionist" account of this principle, according to which:

X treats Y as an individual if, and only if, X's treatment of Y is informed by all relevant information, statistical or non-statistical, reasonably available to X.[16]

Like Arneson's account of wrongful reliance on generalizations, however, this seems to reduce a concern about a very particular way of misrelating to another person to a much more general requirement of epistemic conscientiousness. If an agent fails to take account of some piece of statistical information about a person that is both relevant and reasonably available, we often would not describe that as a failure to treat anyone as an individual.

Here is an example. Suppose that the academic record of a child's older siblings (if he has any) is a significant predictor of his own academic achievement. Imagine, then, that the Achievement Academy is a school with competitive admissions, and that its guiding aim in selecting among applicants is to pick those who will be the most successful. Nonetheless, it gives no weight to the academic records of an applicant's older siblings in making decisions—even though in many cases the school has these records on hand, and they would contribute non-redundant information relative to the school's other metrics. Moreover, let us assume that the school's failure to consider this information is simply an oversight, not a consequence of a principled commitment of any kind.

Now suppose that a child is rejected despite his sister's record of achievement, and that he would have been accepted if that data point had been given its due statistical weight. Nonetheless, I think it would be bizarre for this applicant (or his parents) to complain that the school's procedure had failed to treat him as an individual. To be sure, if the applicants who are most qualified (as judged by all of the available evidence) have a claim on the available spots, then he has a claim that the school has failed to satisfy. This failure might be morally impeachable, insofar as it is traceable to negligence on the school's part. But whether or not there is a genuine issue here, it certainly does not seem to be the same issue raised by the conviction that people ought to be treated as individuals, as expressed, for instance, in Miller's parental leave case. It is rather an instance of the concern about epistemic conscientiousness that we encountered earlier, which has no particular connection to the morality of generalization (as distinguished from any of the other ways of being unreliable). Cases like this one demonstrate, then, that not all oversights in forming judgments about people constitute failures to treat those people as individuals.[17]

If that is so, when is the specific idea of treating people as individuals implicated, and when is it not? To answer that question, we should first flag and set aside one source of confusion. Sometimes when people say that X treats Y and Z as individuals, they just mean this as another way of saying that X treats Y and Z *individually*. In other words, X, in administering whatever treatment, takes Y and Z one at a time. What exactly this taking-one-at-a-time involves varies with context, of course. But it is essentially a formal property of how X goes about administering treatments to people; it does not normally impose any substantive limits on the treatments themselves.

By contrast, there is another sense in which the idea of treating someone as an individual posits a certain kind of constraint on *how* she is treated. This constraint is rooted in a more basic idea, the idea of *being* an individual. Schematically, to treat someone as an individual is to treat her in a way that befits someone with that feature, whatever it is. In this way treating someone as an individual is like treating her as an end-in-herself, as an equal, and so forth.* As Scanlon writes:

> [T]he idea that we must treat others as ends in themselves can ... be understood as a claim about the attitude we must have in order for our actions to have a certain kind of meaning—namely, for them to express an important kind of respect for others.[18]

My suggestion is that treating someone as an individual is parallel in structure: it is a matter of relating to her in the way required by respect for a certain quality of hers, her standing as an individual. And we can get little purchase on the moral requirement to treat something as an X without a prior conception of what it is to *be* an X.

So rather than directly asking what treating someone as an individual amounts to—for example, whether it means forgoing statistical

---

* Indeed, the distinction I have drawn between treating people individually and treating them as individuals is parallel in form and purpose to Ronald Dworkin's influential distinction between treating people equally and treating them as equals (1985, 190).

evidence in forming judgments about him (what I take to be Miller's view), or appealing to all reasonably available information (Lippert-Rasmussen's), and so on—we should fix on the prior question what being an individual, in a sense that it could be incumbent on others to respect, is. Then we will be in a position to ask what forms of deliberation or action are required or forbidden by due recognition of this quality in a person.

Of course, in a certain literal sense, people are obviously individuals. So too are mosquitoes, cars, and planets. Being an individual in this prosaic sense is simply a matter of being a singleton. But being a singleton is not a distinctive or interesting quality of persons—nor is it a quality of persons that even the most obvious failures to treat people as individuals manifest a failure to grasp. (Somebody who asserts that all Muslims are terrorist sympathizers surely understands that he is talking about multiple numerically distinct people rather than one compound entity; he is just supposing that these separate people have a particular feature in common.)

Once we set aside the bare sense of an individual as a singleton, what is left? In addition to being separate entities, persons are also individuals in the sense that they vary from one to the next in significant ways. Some objects are not like this. Although each car that comes off the production line is a metaphysical singleton, they may all be duplicates of one another; this constitutes a further sense in which they are not individuals. By contrast, something that has no duplicates is an individual not only in the sense of being a singleton, but also in the sense of being unique.

That seems closer to the sense of being an individual that could constitute a morally important feature of persons. But this idea remains underspecified. What are the dimensions of similarity or difference that make for the relevant sort of uniqueness? After all, cars of the same make are qualitatively unique in that they have different imperfections than one another. So to say that persons are unique, without specifying some dimension of similarity, is not to distinguish persons from cars. Moreover, for any given dimension in which objects of some kind are unique, it remains an open question

*but about diff.s
not our choice? i.e. might?
if not, but about diff.s purely our
choice & purely
influenced by weight.*

why uniqueness of that kind is significant—something that demands recognition respect.

Here, then, is the beginning of an answer. People are individuated by their standing as the owners or authors of their respective choices and actions—by their autonomy. That feature makes persons unique individuals in a significant way that other objects are not. Of course, insofar as many or perhaps all persons are autonomous, we are not each, in this very respect, unique. But this dimension in which we are alike gives rise to one in which we are not. By virtue of our standing as autonomous agents, which we hold in common, my choices are mine, yours are yours, and so on. That sets us apart.

To be sure, this brief metaphysical foray takes much for granted and leaves much unanswered. Most importantly, why does the relationship we hold to our choices individuate us in a way that matters? Nonetheless, this idea—that autonomy invests the boundaries among persons with moral significance—has a powerful claim on our thinking and deep roots in the liberal tradition. As Gerald Dworkin articulates this view, "What makes an individual the particular person he is reflects his pursuit of autonomy, his construction of meaning in his life."[19] When we say that persons are individuals in a sense worth caring about—worth *respecting*—I think this is most plausibly the dimension of difference we have in mind. If so, then the objection that generalization-based discrimination sometimes fails to "treat people as individuals" turns out to have little to do with the use of statistical evidence as such, and more to do with the importance of treating people as *autonomous* beings.

5.3 Autonomy and Generalization

Respect for autonomy is often invoked as an explanation for the moral significance of consent (and related limits on coercion or manipulation),[20] or in support of an argument for different kinds of pluralism.[21] I think respecting a person as an autonomous individual grounds a further requirement as well, however: that we form judgments about *what she is like* with due attention to evidence of the ways she has constructed her life, and with awareness of her power to continue to do so. These normative implications of autonomy have attracted less notice, but they contribute a good deal to explaining our unease about the ways in which generalization-based discrimination sometimes seems to disrespect the discriminatee as an individual, and hence as a person. Before developing this argument, I canvass some of the literature on autonomy, with the aim of extracting an ecumenical but substantial view of the concept that we can employ as a point of departure.

5.3.1 What is autonomy?

As Joel Feinberg notes, *autonomy* derives from the Greek for "self-rule," and its application to individuals may have originated as a metaphor rooted in the political independence or sovereignty of states.[22] Fittingly, then, autonomy is widely understood as a matter of self-determination—of governing oneself by means of choices that are one's own, and which cumulatively make a person, in Raz's phrase, "(part) author of his own life."[23]

As a starting point, it is widely accepted that there is an important difference between *personal* autonomy and *moral* autonomy. Moral autonomy has to do specifically with a person *qua* moral agent. In Gerald Dworkin's analysis, it concerns whether a person's "moral principles are his own."[24] Personal autonomy, by contrast, is of more general scope. As Raz puts it, this concept is "essentially about the freedom of persons to choose their own lives."[25] Some disagree about how closely these two notions are connected to one another,[26] but it is enough for us to note that they are not the same, and that we are mainly concerned with personal autonomy.

Personal autonomy has been analyzed in different ways, but these generally revolve around a core of shared images. The autonomous person, Raz says, is such that "[h]is life is, in part, of his own making."[27] Similarly, Gerald Dworkin writes: "Our notion of who we are, of self-identity, of being *this* person is linked to our capacity to find and re-fine oneself. The exercise of the capacity is what makes a life *mine*."[28] These images of autonomy as self-creation or self-authorship make sense because, as Stanley Benn suggests, the very idea of "making a choice," which is at the core of our concept of autonomy, supposes a relationship to one's action that is "more like that between a potter and his pot or an architect and his plan, than like the relationship between a skidding car and the resulting accident."[29]

Before we can consider autonomy more closely, however, we have to recognize another basic distinction. Sometimes "autonomy" names a realized condition, and sometimes it names the capacity for such a condition.[30] Consider, for example, someone imprisoned for much of his life in a very small cell. Although his freedom has been dramatically curtailed, we might hesitate to say that he is therefore less of an autonomous being. For his being autonomous, in one important sense, consists in his possession of a certain faculty—a capacity which imprisonment may suppress but normally does not eliminate. Indeed, it is in part *because* he retains that capacity that his being imprisoned stands in need of extraordinary justification. The primary connection between the imprisonment and the prisoner's autonomy, then, seems to be that the former may fail to *respect* the latter, not that it erases or even reduces it.

At the same time, the prisoner plainly does not live an autonomous life—a life he chooses for himself—at least not nearly to the extent that he could if he were free.[31] As Raz says of a similar case, the prisoner lacks "adequacy of choice," which is a prerequisite of exercising his capacity for autonomy.[32] So he is not autonomous (or his autonomy is reduced) in the sense of an actualized condition. Cases like this one serve to confirm, then, that there are two senses of personal autonomy in ordinary use—one a kind of faculty or capacity, the other a realized state of being.

Let us focus on autonomy as a capacity first. According to Raz, an autonomous person "must have the mental abilities to form intentions of a sufficiently complex kind, and plan their execution."[33] In Dworkin's view, the capacity for autonomy also involves a very particular power of reflective self-criticism.[34] On either construal, then, the core of this capacity is a kind of deliberative agency.

Both Raz and Dworkin recognize other conditions for autonomous choice as well, but I think there is value in distinguishing these from the core of requisite deliberative abilities. In particular, Raz emphasizes the importance of adequacy of options to autonomy, and both Raz and Dworkin suggest that the capacity for autonomous choice is threatened by undue influence from others that undermines one's independence. But the reason for partitioning these conditions off is that the first one—the kind of agency required for making choices which, if they were among adequate options and immune to undue influence, *would* be autonomous—is plausibly viewed as a constitutive feature of persons as such. Some persons will not enjoy autonomous lives; and some will not enjoy such lives because they lack adequate options, or because they are subject to undue influence. But these failures do not threaten their very standing as persons. Lacking the deliberative abilities required for autonomy, by contrast, seems different in this respect. To the extent that one is not an agent of the relevant kind, one is that much less a person. That distinction is potentially significant for a theory centered on respect for the moral attributes of personhood.[35]

Together, agency and the other conditions make up an account of what it takes for a person to make a choice in a manner that renders it authentically *her* choice. It is the cumulative accretion of such choices that defines a person's life as her own, and thereby qualifies a person as autonomous in the sense of an actualized condition. We might say that to be autonomous in this latter sense is not merely to possess a certain kind of agency, then, but, as Dworkin puts it, to have a certain *character*.[36]

When we talk about autonomy as something that demands recognition or respect, which of these two dimensions of the concept do we have in mind? Both, I think. There is normative significance to a person's being an agent of the sort required for autonomous choice (and indeed for personhood), and to her being in part the cumulative product of such choices. Moreover, both of these should cast light on what it means to treat someone as an individual.

5.3.2 *Generalization and respect for autonomy*

As I noted above, many normative appeals to respect for autonomy have a common structure. In one way or another, they demand that we not supplant a person's distinctive role as the controlling force in her own life. That is what we are doing, for instance, when we forbear from imposing a blood transfusion on someone out of respect for her autonomy. We recognize that her scheme of values, commitments, and projects differs from our own; and we recognize that, when it comes to *her* life, it would be wrong for us to pursue ours at the expense of hers.

Respecting someone's autonomy in this way is primarily a matter of allowing her to shape her own life and only secondarily involves attending to the *way* she shapes it, with an eye to avoiding wrongful interference with the self-regarding commitments she makes. But this second aspect of respecting someone's exercise of autonomy—seeing her as the person she has made herself—is also of significance in its own right. It would seem patently contradictory, after all, to commit oneself to respecting someone's autonomy, but then, when called upon to make certain judgments about what she is like, to willfully pay no heed to the ways in which she has contributed to determining that for herself.

The kind of self-authorship involved in an autonomous life seems quite distinctive relative to other forms of authorship, so we should be wary of taking this metaphor too literally. Nonetheless, it is a helpful device, and it may help to illustrate the point I am trying to make. Suppose, for instance, that I have crafted a sculpture through successive deliberate choices over a period of years, and that you know this. You view the sculpture, and I ask for your honest critical assessment of it. In appraising the work, however, you consider only the texture of the material with which I began, and which you know I did not choose. It is not that you dislike my artistic choices; you simply disregard them.

Of course, I would feel slighted by this, and not only because your assessment was in some way unfair to me or to the merits of the sculpture. My complaint would be more basic: that you had cut the elements of *me* out of my work, for better or worse, altogether. In other words, your mode of engagement with the sculpture does not manifest appropriate recognition of my authorship of it. To respect or duly recognize me as the author, I think, you have to do more than acknowledge the fact of my authorship abstractly; you have to attend to the differences my authorship made to the product in confronting it.

To be sure, it is an open question whether respect for an artist's standing as the author of his work is morally obligatory in any given context, or whether it is of much importance. But respect for a person's standing as the author of her *life* is obligatory and important. For I take it to follow from our analysis of the concept of autonomy that to respect a person's authorship of her life is at least part of what it means to respect her autonomy.

The upshot of this preliminary argument is that we respect a person's individual autonomy in part by attending to the influence that her exercise of autonomy has had on who she, individually, is.[37] We can approach the same idea from another angle by considering a linguistic ambiguity implicit in the notion of treating people as individuals. When I demand to be treated "as an individual," this might be viewed as a demand to be treated in a manner that accords with a general quality—being an individual—that I am claiming to possess (and which is possessed equally by other people, if they too are individuals, as well). But my demand could also be seen differently: it could be viewed as insisting that I be treated as the particular individual that I am. In either case, I am in some sense demanding recognition. But on the latter interpretation, I am demanding that I be recognized not under the general description of "an individual," which is one thing that I am, but rather under whatever description makes me the *particular* individual, distinct from others, that I am.

Now, these are not competing interpretations of my demand if the general quality of being an individual, in the relevant sense, is such that what recognition respect for it requires is at least in part that one treat a person as the particular individual that he is. Then it would be natural to understand me as essentially making both demands at once: I am demanding to be treated in a manner befitting my standing as an individual, which is (in part) to say, to be recognized as the particular person I am.

That dual interpretation coheres well if individuality of the relevant sort is understood in terms of autonomy as we have analyzed it. In our opening discussion of what it might mean to be an individual, I suggested that autonomy is both a quality we share, and a quality that grounds the morally important ways in which we differ. Respect for autonomy partakes of this dualism as well. On the one hand, respecting someone's autonomy means taking account of his choice of commitments, values, and projects; it is these which, in different ways and to different degrees, define his character and constitute him as *the* particular individual that he is. On the other hand, respecting his autonomy also means recognizing that, whatever his past may suggest, insofar as he is *an* autonomous individual—an agent of a certain kind—he has some ongoing capacity to chart his course for himself.

Let me suggest, then, the following more formal account of treating people as individuals, which we can call "the autonomy account" for short.

In forming judgments about Y, X treats Y as an individual if and only if:

(*Character Condition*)   X gives reasonable weight to evidence of the ways Y has exercised her autonomy in giving shape to her life, where this evidence is reasonably available and relevant to the determination at hand; and

(*Agency Condition*)   if X's judgments concern Y's choices, these judgments are not made in a way that disparages Y's capacity to make those choices as an autonomous agent.

This formula is meant to give content to the idea that treating a person as an individual involves recognizing her both as an individual (an autonomous agent) and as the particular individual that she is (as this is constituted from the choices she has made, the projects she has undertaken, and so on).

According to this account, therefore, treating someone as an individual demands two things. First, it means paying reasonable attention to relevant ways in which a person has exercised her autonomy, insofar as these are discernible from the outside, in making herself the person she is. Second, it means recognizing that, because she is an autonomous agent, she is capable of deciding how to act for herself. When we act in accordance with these requirements, we deal with people in a way that respects the role they can play and have played in shaping themselves, rather than treating them as determined by demographic categories or other matters of statistical fate.

Put another way, the relationship between these two conditions reflects the interplay of self-definition and freedom in the exercise of autonomy. The character condition enjoins us to pay attention to a person's past choices in making sense of who he now is, and hence also in forming judgments about how he is likely to behave in the future. Metaphorically, it presses us to see his life as an unfolding narrative he is writing, and to look at what he has written thus far, to the extent he shares it with us, in predicting what will happen next. The agency condition insists that any such predictions not only take account of evidence of his past choices, or the scheme of incentives or first-order desires he now confronts, but also recognize his capacity as an autonomous agent to continue to make his own choices through an exercise of reflective judgment.

We can get an initial sense of how the autonomy account works in practice by considering the parental leave case once again. Here the account implies that there are two distinct ways in which the employer's procedure may fail to treat candidates as individuals. First, it is significant that the employer makes his prediction by appeal to a reference class—women—which a person has essentially no say in belonging to. Information about the tendencies of that class is genuine information about its members, but it is not information that reflects their own autonomous commitments.

Now according to the autonomy account there is nothing wrong per se with making use of such information. What the character condition requires is simply that one also consider information that *does* manifest a person's self-authorship. The first way in which the employer may fail to treat a female candidate as an individual, then, is that he fails to give due evidential weight to the manner in which she has constructed her life, as this bears on the judgment he must make. Perhaps she has a clear history of always putting her career ahead of her personal life, for instance, or disclaims any interest in children. More broadly, the predictive relationship between sex and taking parental leave is no doubt sensitive to many other variables, some of which are markers of the kind of a life an individual person is in the course of constructing for him or herself, and some of which should be evident to a socially competent interviewer. To disregard that evidence, when it speaks both to a person's particular character and to her future performance, would be to fail to treat her as an individual.*

Before we turn to the second condition, certain features of this judgment bear noting. First, it is clearly a contingent indictment of the employer's conduct. It finds no fault in the skeletal description of the case with which we began; for what is wrong is not his use of the statistical evidence about women in assessing female applicants, but his (possible) failure to attend to certain other evidence as well. Similarly, what is disrespectful of me as the author of my sculpture is not taking your view of the material into account in assessing the piece, but rather ignoring everything else.

So the autonomy account regards a discriminator's reliance on unchosen traits as only a cue of possible failure to treat a discriminatee as an individual. Importantly, even that contingent cue is absent in many other cases of reliance on statistical reference classes. Suppose, for example, that an employer disfavors an applicant because she states an intention to take parental leave.[38] Even in that case the

---

* To be clear, there is also an important objection to what the employer in Miller's case does which has nothing to do with the predictive judgment that women will take parental leave. People should normally be able to take parental leave without fearing professional repercussions. That objection is not relevant here, however, because it does not concern the morality of discriminating against women on the basis of a generalization. It would equally apply to disfavoring all and only the people who volunteer that they intend to take leave, or to firing people when they do take it.

employer's decision involves the tacit application of a statistical generalization about the odds that a certain class of people will take parental leave: the class of people who avow an intention to do so. This suggests that an objection pitched at the use of statistical evidence as such will not fare well as an explanation of how the employer fails to treat a woman as an individual in the original parental leave case.

From the perspective of the autonomy account however, there is a clear difference between these two scenarios. In one the employer's reference class ranges over people who have made the choice to avow a certain intention. Reliance on evidence about that class is not even a contingent mark of possible failure to attend to the ways in which a person has exercised her autonomy, for it is itself an instance of such attention. My hope, then, is that the character condition can vindicate the instinct that leads us to invoke a distinction between "individualized" and "group-based" or "statistical" evidence—the instinct that people should be treated as individual persons with their own individual characters—without pressing us to eschew relevant information or adopt a general skepticism about statistical generalization.

This feature of the autonomy account also furnishes a plausible explanation of the fact that the applicant's complaint against the Achievement Academy seemed to fall flat. According to the character condition, respect for a person as an individual requires seeing him through the lenses provided by his own autonomous choices and commitments rather than only through the lenses of the various other predictive classes in which he falls. Ignoring an applicant's sister's academic records in appraising his fitness does amount to excluding relevant information, but it plainly does not infringe this requirement.

What about the second, agency-centered condition of the autonomy account? Returning to the parental leave case, it is significant not only what reference class the employer invokes, but also what he is using it to predict.[39] He is making judgments about the choices that a candidate will make. According to the agency condition of the autonomy account, then, he can also fail to treat a candidate as an individual by forming these judgments in a way that treats her as determined by statistical tendencies, rather than as an autonomous choice-maker who can make decisions that are her own.

Once again, this is not to deny that sex may be predictive of whether a person will choose to take parental leave, or that the employer can reasonably take account of that fact. One can perfectly well acknowledge that this choice is each individual's to make, while predicting that some are more likely than others to make it in a certain way. Recognition of a person's autonomous agency, in other words, does not require us to forbear altogether from making predictions about how she will exercise it. But to be consistent with respect for her autonomous agency, our predictions about what she will do must take precisely that form: they must be predictions about how she will exercise her agency, rather than tacit denials that she *has* a full measure of such agency.

To respect her as an autonomous agent, that is, one must not misrepresent the nature of her decision-making process by understating its measure of autonomy. This requirement is violated, for instance, if the employer considers a woman's decisions excessively by appeal to the first-order desires he ascribes to her—the maternal drive to nurture one's children, say—with little attention to the ways in which she may exercise reflective choice among such desires. That is to treat her as less of a person than she is, and more as a stimulus-response machine of some kind.[40]

It is a difficult question just when deliberation about someone's choices abridges this requirement. People *are* subject to first-order desires of various kinds, and respect for persons as persons should not be taken to require idealizing these away, or supposing that they are all of equal strength (so we would simply be at a loss to predict which will win out). But there is a comparative question that is happily more straightforward. The employer certainly disrespects women as full and equal persons if he predicts their choices on the basis of a narrow band of simple desires that he believes will very likely "out" in their eventual choices, but affords a greater role to autonomous reflection in considering the choices of men.

This sort of disrespect for the agency of some people is an important aspect of many traditional group stereotypes. When people subscribe to gross cultural generalizations—"Jews are pushy," "Hispanics are lazy," and so on—and avow or act on these, they often fail to regard Jews or Hispanics as individual autonomous persons who are just as capable of choosing whether to act pushily or lazily as others are. What is significant about these attitudes, in other words, is not only the character of the traits that are being ascribed but the constriction of agency that ascribing them to whole groups often implies. Acting on these attitudes very often involves a related failure to abide by the character condition of the autonomy account as well. For these generalizations, when applied as cavalierly and unscrupulously as they usually are, crowd out attention to the characters of individual group-members, as these are constituted by their cumulative autonomous choices.[41]

Indeed, these two forms of disrespect for autonomy also ably explain what is often common, morally speaking, to reliance on pejorative and nominally laudatory generalizations about social groups. Antebellum abolitionists in the United States who "ascribe[d] fancifully noble qualities" to black slaves, for instance, may have failed to appreciate the autonomy of individual black people just as much as contemporary racists do.[42] Like those who regard black people as prone to violence, those who took them to be loyal or compassionate by nature thereby demeaned their standing as autonomous agents. These same attitudes surely involved and encouraged a failure to attend to the characters of individual black people, as constituted by their autonomous choices, in forming judgments about them.

Finally, with respect to both the agency and the character conditions, we might wonder what is the proper *object* of the moral indictment we have been discussing. Is it forming one's beliefs or judgments about people in certain culpably defective ways, that is, or is it engaging in differential treatment on this basis (or is it both)? As formalized above, the autonomy account imposes certain restrictions on how one must act "in forming judgments about" another person. But perhaps what is morally wrong is only *acting* on judgments formed in this defective way—not simply forming beliefs about people in the abstract. Seen another way, the very idea of making a "judgment" about someone may be ambiguous between thought and action.

This question of moral object is certainly an important one, but because it turns on difficult issues about the ethics of belief in general, I am wary of pursuing it too far here. My focus is on the ways that discriminatory differential treatment may manifest disrespect for persons as individuals; in particular, I am arguing that differential treatment is morally defective in this way when it rests on certain defective ways of evaluating or engaging with the evidence about what people are like. While I think it is natural to describe the relevant beliefs about individuals and belief-forming processes as themselves involving disrespect for those people, I will stop short of the question whether it is right to see these as morally culpable in themselves.* It is enough for us to conclude that treating someone a certain way because of a failure to duly attend to her self-defining choices, or because of a failure to take account of her standing as a reflective choice-maker in anticipating her behavior, represents a failure to heed the moral reasons given by her standing as an autonomous person.

5.3.3 Respect for autonomy and the harm of lost autonomy

As I have described it, the autonomy account aims to identify and characterize a requirement of recognition respect for a morally salient property of persons. But autonomy is not only a static property, which, taken as given, we ought to recognize or respect. It is also a valuable dimension of people's lives that we ought to avoid undermining—or which, indeed, we may bear a collective obligation to promote. It is therefore significant that, in respecting a person's autonomy in the manner required by the character condition, we

---

* I thus set aside the questions posed by a growing body of important work on epistemic injustice and epistemic discrimination as such. See, e.g., Fricker (2007); Anderson (2012); Medina (2013).

often *further* his actual condition of autonomy as well—or, perhaps, forbear from constraining it—insofar as we allow his choices to influence his treatment by us in fitting and predictable ways. That is, we promote his control over his life in allowing or enabling his plans to come off, and we do that by being appropriately sensitive to the evidential significance that his choices have with respect to questions we are called upon to judge. By contrast, if a person invests in shaping himself in certain ways, but we are insensitive to the effects of this endeavor on who he is—adverting instead to aggregate evidence regarding people of his race, sex, nationality, or the like—we undercut the efficacy of those efforts on his part as a means of charting the course of his life.

There is an important point of contact here between my suggestion and John Gardner's proposal that "duties of non-discrimination, whether on ground of immutable status or on ground of fundamental choice, are alike in being autonomy-based duties."[43] In the former case, Gardner explains:

[T]he familiar liberal ideal of an autonomous life... is the ideal of a life substantially lived through the successive valuable choices of the person who lives it, where valuable choices are choices from among an adequate range of valuable options. Discrimination on the basis of our immutable status tends to deny us this life. Its result is that our further choices are constrained not mainly by our own choices, but by the choices of others. Because these choices of others are based on our immutable status, our own choices can make no difference to them.[44]

Like my proposal, Gardner's appeals to what we might call the *negative* significance of a trait's being unchosen. Discrimination on the basis of such traits is concerning because of what it suggests a discriminator is *not* being sensitive to—our autonomous choices. To whatever extent our treatment is determined by these traits, in other words, "our own choices can make no difference" to that treatment.

My account approaches this negative significance differently than Gardner's, however. It requires a decision-maker to give reasonable weight to a person's own choices in deciding how to treat him—that is, not to discount these when they are epistemically relevant. That is incumbent on the decision-maker, I am suggesting, simply as a matter of respect for a person's standing as part author of his life. It has the significant but ancillary effect of securing us the possibility for our choices to affect our treatment (to the extent that they are epistemically relevant to the decisions in question). But this requirement plainly allows that our unchosen traits may often be relevant to judgments about us as well, and it does not forbid affording these their epistemically appropriate weight. So my account offers no guarantee that there will not be judgments about us for the purposes of which our unchosen traits are very telling, and it furnishes no ground of objection when those decisions are made accordingly.

This is not to deny that when our fates do turn out to rest on our unchosen traits, our condition of autonomy may thereby be threatened. Within certain limits, of course, this is not a serious concern. I will never be a professional musician, no matter what I do, because of traits that I did not choose and cannot change. But Gardner is rightly concerned that discrimination on the basis of certain immutable statuses, if it is "endemic enough," leaves us with "too few valuable options to choose among, and we are deprived of valuable choice over large swathes of our own lives."[45]

A powerful case can be made on this basis for prohibitions on particular kinds of discrimination in certain spheres of life, even where they might otherwise be epistemically appropriate. But it is important to see that this is a sophisticated rendition of a contingent, harm-based objection to discrimination. Being denied an autonomous life is simply an especially severe harm. Indeed, part of Gardner's project is to explain how antidiscrimination laws can be squared with a liberal theory of the legitimacy of state action for which the prevention of harm is a touchstone. As he says, that is quite a different question than what makes discrimination wrong in the first place.[46]

By contrast, I do not mean to tackle here the question how a harm-based objection to discrimination is best formulated. My point, rather, is that there are important moral reasons against much discrimination that are not harm-based at all, but rather are rooted in the importance of respecting persons as persons. And one of these, I have been arguing, is that the discrimination in question fails to treat people as individuals, in the sense that it fails to recognize them as the autonomous beings that they are.

Anthony Walton's 1989 essay "Willie Horton and Me" offers another useful test case for this account, and illustrates how it is intertwined with, but distinct from, concern for the harm of a loss of autonomy.[47] The essay recounts Walton's experience of the use of Willie Horton, a convicted murderer and rapist, in an influential political advertisement in the 1988 U.S. presidential election. The ad recounted the gruesome details of Horton's case—voiced over a grainy photo of his black face—to accuse the more liberal candidate of being too lenient on criminals.[48]

In the essay, Walton describes a wide range of indignities and frustrations that confront black men in the United States, such as standing "in blazer and khakis, in front of the New York University Law School for 30 minutes, unable to get a cab." More broadly, he writes:

> I must battle, like all humans, to see myself. I must also battle, because I am black, to see myself as others see me; increasingly my life, literally, depends upon it. I might meet Bernhard Goetz on the subway; my car might break down in Howard Beach; the armed security guard might mistake me for a burglar in the lobby of my building. And they won't see a mild-mannered English major trying to get home. They will see Willie Horton....
>
> I think we, the children of the dream, often feel as if we are holding 30-year bonds that have matured and are suddenly worthless. There is a feeling, spoken and unspoken, of having been suckered.... I know that I disregarded jeering and opposition from young blacks in adolescence as I led a "square," even dreary life predicated on a coming harvest of keeping-one's-nose-clean. And now I see that I am often treated the same as a thug, that no amount of conformity, willing or unwilling, will make me the fabled American individual. I think it has something to do with Willie Horton.[49]

When cab drivers pass Walton by out of fear, because he is black, they rely on a tacit statistical generalization about black men that is unwarranted—not just incorrect as applied to Walton, but unjustified as such. But, as Walton implicitly argues, they do something more than that as well: they disregard and undercut a lifetime of choices and efforts on his part, aimed at distinguishing himself from the others who lend the generalization whatever plausibility it may appear to possess.

Those choices, Walton is suggesting, are manifest in his clothes, his manner, his location at the moment, and so on. The cab drivers disregard this information about him. That means, for one thing, that they apply their generalization about black men far more indiscriminately than is warranted, using overly coarse-grained categories.[50] But the information that they disregard is not just *any* information that distinguishes Walton from the class of people whom they fear. Walton's complaint is not the same, for instance, as that of a black woman who is passed by out of fear when in fact (let us imagine) the rate of taxi-driver robbery is elevated only for black men. For the information that is disregarded in Walton's case is the material expression of his efforts, as an autonomous agent, to be and to be seen as a certain kind of person. When they proceed to treat him simply on the basis of their generic attitudes towards black men, the cab drivers fail to respect that aspect of his nature—the fact that he has an individual *character*—by refusing or otherwise failing to see him as the person he has made himself. That is an important part of what we would mean, I think, in saying that they fail to treat or respect him as an individual.

That objection is closely related to, but not the same as, the concern that his project of self-authorship has been undermined or rendered inefficacious. Walton voices that concern as well when he describes feeling "suckered." The success of our efforts to construct particular lives for ourselves, valorized in our culture, partly rests on others recognizing us as the individual people we come to be and responding appropriately—just as the autonomy of a Jehovah's Witness rests on a doctor's correctly interpreting and honoring her decisions. So there are at least two different moral concerns here, both sounding in the value of autonomy. First, when a person treats Anthony Walton as if he were Willie Horton, despite the obvious evidence of their differences, that fails to respect Walton as an autonomous individual.

Second, if this reaction is widespread, then in the aggregate it may
also deny him the chance to effectively exercise autonomous control
over his life.

5.4 Clarifications and Applications

Both conditions of the autonomy account require some further
clarification.

5.4.1 The character condition

First, I have said that one fails to treat someone as an individual by
disregarding some evident exercise of her autonomy—in the form of
her choices, projects, and so on—despite its availability and informa-
tional value relative to the question at hand. Importantly, this means
that one can fail to treat someone as an individual even if *all* one
considers is an exercise of his autonomy, if one also fails to consider
other available information of the same sort.

Suppose, for instance, that an employer rejects everyone with a
criminal history. Let us grant for the sake of the example that
applicants come to have this history by virtue of their own autonomous choices. Nonetheless, some go on to make other choices that
bear materially on their fitness for a job later in life. Insofar as
evidence of such choices is reasonably available to an employer and
he disregards it, he fails to treat an applicant as an individual, even
though he is judging the applicant's fitness on the basis of *a* choice the
applicant made. Put another way, the applicant could still legitimately
claim that the employer has failed to recognize him as the individual
person that he is, and that the employer ought to have made more of
an effort to do so.[51]

Second, the character condition is compatible with the recognition
that our exercise of autonomy is dynamically related to aspects of
ourselves that we do not choose. A person exercises his autonomy not
only in making "unencumbered" choices, but also in determining
which of his antecedent traits to identify with and embrace, although
he did not choose them, and which others to do his best to sand down

or eschew. Thus, for instance, I did not choose my sex, but I do choose to what extent to self-identify as male. Such identification does not consist primarily in the literal self-application of the predicate "male," but in a complex of tastes and behaviors through which I embrace or reject masculinity.[52] Like other choices, these will normally manifest in a variety of self-presentational behaviors. Forming judgments about me on the basis of my race or sex, to the exclusion of relevant evidence that reflects my exercise of autonomy, infringes the character condition. But appropriate attention to the ways in which I *perform* my race or gender will, on the contrary, sometimes be required by it.

Third, some bits of information are obviously more probative than others with respect to a given question, and some are more costly than others to ascertain. In deciding what information to procure or attend to in making some judgment about someone, it seems reasonable to take both of these considerations into account. Thus whether a decision-making procedure respects someone as an autonomous individual should be taken to rest on the agent's "value-adjusted" investments in different bits of information. Part of what is egregious about Walton's treatment by the cab drivers, for instance, is that the information that reflects his autonomous choices is neither less visible nor less telling than his race.

To be sure, going out of one's way to understand a person's autonomous choices before forming judgments about her is often admirable, since it is likely to facilitate her self-determination, and in any case makes it more likely that she will be more fully recognized as the individual person that she is. But there must be limits to what is morally obligatory as a matter of respect. I will leave the question of these limits unresolved—though not without some regret—and rely on the unanalyzed notion of information that is "reasonably" available to a decision-maker, asking whether it is given "reasonable" weight. Note that even this modest requirement surely implies that one ought not to discount information that (1) appears to reflect a person's autonomous choice and (2) is not less available or less probative than other information that one *does* take into account.

The reasonableness condition embedded in the autonomy account has the interesting consequence that one can sometimes decline to treat people *individually* without failing to treat them *as individuals*. Similarly, as Ronald Dworkin observed, "[s]ometimes treating people equally is the only way to treat them as equals; but sometimes not."[53] As we saw above, treating people individually is a formal property of a procedure, whereas treating people as individuals is a matter of according people the respect befitting their standing in a certain dimension. My account of the latter suggests that when the information required for assessing people on the basis of their autonomous choices is not reasonably available, there is no disrespect in declining to treat them individually—that is, in employing gross statistical categories or blanket policies. Of course, certain ways of going about this may be objectionable on grounds of fairness or reliability nonetheless.

Fourth, although my analysis implies that we always ought to treat people as individuals, we should also recognize that failure to do so is a moral offense that comes in degrees. As I have just noted, sometimes what looks like a violation of this norm is not really, because the reasonableness requirement of the character condition provides a kind of built-in flexibility. What constitutes reasonable availability, in particular, will naturally vary across contexts.* But even among genuine failures to treat people as individuals, some may well show greater disrespect for a person's autonomy than others—for instance,

---

* Lawrence Blum suggests that "[t]reating or seeing others as individuals is not always a required or appropriate standard of conduct," because "some interactions with others are too fleeting for the idea of treating as an individual to get any traction" (2004, 272). Since respect and disrespect are jointly exhaustive, and since treating someone as an individual is a facet of treating her respectfully as a person, I hesitate to put the point that way. From the perspective of the framework I have described, it is more natural to say that in many situations one simply discharges one's obligation to treat others as individuals with ease—either because one is not really engaged in the business of forming judgments about those one interacts with in the first place, or because the interaction is too fleeting to give one the kind of information that, if it were available and relevant, respect for a person's individuality would require one to consider in making the judgments one does.

because what is disregarded about a person is more obviously central to the life he has made for himself.

Let me make one final point about the character condition. This condition has the effect that whether people are responsible for possessing a trait is often relevant to the morality of discriminating on that basis, since it is regard for the evidential significance of a person's autonomous choices that is required. But it is important to see that responsibility is relevant here in quite a different way than we might at first have imagined. In particular, non-responsibility for a given trait is sometimes offered as a reason why people should not be burdened on its account, drawing on broadly "luck egalitarian" theoretical commitments.[54] The character condition yields a different prescription, and it rests on a different foundation. In particular, it simply says that we are obligated to attend to a certain kind of information when it is reasonably available, namely, information about reference classes that a person has autonomously joined. The rationale is not that a person should be insulated from the consequences that come with the predictive significance of categories to which she belongs through no fault of her own, then, but rather that she ought to be seen as the person she has made herself as well.

5.4.2 The agency condition

Turn now to the agency condition of the autonomy account. This condition is partly modeled on a proposal of David Wasserman's in the context of the problem of "merely statistical" evidence in philosophy of law. One standard example of that problem, offered by L. Jonathan Cohen, goes as follows:

[There is] an imaginary rodeo where it is known that only 499 have paid for entry, but 1000 people are on the seats. The management picks one person at random off the seats and sues for non-payment. A ... [standard] analysis would indicate that, if those are the only facts before the court, the balance of probabilities lies in favor of the plaintiff. Yet our intuitions of justice revolt against the idea that the plaintiff should be awarded judgment on such grounds.[55]

Why does it seem wrong to hold this person liable, even though he is more likely than not to have snuck in without paying? Wasserman suggests that

> what is objectionable is the reliance on others' conduct, or the defendant's past conduct, to infer his commission of a wrongful act. We object to this inference because it ignores the defendant's capacity to diverge from his associates or from his past, thereby demeaning his individuality and autonomy.[56]

Wasserman says that such inferences "are felt to be inconsistent with *the law's* commitment to treat the defendant as an autonomous individual."[57] But insofar as autonomous agency is an important attribute of personhood, and we owe recognition respect to other persons *qua* persons, there is little reason to suppose that this commitment lies in the particular province of the law.* We all ought to treat others as autonomous individuals, in other words, setting aside the exceptional cases in which they truly are not (about which more in a moment).

I have proposed, however, that this commitment grounds a somewhat different moral requirement than the one Wasserman is arguing for, or at least attempting to account for, in the legal context. One does not deny or disregard a person's autonomy simply by taking account of certain evidence in making judgments about how she is likely to exercise it, or by acting on such a prediction. Not everything that is telling about us is up to us, and recognizing that reality is fully consistent with acknowledging our autonomy. What respect for a person's autonomy requires, rather, is that one be appropriately sensitive to the ways she has authored her life and recognize her capacity to continue to do so.

---

* Wasserman argues that judgments of liability are distinctive in not leaving people free to "vindicate" their autonomy by defying the prediction that is made about them (1991, 947–8). I don't think whether one furnishes someone such an opportunity determines whether one's manner of forming judgments about him respects his autonomous agency.

5.4.3 Where the autonomy account does not apply

The fact that many creatures, including some human beings, are *not* autonomous suggests a kind of natural experiment for testing an autonomy-based theory of treating people as individuals. If the theory is right, the idea of treating people as individuals should have no purchase in those cases. Indeed, Lippert-Rasmussen has argued that a view like mine would fail on just this ground: the distinctness of our concerns about respect for a person's autonomy and about whether she is treated as an individual, he says, is revealed "in cases involving treating non-autonomous minors on the basis of coarse-grained generalizations."[58] Although Lippert-Rasmussen does not discuss any specific cases involving non-autonomous minors, I suspect that the appearance that they pose counterexamples to the autonomy account reflects too demanding a conception of the relevant kind of autonomy. To object to the autonomy account on this ground, one would have to think either that young people lack an individual character that demands recognition in forming judgments about them, or that they do not make choices in the reflective manner that constitutes autonomous agency. Neither view strikes me as very plausible. Presumably these features develop gradually in child-hood, and are, to a significant degree, present at least in most teenagers.[59]

By contrast, if we focus on beings that *really* are not autonomous, I think this test buttresses the plausibility of the account. We can disrespect infants or non-human animals if our action manifests a failure to weigh their interests at full weight, for instance. But it would indeed seem strange to say that we disrespect them by failing to treat them as individuals. Of course, out of concern for their interests, we ought to be epistemically conscientious in making decisions that affect them, including by being sensitive to their relevant differences. But the inaptness of the *specific* requirement to treat them respectfully as individuals is plausibly explained by the fact that they simply are not (or, in the case of infants, are not yet) individuals in the sense that is relevant to this requirement. There are no autonomous commitments of theirs, the significance of which we could be obligated to respect; and there is no possibility of failing to recognize their standing as reflective choice-makers, which they are not.

A similar test case is posed by judgments about autonomous persons to which their autonomy simply couldn't be relevant. Here, too, the autonomy account fares well. If an action depends solely on an estimate of the odds that a person is a genetic carrier for some trait or disease, for instance, it makes no sense to worry about treating her respectfully as an individual in forming that judgment, precisely because the question implicates her only as a biological entity.

More broadly, the autonomy account implies that assessing people on the basis of group generalizations, and discriminating as a consequence, often involves no wrongful lapse of recognition respect. As a rough summary, we can say with confidence that such discrimination is not disrespectful if it (1) is not coupled with unreasonable *non*-reliance on other information deriving from a person's autonomous choices, (2) does not constitute a failure to recognize her as an autonomous agent capable of making such choices, (3) lacks an origin in disregard for her value as a person, and (4) reflects an appropriately diligent assessment given the relevant stakes. On the face of it, this seems likely to imply that many controversial acts or policies that involve reliance on group generalizations, from some forms of employment discrimination to racial profiling in law enforcement, could in principle be implemented in a manner that allows no objection from respect (so long as the agent goes about doing them in the right way).

To make this point vivid, consider the following example. You own a clothing store. You've observed over time that black teenagers are more likely than white teenagers to buy one brand of clothing (Brand X), and white teenagers are more likely than black teenagers to buy another (Brand Y). You don't doubt, however, that individual teenagers make these choices in an exercise of their individual autonomy. One afternoon, you realize that someone must have just stolen a Brand X t-shirt, and you see two teenagers—one black and one white—leaving the store. You can only stop and question one of them. Acting rationally, you stop the black teenager.[60]

My view implies that you have not failed to treat the black teenager as an individual—even though you acted on an inference about his conduct that you drew entirely from your beliefs about others who share his racial identity. The reason is that you did not efface his agency or unreasonably disregard other probative evidence about him that reflected his exercise of autonomy. Put another way, although we might colloquially describe your use of a racial generalization as, by definition, not "treating him as an individual," that usage is misleading because your treatment of him is in no tension with full recognition of his moral standing as an individual. What you did may have been wrong, but if it was, it must be for reasons that lie beyond the ambit of the disrespect account—an issue we will explore in depth in the next chapter. Before turning to that question, however, we should consider both (1) the connection between respect for autonomy and distinctly comparative forms of disrespect and (2) the special issues posed by unconscious generalization and implicit bias.

5.4.4 Respect for autonomy, respect for persons, and comparative disrespect

I have been arguing that discrimination is characteristically and intrinsically wrong when it disrespects people as persons. But I have now analyzed failing to treat people as individuals in terms of a failure to respect them as autonomous beings. To bridge this gap, we need to connect autonomy to personhood.

In the last chapter, I simply took as given that persons have a certain equal value *qua* persons. The relationship between autonomy and personhood requires only slightly more attention. What I have called autonomous agency—the faculty of reflective choice—is plausibly understood as a constitutive attribute of personhood, and this is the ground of what I have called the agency condition of the autonomy account.

Autonomy in the sense of an actualized condition may not be something that all persons enjoy, however. So my account seems to rely on a further claim: respect for someone as a person requires respect for her as autonomous, i.e., as part author of her life, if she is such. In fact, another adequate approach would be to say that every person actually is autonomous to some degree, and that respect for persons as such requires respect for this feature in whatever concentration it appears. Or perhaps respect for persons requires us to extend them a *presumption* of autonomy: to treat them as if they are leading autonomous lives, and to treat their choices with the significance this status would afford them, in the absence of good reason to think otherwise. Any of these connections between respect for autonomy and respect for personhood would suffice for our purposes.

Finally, our analysis of the morality of discriminating on the basis of generalizations in terms of treating people as individuals highlights that this sort of discrimination, unlike discrimination from differential concern, may or may not involve comparative disrespect. If one discriminates on the basis of race from differential concern, in a manner that does not respect people's equal value as persons, it is hard to see how that could be anything but *comparatively* disrespectful (or, as we have defined the term, racist). But the same is not true here.

As we have seen, one can disrespect a person as an autonomous individual by ignoring evidence of his character and assessing him simply on the basis of his race. Although this constitutes racial discrimination in the dimension of whatever is being assessed, it may not constitute racial discrimination in the dimension of respect. In particular, it will not be such if one is consistent in attending to race to the exclusion of other evidence, whomever one is assessing. The discrimination will then not be racist (or at least not on the definition we have adopted). It may rather reflect a commitment to what Kwame Anthony Appiah calls "racialism," the view that races are real and explanatory categories, that is so severe as to disrespect people's standing as distinct and autonomous individuals.[61]

Sometimes, of course, failure to treat people as individuals *is* comparatively disrespectful. It is sexist of an employer to predict a female candidate's decisions on the basis of sex, to the exclusion of evidence of her self-authorship, when he would not do so in assessing a man. Similarly, it is sexist to take a woman's future decision-making as less the product of reflective deliberation than a man's.

Disrespect for someone as a person is wrong whether or not it is comparative, and perhaps it is equally bad in either case. But even if so, attention to this distinction may help us to see more clearly the variety of ways in which people can show disrespect for one another, and how traits such as race and sex may be involved differently in each. It also suggests that if one understands the narrow, moralized sense of "discrimination" as I suggested in Chapter 3—as referring to discrimination in the dimension of respect for persons—much discrimination that is disrespectful of people as persons is actually not "discriminatory" in that peculiar sense.

5.4.5 Unconscious generalization and implicit stereotyping

I argued in Chapter 4 that the disrespect-based account of wrongful discrimination explains why discrimination from differential concern can be wrong independent of its contingent effects, even if one is unaware of one's bias. What should we make of discrimination on the basis of generalizations about groups of people, when one is similarly unaware of relying on them—or, indeed, of holding the cognitive associations in one's mind at all?

It may help to begin by drawing a distinction between two kinds of cases that are easily run together. In the first kind of situation, you reach a conclusion about someone—about her suitability for a job, say—in part on the basis of a belief you hold about people who fall under some more general description. You do not realize, though, that you are relying on that belief in forming this judgment. Still, if you were asked whether you hold the belief in question—and if you answered sincerely, with sufficient powers of introspection—you would acknowledge that you do.

In a second kind of situation, your judgment about a person may be shaped by an implicit stereotype or mental prototype that you not only don't mean to invoke, but also sincerely disavow. In particular, an influential picture of the mind depicts it as encoding associations among concepts, such that the activation of one of the related notions triggers, or renders more salient or accessible, the other. The well-known Implicit Association Test (IAT), which gauges the speed with which subjects can apply different pairings of concepts, helps to map these relationships. Importantly, to have one's mind organized in this way is not to hold a propositional attitude, such as believing that the two phenomena actually tend to co-occur in the world. For even if one disbelieves that proposition, mere knowledge that *others* think the concepts are related, or exposure to cultural materials depicting them as such, can foster and deepen the relevant cognitive associations.[62] This second kind of situation, then, involves not unconscious reliance on a generalization, but unconscious reliance on something we might hesitate to call a "generalization"—a kind of proposition—at all.

What does respect for a person's individuality require in each of these contexts? The application of the autonomy account to the first kind of situation is, I think, relatively straightforward. Specifically, it seems that the same fundamental analysis developed in Chapter 4 applies here as well. Insofar as disrespect consists in a failure of recognition, that is, the onus is placed on each of us affirmatively to appreciate certain elemental facts about one another, in the sense of taking account of the reasons they furnish for acting in some ways rather than others. The autonomy account specifies a certain understanding of what recognizing someone as an individual, in particular, entails. Conscious awareness does not seem to be of any basic significance to that requirement.

In other words, *unconsciously* placing excessive reliance on certain group generalizations—to the exclusion of the information provided by a person's manifest choices—does not constitute an exception to what would otherwise be a failure to treat people as individuals. But neither is the unconscious use of generalizations itself a mark of failing to treat people as individuals. What matters is simply whether certain kinds of evidence about people are given morally adequate weight in forming judgments about them. Thus, just as we may unconsciously rely on racial or gender-based generalizations in forming judgments about people, much of the time we may take account of their own autonomous choices intuitively and unreflectively as well. If our judgments about people are appropriately sensitive to the ways they have defined themselves as individuals, that is sufficient to treat them as individuals, even if we do not *consciously* advert to beliefs about the various reference classes they have joined.

To the extent that unconscious generalization is distinctly problematic, then, it is because it makes *regulation* of one's judgment-forming procedures more difficult. As I noted in §5.1, failing to guard against various cognitive biases that exert an unconscious pull on us is often a manner of failing to exercise due care in forming reliable judgments. That particular concern only applies in contexts where, and to the extent that, one is morally required to make reliable judgments. The domain of the autonomy account is, by design, more general. But the same basic point applies: it will be difficult to monitor whether one is treating people as individuals if one is unaware of the various ways in which one relies on different beliefs. That is an important *instrumental* reason for being introspective about the way we form judgments about people. It allows, however, that some people may have dispositions such that they can safely take a more hands-off approach. Conversely, some of us should realize that we have to be especially cautious about the generalizations we employ—particularly concerning social groups that are the subject of entrenched stereotypes—in order to ensure that we treat persons as individuals.

Where "brute" implicit associations fit in this picture is admittedly a harder question. Nonetheless, the most reasonable response, I think, is simply to count these among the potentially distorting influences that we may be obligated to endeavor to steel ourselves against where reliability is morally required, and also among the factors bearing on our judgments about individuals—factors relative to which we may be required to give certain evidence reasonable weight. Someone can complain equally that he has not been treated as an individual, in other words, whether his individual qualities have been discounted in favor of *beliefs* about people who are like him in some respect beyond his control, or in favor of more bare cognitive associations that prevented his counter-stereotypic features from being afforded their due evidential weight. Either way, his autonomous individuality has not been respected. The theory is thus "medium neutral" with respect to different cognitive processes.

At the same time, action that fails to treat people as individuals by dint of implicit biases is likely to be less blameworthy for the simple reason that such biases are more difficult to control.[63] It is natural to suppose that the measure of blame one bears for a wrong is related in part to how difficult it would have been for one to avoid it. As we fill in more details about these kinds of cases, we might sometimes blame the discriminator for negligence that explains his failure of self-awareness; we might not see this failure as negligent in other cases; and so on.

In addition, the distinction between ordinary disrespect and contempt, drawn in Chapter 4, is relevant here as well. As I argued above, actions show contempt for a person's equality when they spurn or repudiate the moral claims this normative attribute makes on them. One can show contempt for a person's autonomy or individuality as well as for her equality. Imagine a person who, faced with the material expressions of another's efforts at self-definition, willfully decides to cast these aside and instead reduces the other to a token of an unchosen class. Or, drawing instead on the agency condition, imagine a person who relates to another in a manner that knowingly erases her forward-looking freedom to adjudicate among her desires. Think, for instance, of the racial slurs that begin, "You can always tell a. . . . " These jokes function by positing some reflexive, sub-agentic behavioral marker of an imagined racial essence. The dehumanizing images considered above—of Jews as vermin, or Tutsis as cockroaches—are also illustrative in this regard, for they portray the stigmatized group not only as lacking interests of moral value, but also as a horde of fungible entities with neither individual characters nor individual wills. Such contempt for a person's autonomy is clearly not manifest in actions that fail to treat her as an individual merely in virtue of unconscious reliance on either group generalizations or implicit stereotypes.

5.5 Conclusion

In this chapter, I have argued that treating people as individuals is an important facet of treating them respectfully as persons. This is not a matter of eschewing statistical evidence about them, however, but rather of paying attention to their own roles in determining who they are and respecting their capacities to make choices for themselves as autonomous agents. This analysis may not suffice to work out the concrete demands of respect for individual autonomy in particular cases, but it gives us a conceptual framework for thinking through one dimension of that question—a dimension that is easily lost amidst concerns of procedural fairness, distributive justice, and the ways in which some people's well-being may be improperly discounted in an agent's decision-making. Central among the various moral problems with much discrimination is a distinctive failure to engage with the person who is discriminated against in the right way—including by failing to treat him as in part a product of his own past efforts at self-creation, and as an autonomous agent whose future choices are his own to make.

This chapter also concludes Part II of the book, which has developed a disrespect-based theory of when and why discrimination is intrinsically wrong. A fundamental question about the morality of discrimination is what could unify the apparently quite disparate cases that arouse our unease—from outright bias in the valuation of people or their interests, to reliance on certain kinds of generalizations in forming judgments about what they are like. I have argued that the unity we perceive in these offenses reflects the fact that they are manifestations of a failure to recognize different aspects of the same thing, to wit, the discriminatee's standing as a person.

A second basic question is what special significance, if any, attaches to the familiar *grounds* of discrimination—race, sex, religion, and so on. A good deal of discussion has thus focused on whether something essential distinguishes these paradigm cases of societal discrimination, on the one hand, from an individual's idiosyncratic differential treatment of different people—say, those with green eyes or large earlobes—on the other.[64] Andrew Koppelman, for example, has argued that "[a]ny account of discrimination that does not rely on history or culture will be a poor tool for the job of identifying wrongful discrimination."[65] That seems basically sound; but nonetheless there is an undeniable, if partial, intuitive continuity between racism and "earlobe-ism."

One strength of the disrespect account I have advanced here is that it offers a plausible reconciliation of these different impulses. On the one hand, in principle one can commit the wrong identified here by discriminating against someone because of her race, sexual orientation, weight, favorite color, or nearly anything else. Indeed the central focus is placed not on what one does and why, but on what one *fails* to do: respect a person by recognizing her for what she is and deliberating accordingly. So it makes no difference what feature of a person one is reacting to in failing to satisfy this obligation—including whether one is biased against a group that is socially salient or historically stigmatized, or whether concordant discrimination is widespread.

At the same time, my account implies only that racist and "earlobe-ist" discrimination are alike in respect of *intrinsic* moral status—since both manifest the same moral failing on the part of the agent—while leaving open how harmful each may be. In fact, racism is doubtless far more destructive, because of the distinctive context of racial stigma and other considerations to be discussed in the next chapter. But if we see the fact that racist discrimination is much worse than earlobe-ist discrimination as a reason to define discrimination itself in terms that separate the two,[66] or to require that any proposed moral objection to discrimination reproduce this hierarchy, we lose sight of an essential constituent of the wrongness of racist and earlobe-ist discrimination alike, namely, the disrespect they both show for the equal personhood of some people.

A third basic question, related to the last one, is to what extent there even *is* a distinctive morality of discrimination. Matt Cavanagh has argued that at least one desideratum for a moral theory in this area is that it should "capture what is *distinctively* wrong with discrimination."[67] My account fails this test, for it grounds what is characteristically and intrinsically bad about much discrimination in a principle of much wider relevance—the principle that it is wrong to show disrespect for people's standing as persons. It is wrong to do that whether one does so by discriminating or not, so my theory does not reveal anything to be distinctively wrong with discrimination. But so far as I can see, there is little reason to accept Cavanagh's test.

On the contrary, I think it would be surprising if the badness of wrongful discrimination as such turned out to figure in a complete moral theory at a fundamental level. What we should expect of a theory of wrongful discrimination, rather, is that it ground the apparent wrongness of paradigm cases of wrongful discrimination in the *right kind* of more basic norm. That is, a satisfying theory should characterize the wrongness that is typical of paradigm cases of wrongful discrimination in a way that resonates with our intuitive sense of which, of the various more fundamental ways of acting wrongly, such discrimination instantiates; and it should show how attention to that basic moral concern helps us to better understand the overall shape and internal complexities of the phenomena. On this score, I think the disrespect account performs better than the alternatives.

Having now explored the connection between discrimination and disrespect in some depth, however, it is clear that much discrimination is not or need not be disrespectful of the personhood of those who are disadvantaged by it. In employment, law enforcement, or private life, one can often recognize a person for what she is, morally speaking, and discriminate against her nonetheless. In such cases the practices must be bad, if they are, for other reasons. Given the nature of this terrain, the morality of non-disrespectful discrimination can only be sorted out in the trenches of particular acts or policies, on the basis of the particular effects that they are likely to have. In the next chapter, I turn to the work of sorting through these different normative factors in one setting of particular interest: programs of statistical discrimination, such as racial profiling in law enforcement.

PART III

Contingently Wrongful Discrimination

6

A Case Study
Racial Profiling

In Part II of the book, I proposed an account of why discrimination is sometimes intrinsically objectionable, or objectionable independent of its contingent effects. Roughly, I suggested that paradigm cases of wrongful discrimination are objectionable in this way because they manifest a failure to appropriately recognize the standing of some people as persons. When that failure is explained by how a discriminator regards or perceives a discriminatee P-wise, it is itself discrimination in the dimension of respect, and it is rightly described as P-ist. This account aimed to make sense of our intuitive convictions about some paradigm cases of wrongful discrimination, as well as to furnish valuable clarification with respect to cases about which our pretheoretical judgments are somewhat more conflicted.

One important consequence of this view is that much discrimination, and even much discrimination on the paradigm grounds of race and sex, may well *not* be intrinsically objectionable, because it does not manifest such disrespect. For example, discrimination is sometimes employed as part of a good-faith effort to achieve valuable goals by capitalizing on genuine statistical patterns. Practices fitting this description can evince a failure to respect the discriminatees as persons, but they need not do so. In this final chapter, therefore, I ask when and why discrimination of this kind might be bad for other reasons.

I have in mind questions such as these. Is racial profiling acceptable in contexts where racial appearances are truly correlated with patterns in crime? May the military assign different roles to men and women, if sex is shown to be a genuine predictor of relevant qualities or aptitudes? Could the U.S. and U.K. health agencies be right to refuse blood donations from all men who have recently had sex with other men, on the ground that HIV is more widespread among that population?

The policies at issue in these various debates have two key features in common. First, even if they are morally wrong, they cannot be rejected out of hand as necessarily manifesting a failure to take account of the moral standing of some persons. Of course, one *could* adopt a racial profiling policy by virtue of a failure to afford equal weight to people's interests (e.g., in avoiding the burdens of law-enforcement scrutiny), or because of statistical beliefs that are tainted by disrespect for certain people. Similarly, one could implement such a policy in a way that infringes the requirement to treat people as individuals: for instance, if race alone is taken into account, without regard for other aspects of a person's self-presentational behavior.[1] But in principle a policy of considering race in allocating scrutiny could avoid treating anyone as less than a full and equal person. The same is true, I think, of the military and health policies described above.

Besides being at least potentially respectful, these examples are also alike in that they each propose a form of *statistical* discrimination. When people oppose an instance of this kind of discrimination, they often argue that the apparent statistical relationship at issue is actually spurious on closer inspection. In so doing, they effectively graft these practices onto the familiar model of baseless prejudices, which can be discredited simply by exposing their unsound foundations. But, when it is pushed too far, this argumentative strategy carries distinct dis-advantages. Philosophically, of course, it skirts rather than engages the most difficult moral issues. And even from a purely tactical point of view, this approach risks fostering the impression that the critics of discrimination are naïve utopians who insist on denying common-sense realities that do not conform to their own egalitarian world-views. Consequently, this line invites proponents of discrimination to present themselves as the realists in the debate—the only ones willing to acknowledge apparent patterns that may not be "politically correct," but which most people suspect are better grounded in reality than the opponents of discrimination would acknowledge.

This dynamic has been especially clear in public discussion of racial profiling in law enforcement. Consider, for instance, former New York City mayor Michael Bloomberg, who defended his opposition to racial profiling in anti-terrorism efforts by asserting that, "if we've learned anything, it's that you can't predict what a terrorist looks like. Terrorists come in all sizes and shapes and forms."[2] Of course, it's true that you can't predict with confidence what a terrorist will look like, and a policy that focused police searches exclusively on members of one racial or ethnic group would plainly be misguided. But Bloomberg's argument invites the reply that you can indeed make certain rational predictions about whether a person who looks a certain way is on that account *more or less likely* to be a terrorist. This is a simple matter of statistical inference. Similarly, as a conservative television pundit said of profiling Hispanics in a crackdown on unauthorized immigrants in the United States, "you're not looking for a blond-haired, blue-eyed Swede most of the time."[3]

Disputing this empirical reality is a losing strategy for critics of racial profiling in immigration enforcement. More generally, it seems foolish to deny that there are often genuine correlations between certain perceptible features, such as race or sex, and other relevant traits, including some forms of criminality. Indeed, in light of the many correlations that traits like race and sex bear to other aspects of our lives, it would be surprising if there were *not* such relationships— if only because of the inequalities wrought by past and present discrimination on the basis of these same traits.[4] The task facing critics of much statistical discrimination, then, is to explain why discrimination may be wrong *even if* it manifests no disrespectful attitude and constitutes an effective means to a legitimate goal.

I will focus on the case of racial profiling here, both because it is of significant intrinsic interest and because it poses the broader question of the morality of respectful statistical discrimination in an especially clear form. Few deny the importance of the ends purporting to justify discrimination in this case: combating crime, preventing terrorist attacks, and so on. Moreover, racial profiling quickly brings to the surface the central challenge for developing a moral account of statistical discrimination that is not disrespectful: explaining what it is about particular *grounds* of discrimination that might rule them out of bounds.

Consider another example. On Christmas Day 2009, Umar Farouk Abdulmutallab attempted to detonate explosives on an American airliner headed to Detroit, with 289 other people aboard. After the failed attack, media reports described "a raft of potential red flags that were somehow missed."[5] For example, Abdulmutallab had paid nearly $3,000 in cash for a plane ticket and checked no bags for a scheduled two-week trip. The widespread embrace of the idea that Abdulmutallab ought to have been subjected to additional scrutiny on account of these "red flags" reflects, implicitly, a widespread approval of a kind of statistical discrimination in airport security. For if either of these traits were employed as bases on which to allocate extra screening, that would plainly constitute a kind of discrimination, predicated on the hypothesis that these properties, though not themselves objectionable, are correlated with the intention to commit acts of terrorism.

Examples like this one suggest that the pressing question is not *whether* statistical discrimination is objectionable when it does not manifest disrespect—for we all take for granted, at least implicitly, that very often it is not—but when and why it sometimes might be. By working through possible reconstructions of the rationale for opposing racial profiling, we will necessarily also be considering what it is, in general, about reliance on particular generalizations that could render them troublesome though others are not. We will also consider some factors of narrower relevance to the profiling case, which is of significant interest in its own right.

This project involves several distinct threads of positive and negative argument. After offering a conceptual account of profiling, I will first consider appeals to the normative significance of whether a person is responsible for a profiled trait or whether the trait bears a certain kind of explanatory connection to crime. I then turn to the possibility that some forms of profiling simply impose morally unacceptable harms on the people who are singled out for scrutiny. Finally I consider the possibility that we should forgo certain kinds of profiling not simply because of direct injury to people who would be subjected to extra scrutiny, but because these practices undermine the larger project of forging and preserving a community of mutual respect.

In my view, this last argument is the most promising. Opponents of racial profiling often urge that it wrongs those who are subjected to extra scrutiny by forcing them to bear more than their fair share of the costs of law enforcement or public security. But I suspect that the strongest case against racial profiling lies elsewhere. The practice is most troubling because of its potential to inadvertently legitimate pernicious stigmas and hostile attitudes in social life writ large—a concern that extends well beyond the specific contexts in which profiling occurs, or the particular individuals who are subjected to it. Racial profiling, and other practices like it, are very often *contingently* bad because of their *conventional* meanings.

In considering racial profiling, we should begin by making two explicit assumptions. First, as I noted above, we are interested only in cases that satisfy the strictures of the disrespect account. In adopting this restriction, I make no conjecture about the motives of actual profilers. Second, we are interested only in cases where racial profiling is instrumentally valuable as a means to important goals, such as thwarting or punishing non-trivial crimes. Although there are powerful arguments against profiling on grounds of efficacy alone, I assume that these are at least not universally availing.[6]

6.1 What is Profiling?

Although racial profiling has attracted increasing interest from philosophers in recent years,[7] this discussion has neglected a distinction that is commonly drawn outside the philosophical literature.

Specifically, lawyers, judges, and participants in the public debate regularly distinguish racial *profiling* from the use of race in *suspect descriptions.*[8] Moreover, they often invest this distinction with moral or legal significance: whereas racial profiling is widely condemned, at least by scholars writing on the topic, the use of race in suspect descriptions is generally regarded as unproblematic, including by the very same people.[9]

In this section, I investigate both the conceptual contours of this distinction and its putative moral significance. I argue that a precise account of the nature of the distinction brings to the surface why it appears morally important, and that this in turn sheds some preliminary light on the source of moral unease about racial profiling. In particular, racial suspect descriptions strike us as comparatively benign because they do not rest on the inference that defines profiling: that being of a given race makes one at least epistemically more likely to be a criminal. This is an early clue that it may be the invocation and expression of that basic inference—not unfairness that may result, or direct injury to those who are profiled—that lies at the heart of the case against racial profiling.

6.1.1 Defining profiles and suspect descriptions

We might put a first statement of the distinction between profiling and suspect description reliance as follows. Police engage in *profiling* when they use traits that they take to be associated with the commission of some kind of offense as sorting criteria to allocate investigative resources more efficiently, with the aim of thwarting, detecting, or solving crimes of that kind. By contrast, police apply a *suspect description* when they use traits thought to be possessed by a specific suspect as criteria for allocating investigative resources more efficiently in an effort to identify that individual. As R. Richard Banks puts it, "Whereas a racial profile is used to catch any of many perpetrators, a suspect description is used to apprehend a particular assailant."[10]

Although this seems to be the most common account of the distinction between profiling and suspect descriptions, I will suggest that it does not capture the conceptual structure of these categories accurately. As a consequence, it also fails to explain the moral significance many attach to the difference between profiling and suspect descriptions.

First, however, there are a few confounding factors that should be explicitly distinguished from the distinction between profiling and suspect descriptions. For one, it can sometimes sound as if suspect descriptions are always retrospective, aimed at identifying past offenders, whereas profiling is aimed at preempting future offenses (e.g., in airport security). Annabelle Lever, for example, does not use the label of "suspect descriptions," but says that "post-crime profiling departs from a witness's description, however vague, of a suspect who has actually committed a crime," whereas "preventive profiling creates a profile based on statistical evidence of who is likely to commit a crime."[11] There is nothing inherent or natural about these pairings, however. Even in the paradigm cases of suspect descriptions that involve witness observations, the person described can be a person believed to have a certain intention—rather than to have committed a certain crime in the past—and the point of employing the suspect description can be to prevent the person from carrying out an offense. Conversely, "a profile based on statistical evidence of who is likely to commit a crime" can be (and often is) employed to cull lists of possible suspects when investigating crimes after the fact, not merely for the sake of crime-prevention.

Second, sometimes suspect descriptions are effectively equated with reports by witnesses or victims.[12] The word "description" certainly can be understood in this narrow way, but I think that is unhelpful if our aim is to mark the boundary between two reasonably fundamental kinds of investigative techniques. For example, if the police focus their investigation of a crime on red-haired suspects because a red hair fiber was found at the scene, I take it that they are operating from a suspect description, even though no witness or victim report is involved.

Third, it can appear as if suspect descriptions are by nature more accurate, or more efficient, than profiles. Examples of suspect descriptions often suggest nearly complete confidence that the suspect is as described—perhaps because he or she was clearly seen at the crime scene—whereas we know that profiles, at their best, offer only probabilistic information. But this too is not fundamental to the difference between these categories. Actual witness reports normally imply only that a person is *more likely* to have one trait or another, and we might receive conflicting witness reports in a single case.

Mathias Risse and Richard Zeckhauser offer a helpful example. If eyewitness reports indicate a 60 percent chance that a crime was committed by someone of a certain description, and people of that description make up 25 percent of the general population, a random person fitting the description is 2.4 times as likely to be guilty as someone drawn at random from the general population.[13] Though this case involves a suspect description, the very same efficiencies could be due to profiling. Suppose, for instance, that 2.4 percent of people fitting a certain description commit a certain offense, and 1 percent of the population at large does so. Then screening only people of that description will yield 2.4 times as many offenders per search as a policy that screens at random.[14]

Let us turn, then, to formal specifications of the distinction between profiling and suspect descriptions. As we have seen, the most obvious account points to the difference between searching for members of a broad class of people—the people who have committed or will commit some crime—and searching for a determinate individual. In a slight variant on this approach, some distinguish the two categories by the specificity of the *offense* that is being investigated rather than that of the *perpetrator* who is being pursued. Samuel Gross and Debra Livingston, for instance, say "[i]t is not racial profiling for an officer to . . . investigate a person because his race or ethnicity matches information about a perpetrator of a specific crime that the officer is investigating."[15]

Despite their intuitive appeal, there are powerful counterexamples to both the "specific individual" and the "specific crime" accounts of the boundary of profiling. Suppose, for instance, that the police receive a credible tip that a one-person terrorist attack will be attempted on

Flight 555 today. It may be efficient to investigate particular passengers on that flight more than other passengers, in accordance with rational predictions about traits that the terrorist plotter will possess. If so, that investigation will aim at the identification of a specific individual, viz. the terrorist in waiting, in order to prevent a specific event, viz. the looming attack on this flight.

But if nothing further is known about the terrorist, the criteria used to identify him *in particular* may derive all of their force from generalizations about *the whole class* of people who commit terrorist attacks on airplanes. Suppose that is so: in particular, a security officer chooses passengers of Middle Eastern appearance for special scrutiny because he believes that this suggests they are more likely than others to be the terrorist. There would be little doubt that the officer is engaged in profiling in this case, not the use of any suspect description, even though he is looking for a specific person with respect to a specific crime. It follows that the two accounts we have identified thus far cannot be correct.

What seems to distinguish this case from the use of a suspect description is that, notwithstanding the specificity of the crime and the perpetrator being investigated, the *evidence* against certain passengers consists of information about terrorists in general, rather than something "individualized" to the people or the incident in question. This notion of "individualized" evidence is not transparent, however. After all, if a red-haired man is stopped for questioning because of a witness's description of a red-haired assailant, there is a clear sense in which this evidence is not "individualized" to him either: it is evidence against red-haired people in general, and not against him individually.

One analysis of the notion of "individualized" evidence has been offered by Judith Jarvis Thomson in the context of the problem of statistical evidence in philosophy of law. Specifically, Thomson understands "individualized evidence" as "appropriately causally connected evidence."[16] For example, she says, the mere fact that one company, called Red Cab, operates the majority of cabs in an area is inadequate to hold that company liable for any particular accident involving an unidentified cab, because this fact does not constitute "individualized evidence" against Red Cab. The reason for that, she says, is that the company's market share does not explain, is not explained by, and shares no common explanation with the putative fact that one of its cabs caused the accident.[17] By contrast, Thomson explains,

if a [cab operated by Red Cab] . . . crashed into a parked car shortly after Mrs. Smith's accident, and four blocks past the place of it, the driver giving all signs of being drunk, then that . . . would be called individualized evidence against Red Cab; and my suggestion is that that is because that driver's having been drunk would causally explain both his crashing into the parked car and his (and therefore Red Cab's) having caused Mrs. Smith's accident.[18]

Whatever its independent merits, Thomson's proposal cannot be adopted to ground the distinction between suspect descriptions and profiling. To take a simple counterexample, suppose that baldness shares a common explanation with the disposition to commit assaults (perhaps both traits are influenced by the same hormones). If the police subjected bald people in the vicinity of an assault to extra scrutiny because of this correlation, they would surely be engaged in profiling, notwithstanding the causal connection. By Thomson's account, however, the causal relationship between baldness and assaults would apparently suffice to render the evidence against bald people "individualized." The hormones parallel drunkenness, as a contributing cause of both the evidence (baldness) and the hypothesis it is evidence for (committing the assault).[19]

Although the notion of "individualized" evidence seems to be a useful one, then, we need a different account of what it means in this context. Whether evidence is "individualized" in the relevant sense, I think, is really a question about the structure of the inference in which it figures. On the one hand, fitting a terrorist profile simply raises the (epistemic) probability that a person is a terrorist. If a profile can help to catch an individual terrorist—as in the Flight 555 case—matching the profile must also render a person more likely to be the unidentified subject of the investigation; but it will do this *by virtue of* the more general effect, that is, by increasing the probability that the person is a terrorist.

By contrast, a suspect description works in the opposite direction. If a red-haired person is seen fleeing the scene of a mugging, then a person's having red hair raises the probability that he was the person who was seen fleeing, and thus that he was the particular mugger in this case. As a consequence, his having red hair may also raise the probability that he is a mugger, full stop. This further inference is not essential to the suspect description, however. Indeed, it may not follow at all. For even if having red hair increases the odds that a person is *that* mugger, it could be that red-haired people commit fewer muggings than other people, in which case the property of having red hair may negatively predict the property of being a mugger, this particular crime notwithstanding.

Formally, then, we can define profiles and suspect descriptions by adapting a distinction between "component effect along a causal route" and "net effect" described by Christopher Hitchcock in the context of analyzing causal pathways. Hitchcock puts the distinction as follows:

C has a [component] effect on E along a particular causal route when C makes a difference for E in virtue of being connected to E along the route in question. C has a net effect on E if it makes an overall difference to E taking into account all of the routes that connect them.[20]

We can draw the same distinction in terms of evidential pathways rather than causal ones.

First, let T be the hypothesis that a person is a target of a particular investigation, and let F be the hypothesis that he possesses some specified trait, such as a race or hair color. Then we should judge people who we believe to possess that trait more likely to be targets of our investigation just in case there is a positive *net effect* of F on T, in terms of evidential support: that is, if $p(T \mid F) > p(T)$.

Let us say that there is a *component effect* of F on T along the evidential pathway given by some third variable M if and only if $p(M \mid F) \neq p(M)$ and $p(T \mid M) \neq p(T)$. When such an effect exists, we can call it *F-M-T*. Then we can define a profile as a component effect *F-M-T* in which *M* is the possession of a disposition or propensity to commit some type of crime, such as "muggings" or "terrorist attacks on airplanes."* A person *engages in* profiling when his degree of belief in *T* is influenced by such an effect. Other component effects of *F* on *T*, by contrast, represent suspect descriptions. Finally, a racial profile is simply the special case of a profile in which *F* refers to a racial category.[21]

If we define profiling this way—as a pattern of relations among beliefs of a certain kind—it will not be accurate to say that an inspector who mechanically applies a profile handed down from above engages in profiling. That is not surprising, however. Sometimes profiling is simply done by the people or institutions that establish relevant systems of rules, rather than by officials who interact with the people who are, in either case, being profiled.

The graph below depicts how profiles and suspect descriptions, understood as different kinds of component effects, may figure in an investigative judgment. In this case, suppose that the police are seeking the perpetrator of a particular assault and must decide whether to treat a person *X* as a suspect. The police know that a witness described the perpetrator as female, and that being male predicts committing assaults.

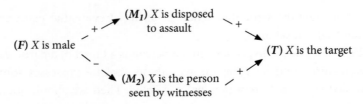

Figure 1 Competing component effects—one a profile and one a suspect description—bearing on an investigative judgment.

---

* The ascribed disposition need not reflect an "internal" propensity. Indeed, one need not adopt any theory about what grounds the disposition at all in order to engage in profiling; it can reflect a bare assessment of probability.

This case demonstrates the familiar but neglected proposition that one cannot simply assume the transitivity of evidential support. Here it is true both that $p(M_1 \mid F) > p(M_1)$ and that $p(T \mid M_1) > p(T)$, but it may not be true that $p(T \mid F) > p(T)$. As a rule, that can be assumed to follow only if M_1 "screens off" F and T: that is, if F and T are probabilistically independent conditional upon M_1 and upon $\sim M_1$.[22] In graphs like Figure 1, this condition would require that there be no evidential pathway from F to T that is not mediated by M_1. To make rational investigative judgments, then, various predictive reference classes—some profiles and some suspect descriptions—must be weighed together and integrated to estimate a net effect.

Before proceeding, let me note one other interesting consequence of these definitions: Understanding profiles and suspect descriptions as different inferential pathways implies that the same pattern of material facts can often be used in either way. That in turn could help to explain why categorizing particular cases as instances of one practice or the other often proves contentious.[23]

Suppose, for instance, that a forensic analyst studies a murder, and judges that the pattern of footprints at the scene suggests that the attacker walks with a limp. It seems most natural to present this as a suspect description: a person's walking with a limp has a positive component effect on the hypothesis that he is the unidentified subject of the investigation. That effect does not appear to be mediated by any hypotheses or generalizations about a type of crime (such as murder) that people with limps are more likely than others to commit.

Even in such cases, however, a transformation from a suspect description to a parallel profile will be possible if we are sufficiently liberal about what we recognize as a crime-type for the purposes of specifying M. In this case, the investigator could take the analyst's conclusion to mean that people with a limp are more likely than other people to commit the particular type of crime that was committed in this case—namely, "murders with nearby footprints patterned this way." He could then reason that any given person's walking with a limp has a positive effect on the hypothesis that he is disposed to commit the relevant category of crime, which in turn has a positive effect on the hypothesis that he is the unidentified subject in the instant case. If the investigator reasons this way, he is employing a profile, albeit a highly unusual one, rather than a suspect description.

6.1.2 The morality of profiling and suspect descriptions

As I noted at the outset, there is a common view that racial profiling is more troubling than the use of race in suspect descriptions. We should certainly be open to the view that this intuition is simply misguided, since the practices clearly have much in common. But I think the characterization of profiling that I have suggested helps to clarify why this distinction seems to carry moral weight, and lends at least some preliminary vindication to that appearance.

In particular, this way of understanding the distinction highlights the fact that, when we scrutinize someone because of a suspect description rather than a profile, we effectively dilute the inference from possessing a particular trait to criminality by introducing a mediating factor of personal identity. Equivalently, only a profile relies on a generalization that people with some trait are more likely to commit some kind of crime. Given the past and present practice of embracing such generalizations out of hostility and prejudice, especially in the context of race, it is natural that they are met with unease and distrust.

This point can be put in terms of the typology of disrespect we developed in Chapter 3. Specifically, affirming the notion that race is predictive of criminality—including by relying upon it as the ground of an inference—is *conventionally* disrespectful. In other words, because this is something people often do out of basic disrespect for others, it has taken on a conventional meaning that has rendered it harmful even in the absence of the underlying disrespectful attitude.

By contrast, suspect descriptions do less to imply or insinuate that possessing the relevant trait, as such, renders one even epistemically more likely to be a mugger, a terrorist, or whatever. Rather, this status merely renders one more likely to be the unidentified subject of some investigation, who is suspected of being a criminal. As Arthur Applbaum puts it, police scrutiny prompted by a suspect description can in principle convey a message like this:

We do not suspect *you* of committing a crime, we suspect someone who resembles you. . . . I am not supposing that individuals with your skin color are more likely to commit crimes, which I can well imagine would be insulting. I simply am supposing that individuals with your skin color are more likely to be the particular person for whom we are searching.[24]

The apparent significance of this difference hints at one important thread in the moral case against racial profiling. Very roughly, it seems that differences in the apparent public meaning of profiling and suspect descriptions could confer different moral statuses on them, even if many of their immediate consequences—in the racial distribution of who is selected for searches, and in the degree of inconvenience these people face—were the same.

Nonetheless, the most familiar arguments against racial profiling are different in character. They urge either that profiling on the basis of race is objectionable in principle, because of something to do with the nature of race—either that one is not responsible for it, or that it is not causally related to crime—or else that racial profiling simply does unjustified harm to the individuals who are selected for scrutiny. I consider these arguments in the next two sections.

There is one way in which the intuitive force of arguments against racial profiling is often artificially reduced, however, which we should guard against at the outset. The question whether to engage in racial profiling in terrorism cases, for example, is very often presented as a choice between racial discrimination and an increased risk of death and destruction due to terrorist attacks.[25] But if we judge it important to guard against this risk, then even if we rule out racial profiling, we retain the option to do so in other ways—increasing the frequency of random searches for all airline passengers, for instance.[26] In the cases that concern us, these practices will be less efficient than using racial profiling; that is what occasions the moral problem in the first place. But it is a clear analytic mistake to imagine a security regime that employs profiling and achieves some desired level of safety, to simply remove the profiling, and then to count the reduction in safety as the cost of forgoing profiling.

6.2 Arguments against Racial Profiling in Principle

Racial profiling may be bad simply because of the harm it does. But often it is suggested that the practice is objectionable on more "principled" grounds—that, for one reason or another, it is bad in itself to distribute the burdens of scrutiny along racial lines. Steven Durlauf, for example, suggests that "[f]or an innocent individual, complete fairness implies that the conditional probability of the negative outcome of being stopped should not depend on his race."[27] Similarly, Randall Kennedy writes:

When a Mexican-American motorist is selected for questioning in part on the basis of his perceived ancestry, he is undoubtedly being burdened more heavily at that moment than his white Anglo counterpart. He is being made to pay a type of racial tax for the campaign against illegal immigration that whites, blacks, and Asians escape.... Instead of placing a racial tax on blacks, Mexican-Americans, and other colored people, governments should, if necessary, increase taxes across the board.[28]

The challenge facing these arguments is to distinguish *racial* profiling from the many other forms of differential policing that do not seem seriously objectionable. Profiling of people who fidget anxiously in a security queue, for instance, does not seem to raise grave moral concerns—even if only a very small fraction of these people are actually guilty of anything.

What, then, might make a *racial* tax especially problematic? In this section I consider two features of race that could be invoked to ground this distinction: the fact that a person is not responsible for his race, and the nature of the evidential connection between race and crime.

There is another important possibility, however, that I will simply note and set aside here. In particular, there is something undeniably perverse about singling out members of a group for scrutiny, which involves burdening them more than others, when the reason for doing so—putative correlations with crime distributions—is ultimately rooted in the systematic disadvantages *already* wrongfully imposed on members of that group, or in a collective failure to remedy those disadvantages. This is an important concern, although its ultimate upshot is not entirely clear.[29] In any case, I set it aside because it is not common to many cases of racial profiling. If there is a correlation between being of Middle Eastern appearance and committing acts of terrorism, or between being Hispanic and being an undocumented immigrant in the United States, it is an open question whether that is because of past or present mistreatment of these groups. So I will simply acknowledge that this consideration may make a difference in certain cases, for instance with respect to profiling African Americans in the United States, while focusing our discussion on factors of more clearly general relevance.

6.2.1 Responsibility and mutability

Durlauf argues that it is unfair for an innocent person's likelihood of being stopped or searched to be influenced by his race, because race is not something "for which an individual is responsible."[30] Is a person's moral claim against being burdened by policing stronger when he is not responsible for the trait that prompts the police to target him?

We can take for granted that a person does generally have a weaker claim against being subjected to some burden if he shares in the responsibility for that burden.[31] Even when a person is responsible for possessing a particular *trait*, however, it seems unreasonable to infer that he bears any responsibility for the burden he incurs from being profiled on that basis. For one thing, information deficits can easily force a wedge between the two. If I am responsible for a trait, I still cannot normally be held responsible for my being subjected to extra scrutiny on that basis if I could not reasonably have known, at the time that I took on the trait or last had the chance to change it, that profiling for this trait was in effect.

In the absence of transparency about what prompts extra scrutiny, then, the difference between responsibility and non-responsibility for a trait seems irrelevant to one's responsibility or non-responsibility for being encumbered on that basis, and thus to the strength of one's moral claim against being searched. And in most contexts, such as security screenings, opaqueness about just what triggers increased scrutiny is the norm—indeed, opaqueness is essential to the utility of the profiling. In such cases, then, the fact that you are responsible for whether you buy a ticket in cash, but not for your race, cannot ground a moral difference between the two forms of profiling.

This argument may suffice for some practical purposes, but it does not settle the more fundamental question. If everyone *did* know what triggers scrutiny, would it be morally better to profile people on the basis of traits that they are responsible for possessing? The answer, I think, is that it might well be better, but not because those who are scrutinized under this arrangement are partly responsible for the burdens they incur. It would be better simply because traits people are responsible for possessing are more likely to be *mutable* traits, and when that is so, the burdens these people incur are likely to be of lesser magnitude than they would be if the same trait were immutable.*

Specifically, assuming perfect information about what prompts scrutiny, immutability matters in the following way. If a trait is immutable, then profiling for this trait burdens a person if he possesses this trait. If a trait is mutable, then profiling for this trait burdens him if he possesses this trait or *would* do so if not for the marginal incentive, due to the profiling, not to have it. The people who meet the second condition (i.e., when the trait is mutable) have no weaker claim against being burdened for the sake of security than the people who meet the first condition (when it is not). But the burden that people are subjected to by the policy may be *less* in the second case, simply because they are allowed to pick their poison: they can either not adopt (or retain) a trait they otherwise would have, or face an elevated chance of search. *If* not adopting or retaining the trait is the less costly option for someone, then the burden that

---

* Not *all* traits that you are responsible for are mutable, since you can make an irreversible choice to adopt what is then an immutable trait. Past histories have this quality: now that you have read this sentence, you can never shed the property of being a person who has read this sentence.

person is subjected to will be reduced relative to the case in which the relevant trait is immutable.

This interpretation of the relevance of mutability to the fairness of profiling highlights an important point. Sherry Colb argues that racial profiling is distinctly unfair "because race is immutable and therefore cannot be altered to avoid unwanted disparate treatment."[32] But in fact burdening someone on the basis of a trait that she can change is not necessarily *at all* fairer than burdening her on the basis of other traits, even in the context of perfect information: it will be fairer only if the cost to her of abandoning or suspending the trait is less than the cost of the elevated chance of search. In many cases—for instance, those of some people who wear religious apparel—that condition will not be met, so the fact that they can change the trait will make no difference at all to the burden imposed on them by profiling on this basis.

It is also important that what is significant about race here turns out to be a matter of mutability, not responsibility. Indeed, it does not seem that responsibility for a trait itself makes any difference. If a person is aware that profiling is in effect and responsibly adopts or retains a trait anyway, she is responsible for the fact that the burden imposed on her *takes the form of an elevated risk of search*, as opposed to the form of forgoing a trait she would prefer to adopt or retain. But she is not made responsible for the burden itself because she is responsible for choosing its form.

The fact that race is immutable makes a potential difference, then, but this effect is not mediated by the fact that one is not responsible for one's race, and it does not manifest as a weakening in the force of people's claims against the burdens imposed by profiling (when these burdens are taken as a whole). It matters whether you can change a trait simply because this is related to a potential difference in the extent of the burdens imposed on you. I will return to that general idea—that racial profiling is morally worse than other procedures because it simply imposes burdens of greater magnitude—in §6.3 below.

Part of the intuitive appeal of the argument that racial profiling is bad because people are not responsible for their race, I think, may rest on a very simple confusion. People who are subjected to racial profiling reasonably object that, as Kennedy puts it, this "penalizes them for the misconduct of others who also happen to be colored."[33] The apparent force of this objection is that the people who are profiled are clearly not *responsible* for what other people who happen to share this trait do, so it is unfair that they be encumbered on account of that misconduct. But this point actually has nothing to do with the fact that people are not responsible for their *race*. People who buy tickets in cash or dress in particular ways are not responsible for what other people who fit these descriptions do, even though everyone involved is normally responsible for possessing the profiled traits.[34] Thus both kinds of profiling are apparently alike in respect of the kind of responsibility that could weaken someone's moral claim against being burdened by profiling.

6.2.2 Evidence and explanation

What else might render racial profiling morally worse, in principle, than profiling on the basis of other traits? Another salient feature of race is that, unlike many properties, it cannot be a *consequence* of crime, or of the intention to commit a crime. People sometimes buy tickets in cash or fidget in a security queue because they intend to hijack an airplane, for example, but nobody is of a certain race because they intend to do anything. Perhaps this is what is meant by the common claim that race is "no indication whatsoever that [people] have done anything wrong."[35] Could this difference between race and other traits imply that selecting people for searches on the basis of race is especially objectionable?

One way of developing this suggestion would be to require that a fact bear some explanatory connection to a hypothesis in order to count as evidence in favor of it. In discussing the problem of merely statistical evidence that we considered earlier, for instance, Thomson argues that (E), the frequency distribution of cabs operated by Red Cab and other cabs, should not be called "evidence" for (H), the hypothesis that a cab operated by Red Cab caused a particular accident. She writes:

No doubt the truth of (E) is some reason to think (H) true; no doubt you would bet on (H) if told (E); no doubt (E) makes (H) probable. But is the truth of (E) *evidence* for (H)? I think not.[36]

Thomson goes on to say that "it is not terminology that matters to us," but rather "what is wrong with (E) which issues in this disinclination to call it evidence for (H)."[37] The same is true here: whether or not an explanatory connection is required for "evidence," does the presence or absence of such a connection bear on the morality of subjecting someone to scrutiny on the basis of a particular trait?[38]

There are actually three different possible proposals that rely on claims about the moral importance of explanatory relationships in this context. First, the problem with racial profiling might be as I posed it at the outset—that a person's race is never explained *by* the criminality for which it is being taken as evidence. Second, some have made essentially the opposite objection, invoking the fact that *crime* is not explained by *race*. Finally, one could pose a wholesale version of the objection. The actual thesis of Thomson's analysis of the Red Cab case is that something is not acceptable as evidence if it "stands in no explanatory relation whatever" to the hypothesis it is taken to support, including by virtue of a common cause.[39] As applied to racial profiling, this would require the claim that race is neither upstream nor downstream evidence of crime, and shares no common explanation with it. I will briefly consider and reject each of these objections.

First, the fact that a person's race is never downstream evidence of his committing a crime does seem to distinguish inferences on the basis of race from many more ordinary inferences in police work. For example, as Michael Levin points out, "[a] bolt cutter in the back seat of a car is evidence that the driver is a burglar . . . because the driver's being a burglar would explain the presence of the bolt cutter."[40] By contrast, being a burglar cannot explain being of a certain race. Does this make a moral difference?

I think it does not. The most obvious counterexample to this proposal is simply evidence about people's motives. By definition motives explain crimes, rather than being explained by them. Nor is *evidence* of a person's motive normally explained by his committing a crime. But it seems to be perfectly genuine evidence, and it is often admissible in criminal trials. The standard for imposing searches, one would think, should be no more stringent.[41]

So the use of non-downstream evidence doesn't seem especially problematic. Next, then, Michael Boylan suggests that it is bad to employ race as evidence of criminality because, even if racial differences are correlated with crime rates, racial differences do not themselves explain crime. He writes:

> What is germane [to the justification of racial profiling] is the empirical claim that *because* someone is African American—or Latino or white—they are more likely to commit a crime. There are simply no scientific grounds for these claims. This is because there is no biological mechanism that would suggest that this is the case.[42]

It is not clear what principle underwrites this objection. If it were that *only* upstream evidence is morally admissible, it would be very implausible. That would exclude, for instance, the bolt cutter case above. So perhaps Boylan is also relying on the obvious fact that a person's race is not explained *by* a person's crime. That is, perhaps he is suggesting that racial profiling is objectionable because it is bad to use evidence that is of *neither* the upstream nor the downstream variety.

Supposing that the evidence employed in racial profiling is neither upstream nor downstream evidence, however, we should still presume that whatever significant correlations there are between demographic variables and crime patterns are explainable. The remaining possibility would be that racial differences merely share a common cause with the relevant kinds of criminality.* But then to reject the use of race as evidence because it is neither upstream nor downstream

---

* How could this be? Here is a very crude and schematic example for illustrative purposes. A person's race may causally explain both his child's race and his being subjected to discrimination that disadvantages him, and by extension his child, in a way that ultimately contributes to explaining his child's committing a crime. Then the child's race and the child's crime share a common cause: the parent's race.

evidence, we would have to suppose that the use of "common cause" evidence is objectionable.

Once we have abandoned the objection to upstream evidence, however, that seems very implausible. After all, cases of common cause evidence can easily be constructed simply by introducing an observable consequence of something that would otherwise serve as upstream evidence. Here is one such case. On Monday, Jane tells her husband John that she had an affair; on Tuesday, Jane turns up dead. Jane's confession to John is upstream evidence in favor of the hypothesis that John killed her, since it would help to explain that (putative) fact. But suppose the detectives don't know that Jane made this confession—until they find her diary, in which she wrote, on Monday night, that she had just confessed her affair to John. That she wrote this is evidence against John, just as the fact of her actual confession is, although the diary entry does not itself explain his (putatively) killing her. Rather, the diary entry is partly explained by something— her confession—that partly explains his (putatively) killing her. This difference in explanatory structure does not seem to yield any significant moral difference, however, with respect to the fairness of using the evidence against John.

The upshot is that we should not regard any category of evidence, segmented by its form of explanatory connection, as an especially objectionable basis for imposing the burden of being searched or investigated on people. The only version of the objection that remains, then, is that racial evidence is flawed because it has no explanatory connection *at all* to crime, including by way of common causes. This is what Thomson apparently thinks about the connection between the frequency distribution of cabs and the hypothesis that a cab operated by Red Cab caused a particular accident. But whether or not that is an accurate description of that case,[43] it seems very implausible as a view about the relationship between race and crime. As I have suggested, if certain kinds of crime really are not probabilistically independent of race, there should be a strong presumption that *some* explanatory connection, however attenuated, unites the two.[44]

In sum, then, the nature of the explanatory connection between race and crime does not seem to ground a persuasive objection to racial profiling, as compared with other forms of differential policing. Of course, it is certainly worse when people are selected for searches on the basis of less *accurate* forms of evidence rather than more accurate ones. But this does not require attention to how race and crime are causally or explanatorily related, and it is no objection to racial profiling in principle.

6.2.3 Conclusion

It is natural to construe the moral objection to racial profiling in terms of something wrong with it in principle, but this line of argument is less promising than it appears. As we have seen, such an argument requires an explanation of why *racial* profiling is especially objectionable. Claims about the explanatory relationships between race and criminality seem to do little work in this regard. The mutability or immutability of a profiled trait may be relevant to fairness, but only under certain contingent conditions.

In particular, I noted in our discussion of immutability that this factor could well be relevant to the *magnitude* of burdens imposed by racial profiling, as compared to certain other ways of allocating scrutiny. That is not what is normally meant by the claim that racial profiling is distinctly unfair—that it imposes greater costs on members of the targeted group than other practices do on the people *they* burden—but it may well be true. Here, then, we encounter an intersection between objections based in fairness and those that simply indict profiling as especially harmful.

For both kinds of arguments, the key point is that the magnitude of the "tax" that is being distributed by policing is not necessarily independent of who it is imposed upon. This can easily be overlooked. Risse and Zeckhauser, for instance, write: "The screening of individuals from all groups, albeit with different probabilities,... indicates that we are not subjecting specific groups to actions we would not impose on others. Only the *frequency* of the actions differs."[45] Strictly speaking, security searches or highway stops do impose the same "actions" on members of all groups. But the *significance* of those same actions can nevertheless differ across groups in a way that affects how costly or burdensome they are, and this is what matters. In a society thought to practice racial profiling, being pulled aside for extra screening at an airport is surely a different experience for a young man of Middle Eastern descent than for an older white woman. Recognition of these extra costs should give us pause in considering whether we might after all be "subjecting specific groups to [*impositions*] that we would not impose on others," or indeed which we ought not to impose on anybody.

These extra costs could be taken to furnish a reason why racial profiling is more *unfair* than other forms of profiling, or simply as evidence for the claim that its harms outweigh its benefits. The analysis will be much the same in either case. I turn to the latter idea, which I will call the Harm Argument, in the next section.

6.3 The Narrow Harm Argument

The Harm Argument comes in narrow and broad forms. The Narrow Harm Argument claims that racial profiling is unjustified in light of the harm it does to those who are subjected to police scrutiny. The Broad Harm Argument points to both these harms and the broader social costs of profiling, which may injure someone whether or not she ever encounters the police.

I will consider the Narrow and Broad versions of the Harm Argument in turn. Naturally, this is an area in which philosophy can only go so far. We can't weigh costs and benefits against one another without assigning some magnitudes to each, and these will have to be sensitive to a number of empirical contingencies. But we can hope to lay down some useful parameters to guide such an inquiry, and to clarify which sorts of harms are relevant in what ways.

The Narrow Harm Argument, as I have defined it, concerns harm done by racial profiling to those who are subjected to scrutiny by the police. The most obvious harms are psychological: the encounters often provoke feelings of humiliation, resentment, and other forms of hurt. But I do not want to assume that all of the harm done is experiential. For example, when a black man is pulled aside for scrutiny in public, this can have the effect of causing onlookers to view him in derogatory terms, and perhaps being viewed in that way is harmful to him even if it has no effects on his experiences. In addition to the harm that consists in the feeling of humiliation that a person may experience as a consequence of profiling, in other words, there may be a distinct harm in his being humiliated in the eyes of others, similar in kind to the possible harm of being insulted behind one's back. Whether such harms are genuine is a distinct and unsettled question. Although I won't take a view on that question here, what I say below should apply either way.

6.3.1 Belief and the harms of profiling

We should recognize a further distinction among the contingent harms of racial profiling, whether these are experiential or (possibly) not. The proximate cause of some of these harms is the *belief* that a person has been racially profiled, whereas for others this belief is immaterial.

The belief-dependent harms are the most readily apparent. It is normally the judgment that one has been subjected to additional scrutiny on account of one's race that leads one to feel demeaned, stigmatized, or humiliated. It may also be that this belief about somebody else—the belief that she was searched on account of race—affects how one views her, in a manner that harms her in itself.

When we assess these harms, then, we have to look to the number of people who will believe they are being searched because of profiling, or about whom this will be believed—which could either exceed or fall short of the number of people of whom this is actually true. To better define this class, we need to consider how a person forms the belief that she (or somebody else) has been profiled.

A person who is searched is likely to know little about the overall distribution of people searched. After all, at a public checkpoint like an airport, people observe at most the scrutiny applied to the handful of people who pass through before them. In other cases, as when a driver is stopped on a highway, she may know even less. Some people will have better evidence with respect to these questions than others, for instance if they travel frequently and find themselves frequently stopped, or if they are members of communities that report common experiences. But in general, even when people are profiled, neither they nor onlookers will have access to the evidence required to know it.

When someone finds herself taken aside for extra screening at an airport, then, her belief about whether she has been profiled on the basis of her race is more likely driven by her beliefs about the presence or absence of racial profiling in general than anything particular to her experience at the time.* If she perceives the institutions involved to be ones that employ racial profiling, that is, she will often interpret a search as racially motivated, even if it was not; and if she does not think that racial profiling is practiced in general, she will often not interpret her own particular search as racially motivated, even if it was.

These facts matter a great deal for how we should take account of the belief-dependent harms imposed by racial profiling. For example, if a racial profiling policy prescribes that 10 percent of the population at large, and 15 percent of men of Middle Eastern appearance, will be searched—and if the policy will prompt people to believe that profiling of men of Middle Eastern appearance is in effect—then the per-individual risk of belief-dependent harms done by profiling should be multiplied by the full 15 percent of men of Middle Eastern appearance who are searched, not the marginal 5 percent who are searched because of profiling.

This is clear enough when it is made explicit, but it is not always recognized. Risse and Zeckhauser, for instance, note that searching someone because of a profile "often does no harm beyond the inconvenience," but then go on to claim that the "harm is greater only if the characteristic for which a person is targeted" is vested with special

---

* Of course, matters will be different if the search itself is conducted with apparent disrespect, especially racial disrespect; that will certainly be a cue to the person that she was more likely to have been stopped on account of race. But, by hypothesis, we are considering racial profiling that is conducted respectfully.

social or psychological significance.[46] In fact, harm is likely to be greater if the characteristic for which a person *takes himself* to have been targeted carries a special significance. We should be wary of understating the harms of adopting a racial profiling policy by assuming that they are suffered only by people whose targeting is *actually* influenced by race.

This argument suggests that the total harm done by instituting profiling may be greater than is sometimes assumed. But a second effect pushes in the opposite direction. It is not *necessary* that a person actually be profiled in order for him to be the victim of belief-dependent harms, but it is not *sufficient* either. The harms at issue do not arise when a person does not believe that he has been subjected to profiling, even if he has been. This suggests that, if the central moral objection to racial profiling did ultimately rest on the belief-dependent harms involved, certain controversial policies could conceivably be improved simply by making them more discreet.[47]

At the same time, even if we continue to limit our attention to the direct harms done to individuals subjected to scrutiny, not all of the harms of racial profiling *are* belief-dependent. These other harms are subtler but no less important. To bring them out, we can begin from the premise that there are some generic harms to being subjected to scrutiny, regardless of whether profiling is or even is believed to be in effect. Some of these harms are material, such as the delay or inconvenience involved. Others are psychological: a feeling of anxiety, and potentially of humiliation. And yet others may be non-experiential: for instance, possible degradation in the eyes of others.

Racial profiling will prove more harmful than other policing practices, then, if it is simply the case that these harms are greater on average for members of the targeted group than they are for the population at large. Because racial profiling has the effect of concentrating the scrutiny that triggers these harms on this group, it will then do more harm. And that effect may obtain whether or not anybody believes that race figured in the allocation of scrutiny.

This extra harm is a consequence of racial profiling, then, but not belief-dependent. In certain social contexts, there is reason to think it is severe. If African Americans are more likely to feel genuinely unsafe—or to be so—when confronted by police officers in the United States, whether or not they believe they were profiled, that is a harm increased by racial profiling.[48] Similarly, if Hispanics are more likely to be viewed in demeaning terms by passersby when they are questioned in public by the police, that is a potential harm that will be increased by a policy that focuses police scrutiny on Hispanics, whether or not anybody believes Hispanics are being profiled. Indeed, it could be better in this narrow respect if passersby *did* form that belief, rather than assuming that a person is being questioned because he is an undocumented immigrant or a criminal.

This discussion makes clear that the force of the Narrow Harm Argument is highly sensitive to social context. First, the argument rests on nothing that is either intrinsic or unique about race. This means both that racial profiling could sometimes fail to be objectionable on this account, and that other non-racial forms of profiling could sometimes be objectionable as well. This latter point may help to explain why many who object to racial profiling also object to religious profiling: it could be a similarly contingent fact that profiling on the basis of religion is also felt to be demeaning or stigmatizing, for instance. But by the same token, if in some contexts racial (or religious) profiling does not carry these special costs—perhaps because these are not salient social categories in a given society, or because the profiled group is a dominant one, or for some other reason—then profiling will not be objectionable, at least not on this ground.

The context-sensitivity of the Narrow Harm Argument thus implies that in order to make the case for this objection in any given instance, one will normally have to undertake a textured analysis of the actual psychological effects and social meaning of *that* practice. In the case of immigration enforcement in the United States, for example, these might include creating a sense among innocent Hispanics that they are not full members of the community, or cementing the impression that there is a single "American" way of looking (to which they do not conform). But these effects presumably differ from those of profiling blacks in investigating certain kinds of drug crimes, or whites in investigating other kinds of drug crimes, or people of Middle Eastern appearance in devising anti-terrorism measures, and so on. For this reason, the Harm Argument requires a greater sensitivity than the more "principled" arguments against racial profiling that we considered above both to the social context that renders particular practices more or less demeaning or humiliating, as well as to the various traits, beyond race, that may be connected to similar effects in a given setting.

6.3.2 Does it matter if harm is "expressive"?

Risse and Zeckhauser make another point about how we should go about assessing the immediate harms of racial profiling, which is fundamental to their qualified defense of the practice. They emphasize that "the harm attached to profiling per se is *expressive*," by which they mean that "it occurs primarily because of harm attached to *other* practices or events."[49] They identify two ways in which an expressive harm of this kind can come into being:

[H]arm may be expressive if an event or practice is a *reminder* of other painful events or practices . . . or if one event or practice becomes a *focal point* for events or practices, a symbol of structural disadvantage or maltreatment. In addition to whatever harm the practice itself causes, the focal point becomes associated with harm attached to such disadvantage, and that harm plausibly accounts for the lion's share of the harm associated with that practice.[50]

Racial profiling, in their view, is a practice that fits this description; in particular, it "serves as a focal point for the racial injustices of society."[51] Consequently, profiling itself "is not the primary cause of the feeling of resentment and sense of hurt among minorities and the loss of trust in the police that it triggers."[52] This, they say, "affect[s] how the harm caused by racial profiling should be integrated into utilitarian calculations."[53] In particular:

If we are correct, what must enter the cost-benefit assessment of racial profiling is the *incremental* increase in harm those acts impose, not the overall level of harm ostensibly associated with them. So what utilitarians must assess is whether the incremental increase in harm caused by profiling as such, rather than the overall amount that comes to the fore in acts of profiling but is largely caused by underlying racism, outweighs the advantages of crime reduction.[54]

What exactly does it mean for some quantity of harm to "come to the fore in acts of profiling," while being "largely caused by underlying racism"? On one understanding of these notions, the argument seems clearly mistaken; on the other, it is unobjectionable but cannot bear nearly the weight that Risse and Zeckhauser seem to place on it.

The first reading, and the one that would best explain Risse and Zeckhauser's conclusion that "the harm done by profiling per se is comparatively modest,"[55] would be as follows. Racial profiling would not be humiliating, demeaning, or otherwise especially harmful if not for a social context characterized by widespread racial inequality and injustice.[56] Consequently, a proper cost–benefit analysis should not count these harms against profiling, at least not at their full weight, because although profiling "triggers" these harms, they are "largely caused by underlying racism."[57] Thus "[t]he crucial point . . . [is] that profiling *all by itself* does not cause the preponderance of the harm naïve calculation would lead people to think it causes."[58]

As a recommendation about how profiling should be assessed in the real world—which is what Risse and Zeckhauser intend[59]—this seems flatly mistaken. Suppose that a toxic chemical is introduced into a room full of people. I have a container of another chemical, which I can choose to release into the room as well. When this chemical is inhaled by people who have also inhaled the toxic substance already in the room, it will harm them as well. But if they had not inhaled the harmful substance already in the room, this second chemical would be harmless to them. We could say that, in performing the cost–benefit analysis of whether to release the second chemical, I should bear in mind that doing so would not be harmful in the absence of the existing toxic substance. In particular, the harm that would be "triggered" by releasing the second substance, or which would "come to the fore" when I do so, is actually "largely caused" by the fact that people have inhaled the underlying substance already in the room. So that quantity of harm should not count against releasing the second chemical, at least not at its full weight, since doing so would not *in itself* be harmful at all.

Clearly this is absurd. If it is what Risse and Zeckhauser mean, then it should have no bearing on how we count the harms brought about by profiling, at least not in the actual world where these harms will occur. In other words, it does not matter, for the purposes of deciding on the appropriateness of profiling in a world characterized by certain social facts, whether or not those facts are necessary for the causal connection between profiling and harm to obtain.[60]

Since this approach to weighing the harms of profiling seems clearly mistaken—and because, in a response to critics, Risse explicitly disavows the view that expressive harms are not genuine harms[61]—it might be more charitable to understand Risse and Zeckhauser differently. In particular, perhaps they mean the harm "ostensibly associated with" profiling, or "the harm naïve calculation would lead people to think it causes," to be *all of the harm that is due to the conditions in virtue of which profiling is harmful.* They might be saying that we should count against profiling only the harm of which profiling is a cause, and not other harm that is caused by states of affairs that also happen to be contributing causes of the harmfulness of profiling. If so, they are surely correct. Similarly, if I introduce the second chemical into the room, we should not count as a harm of that action the harm that would have been done by the ambient toxic substance anyway. But it is difficult to see why we *would* do that, or how even very "naïve" calculation could lead someone to see the harms of profiling as including harms of which profiling is not a cause.

Although it is inconsistent with some of what Risse and Zeckhauser say,[62] I think this is still probably the most sympathetic reading of their argument. It is buttressed by the fact that Risse and Zeckhauser offer the following thought experiment to support their claim:

[S]uppose we live in a world of racism, race disparities . . . and profiling. (This could be a description of our world.) Then imagine how much better-off, say,

African Americans would be if we just got rid of profiling, *keeping everything else fixed*. We think that the answer is "only slightly so."[63]

Seen in this light, the conceptual machinery of "expressive harm" appears to be doing relatively little work after all. Rather, this assertion suggests that Risse and Zeckhauser simply think that, even in the context of broader societal racism, profiling is not very harmful to members of the group that is profiled. For this reason, perhaps, they think that those who *do* see a significant incremental harm in profiling must be mistakenly counting the general disvalue of racism or race disparities against the practice—and perhaps Risse and Zeckhauser think that we are especially prone to this error because the harm at issue is an expressive one, in their sense.

If this is what they mean, however, I see very little reason to think that the error they have in mind actually plays any significant role in the ordinary judgment that profiling imposes significant harms. By all reports, the belief that one is being singled out for suspicion on account of one's race *is* stigmatizing, demeaning, and humiliating. To take one example, in the words of Christopher Darden, an attorney who is black, the experience of racial profiling "undermines and calls into question everything you've accomplished in your life, everything you've worked for. No matter how hard you've worked, no matter what you do . . . you're treated like a common criminal."[64] So there is every reason to think that, at least in many contexts, the elimination of racial profiling *would* constitute a significant improvement in the well-being of the people affected. Nothing about the expressive character of the harm undermines that judgment.

Even if Risse and Zeckhauser are mistaken, it is evident that the Narrow Harm Argument cannot easily be defended or opposed in general terms. We would need to assess the actual magnitudes of the costs and benefits involved in order to decide on its merits in a given case. I have argued that, in undertaking such an assessment, (1) we should consider both the set of people who may suffer belief-dependent harms *and* the distinct set of people who are actually subjected to scrutiny when they otherwise would not be; (2) we should attend to the social context which gives different profiling practices their meanings for the people affected; and (3) we should not discount the magnitude of the harms in question because they are "expressive."

As a general matter, I suspect that the Narrow Harm Argument is a powerful objection to racial profiling in many cases. For instance, the alienation and stigma experienced by a Hispanic American who believes he has been stopped and asked about his immigration status on account of racially motivated suspicion is likely to be substantial, and it is far from clear that the badness of imposing these costs on people is balanced by the marginal effect on unauthorized immigration in each such case—even if one were to count identifying undocumented immigrants as a significant good. Broadly speaking, then, rather than emphasizing the racial inequality at the core of this policy, opponents might do better to emphasize simply how badly it hurts innocent people relative to the benefits it yields. I think we have still seen only a fraction of the harm done by racial profiling thus far, however. In most cases, the decisive reason against the practice is offered by the Broad Version of the Harm Argument.

6.4 The Broad Harm Argument

Both the Narrow Harm Argument and the "principled" arguments we considered at the outset suggest that racial profiling is wrong because of what it does to people who are searched or scrutinized— if not always on account of their race, then at least by a system which they believe to have targeted them on account of their race, where the practice contributes to sustaining that belief. The moral case against racial profiling is not limited to its consequences for the people it affects directly, however, but also extends to the more diffuse consequences that result from institutionalizing and legitimating certain attitudes and habits of thought. Even if racial profiling imposed no unfair burden on the people it recommends for scrutiny, and even if the harms inflicted on the people who are searched were not so bad as to render the practice unacceptable, it might be objectionable for reasons that extend beyond the situations in which these interactions occur.

Annabelle Lever puts a version of this point this way:

Racial profiling publicly links black people with a tendency to crime. For that reason alone, it is likely to exacerbate the harms of racism. However scrupulous the police, racial profiling is likely to remind blacks, all too painfully, that odious claims about their innate immorality and criminality justified their subordination in the past, and still resurface from time to time in contemporary public debate. So, too, racial profiling will likely perpetuate, as well as reflect, white tendencies to draw invidious and complacent racial distinctions, and exacerbate unmerited indifference and hostility to the legitimate interests of black people.[65]

In this section, I develop a version of this objection and consider some of its theoretical implications. I call this the Broad Harm Argument because it points to a wider array of harmful consequences than the Narrow Harm Argument does. As with the Narrow Harm Argument, much of the determination about the force of this objection will depend on close analysis of particular social contingencies and the magnitudes of different costs, which is beyond my scope here. But we can still hope to clarify the range of relevant considerations and the criteria on which they depend. My overall conclusion is that the Broad Harm Argument likely furnishes a decisive objection against racial profiling in very many of the cases where it might be practiced.

What I am calling the Broad Harm Argument consists of several different concerns layered onto one another. First, a known policy of racial profiling may demean, stigmatize, alienate, or otherwise injure members of the profiled group, even if they are never themselves profiled and never even believe they are being profiled. Consider a recent law in the state of Arizona, which has been criticized for leading police to target Hispanics on suspicion of immigration violations.[66] In assessing such a law, we should consider not only the experience of individual Hispanic people who are subjected to searches (and thereby perhaps unfairly burdened or unduly harmed), but also the effect the policy may have on Hispanic people in general. In this case, the policy may well convey a sense that Hispanic Americans are unwelcome, even in their own neighborhoods, or that they are regarded as alien in the eyes of the law by virtue of their physical appearance. In addition, it may lead innocent people to alter their behavior so as to minimize the risk of confrontation with police whom they expect to stop or question them on account of their race.

Second, besides these first-order effects, such a policy will also have significant consequences for the attitudes of *other* people towards members of the profiled group. Those attitudes in turn may adversely affect members of the profiled group, as well as others, in ways that the policy alone does not. Third, members of a profiled racial group may then react to such harms with resentment or hostility that harms others, or undermines other important social values. All of these diffuse injuries—registering in terms of who gets hired for jobs, who becomes friends with one another, who is subjected to alienating suspicion by peers in daily life, who actively participates in a political system, and so on—fall under the heading of the Broad Harm Argument against racial profiling.

As with the Narrow Harm Argument, then, the social context of a classification will be crucial to determining whether it is morally acceptable. Some of the principles sometimes put forward to distinguish racial discrimination from other kinds of discrimination—such as the significance of historical stigmatization on the basis of race, or the relative power statuses of different groups—can be understood as relevant in this way.[67] For example, if white people are more likely to be drunk drivers in some area of the United States than black people, the Broad Harm Argument against responding with racial profiling would be much weaker than if the same were true of black people, simply because existing social prejudices leave blacks more vulnerable than whites to further harm by being socially associated with particular forms of misconduct. On the other hand, although whites themselves may not be badly injured by such a policy, it would not be surprising if they reacted to being so targeted with racial resentment that ultimately injures non-whites. The Broad Harm Argument should not be limited to assessing the harms inflicted on the profiled group; sometimes profiling one group will be wrong because it will predictably injure another.

Nonetheless, I will focus here on the harms to a minority racial group of being subjected to a known practice of profiling. The key question for us to consider, I think, is what about the social meaning of *racial* profiling renders it especially harmful in the ways I've just sketched. One point of entry into answering this question is the distinction between profiles and suspect descriptions that I argued for at the outset of the chapter.

Suspect descriptions, I proposed, are distinguished by the inferential structure they employ, which runs from the possession of a particular trait, to a judgment about personal identity, to a judgment about criminality. As a consequence, they do less than a profile might to suggest or insinuate a broader connection between the trait in question and being a criminal. Since this is a point about the social meaning of each practice, the significance of that difference should be felt in terms of the force of the Broad Harm Argument as applied to each case. This in turn will help to identify the relevant respects in which profiling on the basis of race may be more troubling than profiling in general.

There are two different levels on which the difference between suspect descriptions and profiling might be felt. First, the utility of a suspect description does not presuppose or rely upon the truth of any generalizations about the relative frequency of a category of crime among those who do and do not possess the trait in question. As I noted earlier, a suspect description of a mugger as red-haired is useful in pursuing the mugger even if red-haired people are in general *less* likely to be muggers than other people. For this reason, the use of the suspect description need not convey to anyone the message that *in general* we should be more suspicious of people with the trait in question than of others (whether or not that message would be a true one).

Second, but related, is that the suspect description is further removed than a profile from any causal hypothesis about the connection between the trait in question and criminality. In reality, of course, the use of a profile does not in any way presuppose that the profiled trait is a cause of crime. For a profile to be useful, the possession of a particular trait must only raise the *epistemic* probability that a person is a criminal. But the distinction between a trait's making one (epistemically) more likely to be a drug courier, and its actually *making* one more likely to be a drug courier, is predictably lost on many people. As a consequence, adopting a profiling policy may encourage the familiar and hurtful biases that attribute differences in rates of crime to deep-seated differences internal to the people involved, rather than to their social contexts.

These points about the social meaning of profiling ground a clear and compelling distinction between racial profiling and profiling on the basis of various other traits—how one pays for an airline ticket, or the kind of car one drives, and so on. There is obviously no serious prospect of fostering distrust and hostility towards the class of people who buy airline tickets in cash. This "identity" is not socially salient, and it carries no pre-existing stigma which profiling could legitimate or exacerbate.[68] By contrast, the social images of young black men as delinquents, or of Muslims as potential terrorists, are persistent sources of animus, contempt, and alienation. A government policy that even appears to vindicate those images would be a serious affront to the groups in question and amplify the harms they suffer.

This objection to profiling will apply to any group, whether racial or not, that is vulnerable to the attendant harms. But research in the social sciences suggests that concerns of this kind may be particularly pressing in the context of race. Specifically, some psychological and anthropological evidence suggests that people are disposed to interpret racial categories as "natural kinds," perhaps by virtue of the same cognitive machinery we employ in categorizing species.[69] According to the "essentialist" folk psychology that is apparently dominant in some cultures, racial classifications reflect inner essences that, like species differences, are robust to a wide range of environmental variations. Just as the Ugly Duckling of the fable—a swan raised from birth by ducks and perceived by all as a duck—inexorably grows into a swan anyway, so too people are disposed to view racial or ethnic categories as stable and highly explanatory, even when social conditions should predict a great deal of variation.[70] In many of the contexts with which we are concerned, those cognitive dispositions are then compounded by the accumulated weight of social prejudices, such as the "age-old, derogatory images of the Negro as criminal, images that have been revived and deployed in all manner of contexts, from popular entertainment, to scholarship, to political campaigns."[71]

Related tendencies also amplify the dangers of racial profiling in particular. Glenn Loury notes that aggregate crime statistics reported at the level of a particular group are always compatible with many different possibilities regarding how the criminal tendency reflected in the statistics is distributed within that group.[72] What we do with that plasticity has important consequences for how we think about the group as a whole. We can illustrate and develop Loury's point by adopting a very simplistic model for explaining crime. Suppose that whether a person x will commit a given crime at a time t is a function of two variables: a stable personal threshold, T_x, which describes how conducive the overall circumstances must be for him to commit the crime; and a measure, $C_{t,x}$, of the crime-conduciveness of his circumstances at the time. So x commits a crime at t if and only if $C_{t,x} > T_x$.

It is important to note that T_x is, aside from its primary role in the model, necessarily also a proxy for various qualities that we approve of as a society and seek in our own friends and associates. Very crudely, to the extent there are "bad people," they have low T_x values. (Remember that a low T_x means not simply that x is more likely to commit a crime than others, but that he is more likely to commit a crime faced with the same circumstances, however that idea is understood.) For this reason, a person will accrue both social capital and self-esteem from others' perception that his T_x value is high (or at least not unusually low).

Suppose, then, that the frequency of a certain crime is 10 percent within one group, and 5 percent within another. There are two questions we might ask about this pattern of facts. First, within each group, what makes the offending 10 percent (or 5 percent) different from the non-offending 90 percent (or 95 percent)? Second, what makes the first group (with its 10 percent crime rate) different from the second group (with its 5 percent crime rate)? The psychological evidence suggests that when these are two *racial* groups, we will be disposed to answer each question in the way that most undermines the social standing of the group with the higher crime rate. That in turn underscores the danger of rendering race a salient factor in the estimation of criminality, as racial profiling by law enforcement officials—the presumed experts on estimating criminality—can normally be expected to do.

Consider the first question. When we explicitly or tacitly choose among explanations for differences in criminality *within* a group, it matters whether we favor those that preserve greater consistency in T_x or $C_{t,x}$ across group members. On this score, the implicit hypothesis that racial categories are robust and explanatory biological types will naturally push in favor of assuming a relatively homogeneous T-distribution within a racial group. Moreover, this will seem especially natural to non-members of the relevant group, because of what psychologists call the "outgroup homogeneity effect."[73] In essence, we normally perceive greater internal variation in groups to which we belong, and more homogeneity in groups to which we do not. So, for example, white Americans are likely especially predisposed to view black Americans as similar in respect of their "basic" properties (T_x), and thus to take the fact that some commit crimes while others do not to reflect mere differences in their circumstances ($C_{t,x}$).

At the same time, the very same tendency to see racial categories as robust and explanatory can also be expected to dispose people to see variation in crime rates *between* racial groups as a reflection of deep-seated differences, traceable to differences in people's basic dispositions (T_x) rather than their circumstances ($C_{t,x}$). This yields, in effect, the least flattering possible portrait of the group with the higher crime rate. An elevated crime rate among black people, for instance, will be seen as explained by fundamental differences in crime thresholds between blacks and whites; but non-offenders among blacks will be seen, especially by whites, as *not* deeply different than black offenders.

In practice, then, these effects can combine to tar many members of a racial group as deeply crime-prone who not only did not commit a crime, but also would not have done so in the same circumstances as those who did. As Loury notes, that encourages the sense that even if particular members of the group in question are not guilty when screened, they are just as deserving of impositions as those who were, because it is only their circumstances that explain the different outcomes between them and the guilty.[74] David Wasserman raises a similar worry:

> A policeman questioning a young black man on an urban street where there has just been a shooting is likely to see him as an entirely appropriate suspect, as someone who probably has engaged, or will engage, in this kind of violence even if he did not on this occasion.[75]

Moreover, as I have noted, the perception of a low T_x value will be a major obstacle to social advancement and individual self-esteem, well beyond interactions with the police. Unfortunately, the twin effects I have described—the disposition to attribute differences in crime rates between racial groups to aggregate differences in character rather than circumstances, and the disposition to assume a relatively uniform distribution of character within a racial group—will press in just that direction.

Our concern here is not with the general psychology of racial prejudice, but with the specific questions whether and why racial profiling in particular might threaten important individual and social goods. The answer, in short, is that we may be especially disposed to interpret the public message made by an institutional practice of racial profiling in a way that facilitates pernicious racism. As Lever puts it, "[r]acial profiling . . . teaches blacks that they are more likely to be viewed as criminals than are whites; and it teaches whites that they have more to fear from black people than from other members of their society."[76] My point is that there is also good reason to fear that this lesson will be received in the most harmful way possible: as a broad-based indictment of blacks in general, and as a reflection of differences in fundamental properties rather than in circumstances or disadvantage.

As should now be clear, the concerns that animate the Broad Harm Argument are also closely related to the theory of wrongful discrimination developed in Part II of the book. My suggestion here is that racial profiling is *contingently* bad; but among the ways it is contingently bad is that it will predictably induce people to act in ways that are *intrinsically* bad. For instance, aside from its clear material and psychological harms, a known practice of racial profiling makes it more likely that members of the profiled group will not be dealt with as autonomous individuals, because judgments about them will be formed simply on the basis of racial appearances. This concern would apply, moreover, even if the practice of profiling were itself highly sensitive to the various factors besides race that make someone a more or less likely suspect with respect to a certain kind of crime.

The upshot of these various considerations is that in many cases racial profiling is objectionable for the simple reason that it encourages racism, and that this harm will often outweigh whatever benefits it achieves. Perhaps the issue only appears more complicated because of certain implicit assumptions which often go unexamined: that a practice must *be* racist to promote racism, for instance; or that even if it is not motivated by racism, it must at least involve the unfair distribution of burdens on the basis of race. On the contrary, it seems clear that in the right social milieu, institutionalizing practices that are themselves innocent can undermine the conditions for effectively realizing a community of mutual respect.

Recognizing this point helps to explain some of the characteristic frustrations of popular debates over racial profiling. Proponents of profiling often find themselves maligned as racists when, they insist, they are nothing of the kind. They mean "nothing personal" by their support for racial profiling, and they don't understand why they are accused of promoting racism when their argument for profiling draws on no racist premises. In fact, however, whether racial profiling *can* be justified without recourse to objectionable assumptions may be of less importance in assessing its moral merits than how the practice will predictably be interpreted, and the justification that will be imputed to it by others.

Similar considerations furnish the response to Risse and Zeckhauser's claim that racial profiling does not constitute morally troubling "pejorative discrimination" because, even in social contexts marred by racism, profiling need not "either intend to or de facto contribute to an oppressive relationship."[77] With respect to the first condition, they rightly say that proponents of profiling need not intend to oppress a racial group. With respect to the second, they rely on their earlier claim that the harm done by profiling is "expressive," and is thus "parasitic on an underlying oppressive relationship that is independently present in society."[78] Consequently:

[W]hile indeed this sort of harm would not arise were it not for that underlying oppressive relationship, *the use of race as such, as opposed to abusive policing and disproportionate use of race,* crucially, does not contribute to that oppressive relationship.[79]

The Broad Harm Argument strongly suggests that this line of thought is misguided. The use of race as a proxy for criminality is likely to be taken as validation for racist assumptions about minority groups, and thereby to nurture the very prejudices which most directly contribute to the oppressive relationships in question.

6.4.1 Profiling and publicity

As I have said, I think the most compelling argument against racial profiling is the Broad Harm Argument. Perhaps the most provocative consequence of this position is that racial profiling might be unobjectionable if it were simply conducted in secret. We have already seen, above, the possibility that some arguments against racial profiling would not apply if people simply did not believe that they were being profiled. By contrast, the Broad Harm Argument would still apply if no particular person thought he was being profiled, as long as people thought that profiling of certain groups, *in general,* was underway. But what if even that could be kept a secret—perhaps precisely in order to meet these moral concerns? Put differently, by the lights of this argument, isn't there a case to be made that government agencies should pronounce that racial profiling is wrong and won't be practiced, and then use it anyway?

Of course, we might oppose such a scheme on general grounds to do with honesty and transparency in government, rather than the morality of racial profiling. In nearly every actual case, moreover, this proposal would be exceedingly unrealistic. Large bureaucracies do not keep secrets well, and the chances of effectively monitoring compliance and rooting out racial abuse would surely be undermined by a culture of secrecy. For all of these reasons, I do not believe there is a persuasive real-world argument to be made for secret racial profiling, even if one takes the decisive arguments against racial profiling to be those that rest on contingent consequences of the attitudes it engenders.

Still, it is a philosophically significant result if racial profiling is not *in itself* objectionable, and this result is not without any possible relevance to the real world. Consider, for example, the Computer-Assisted Passenger Screening (CAPS) system adopted by the United States in the late 1990s. This program was introduced at airports "to select passengers whose checked baggage must be subjected to additional security measures."[80] Specifically, such automated systems use information provided by passengers when they purchase their tickets in order to assess risk, and recommend the baggage of some "selectees" for additional screening. Many would be outraged, I think, if race were included as a factor in this algorithm. The White House Commission on Aviation Safety and Security, which recommended the adoption of the CAPS program, specifically prohibited the use of race, religion, or national origin as factors.[81]

So long as the program is limited to checked luggage, however, and implemented in the warehouses where bags are processed and screened, it seems difficult to mount an objection from fairness or immediate harm. The Broad Harm Argument emphasizes the wider social consequences of institutionalizing negative stereotypes, which might occur even if no particular people believe that they are being profiled, or are encumbered at the time, as long as it is nevertheless believed that racial profiling is practiced. Such concerns ably explain the White House decision to publicly disavow consideration of race in the screening algorithm. But at least in theory, the concerns raised by the Broad Harm Argument could be met in other ways instead, while preserving the racial profiling itself. Perhaps the contents of the CAPS algorithm could simply have been a closely held secret, like many other protocols having to do with national security. Or we could suppose that the choice of "selectees" is made by an exercise of individual discretion at the airport, and that a particular official secretly employs race or ethnicity as one factor in his judgments, to exactly the extent that race or ethnicity is a useful predictor of risk.

In this case, the inconveniences imposed by searches, the harms they sometimes entail, any resulting unfairness, and the possibility of institutionalizing or legitimating social prejudices are all apparently eliminated. So is there a substantial moral objection to what is done here? My treatment of racial profiling appears to suggest that there may not be.

This is not to say that there are no good reasons for being uneasy about this case. We might be suspicious of the motives of the people who choose to include race in the CAPS algorithm or to exercise their discretion along racial lines; or we might worry that they will internalize broader racial prejudices; or we might believe that these practices will ultimately be revealed, inadvertently demeaning many people and deepening racial distrust. But in a contrived hypothetical where we could be assured that nothing of this sort would ensue, I think it would be hard to avoid the conclusion that there is nothing morally wrong with this practice—indeed, we would have to conclude that it is a morally praiseworthy one, if it helped to protect innocent people from harm.

To be clear, what is striking here is not simply that racial profiling could be justified under some hypothetical circumstances—that, for all I have said, could sometimes be true when the various arguments I have canvassed *do* apply—but rather that there might sometimes be no substantial moral objection to it at all. At the same time, it would be a serious mistake for security and law enforcement protocols to aim to accommodate moral concerns about racial profiling in this way. After all, the practical barriers to truly divorcing profiling from its harmful consequences are likely to be overwhelming, and there is good reason to worry that any such effort would succeed at establishing a practice of profiling, but not at doing so in a way that avoids the attendant harms.

Still, the present analysis does cast light on the character of the central moral objections to racial profiling, and on the way the debate should perhaps be carried forward. Concretely, if I am analyzing the moral problems posed by racial profiling correctly, that debate should focus on the contingent harms done by profiling in the context of particular social meanings, and policies should be assessed by reference to those harms. Such a discussion might be facilitated by leaving behind some claims against racial profiling that, I have argued, are unpersuasive: that it is simply more unfair to select people on account of traits they are not responsible for, for instance, or that race cannot be "evidence," in a morally actionable sense, of crime.

Here is one final way of dramatizing the picture of the moral case against racial profiling that has emerged. Compare two states of affairs, each departing from a common baseline society that features both significant racism and the kinds of racial patterns in crime that could potentially render racial profiling efficient. In one case, suppose it is widely believed, by people of all racial backgrounds, that racial profiling of one group is routinely employed in law enforcement. In fact, however, people who believe this are mistaken: racial profiles are never a factor in the decision to subject someone to scrutiny. In the second case, flip these stipulations around: suppose that racial profiling is routinely employed, but for some special reason, nobody realizes this is so.

It seems clear to me that the first case is likely to be much worse from the moral point of view, even though it actually *involves no racial profiling*. In this case, the Broad Harm Argument and the belief-dependent component of the Narrow Harm Argument will apply with significant force—only not as arguments against racial

profiling (since there is none) but as arguments against the arrangement, whatever it is, that allows the impression that racial profiling is
routinely used. In the second case, the principled arguments against
racial profiling as such—to do with responsibility for a trait and
explanatory connections—would apply, as would the non-belief-
dependent component of the Narrow Harm Argument. These latter
objections are by no means trivial, but I think there is a strong case to
be made that the first set of objections is more powerful. This contrast
underscores that the core moral case against racial profiling, in the
contexts where it is normally considered, may not be as it appears on
the surface; strictly speaking, in fact, it may not *be* a case against racial
profiling.[82]

6.5 Conclusion

I have taken racial profiling in law enforcement as an exemplar of the
kind of discrimination that is not condemned by the disrespect-based
objection to core cases of wrongful discrimination, but which may
well be objectionable on other grounds. In a moment I will turn to
considering how these distinct threads of moral analysis relate to one
another. First, however, it is worth seeing to what extent our analysis
of racial profiling can be generalized to other, structurally analogous
cases. My hope is that it at least lays down some markers for considering the morality of statistical discrimination more generally.

Consider, for instance, the policy in some countries of refusing
blood donations from men who have had sex with other men within
the past year as a safeguard against HIV infection.[83] Let us assume
that the relevant agencies could achieve the same level of safety in
their blood supply without this restriction, but only at somewhat
greater expense. It is clear, then, that the policy embodies statistical
discrimination, and that there is at least something to be said for it.
I also think it need not manifest basic disrespect for anyone as a
person. How would we go about assessing whether it is wrong?

Following the model of the racial profiling case, we should first ask
how a policy of excluding people on the basis of sexual activity might

be objectionable in principle. The option to donate blood is presumably a benefit, as most options are, and this policy denies it to some people, including many who are not infected with a communicable disease. But just as we compared racial profiling to other forms of criminal profiling, so we should view the sexual history policy against the backdrop of other exclusions from blood donation.

Some of these exclusions are temporary, such as a waiting period after travel to certain countries. Others are, like the sexual activity exclusion, functionally indefinite or even permanent. For example, people are prohibited from donating blood in the United Kingdom if they are at "familial risk of prion-associated diseases."[84] Suppose, for illustrative purposes, that this exclusion affected roughly as many people as the recent-sexual-history policy does. If we can safely assume that the family history exclusion would still not be gravely unfair, then we should ask why using sexual history to select the people who will be excluded would be *more* unfair than that. This was the role of the discussion of responsibility and explanatory connections in the profiling case, and here again I see no plausible way to make out that objection.

So we should next ask about the Narrow Harm Argument. What does it *do* to particular men to deny them the option of donating blood because they have had sex with other men in the last year? Is there a significant harm beyond what would be done to people excluded for some more mundane reason, like the fact that a relative suffers from a prion-associated disease? It seems very likely that there is. An exclusionary policy alienates gay men from the community of mutual support and civic engagement realized by the blood donation system, and probably constitutes a "focal point," in Risse and Zeckhauser's sense, for broader injustice that involves the deliberate exclusion of gay people.[85] As a consequence, a sexual history exclusion is significantly more harmful than the family history exclusion to those who are turned away. Like in the case of racial profiling, then, it may be not be unfair to screen people on this basis, but it may nonetheless be wrong to do so because of the special harms involved. Or, to put the point somewhat differently, it may be unfair to screen people on this basis only because it is unfair to impose the special costs of being-selected-on-this-basis on some people, when the same goals could be achieved by imposing a lower cost on a larger class of people—not because imposing the costs of search or exclusion on people with this trait, and not on others, would be unfair in itself.

Finally, then, what about the Broad Harm Argument? This also seems to ground a serious concern about the sexual history exclusion. As one critic put it (before the United Kingdom lifted its permanent ban on donations from men who have had sex with men), that exclusion "stigmatise[d] gay men by perpetuating the offensive myth that they cannot be trusted in matters of sexual health."[86] Even the one-year exclusion policy probably also encourages the diffuse sense that gay men are somehow tainted, on a biological level, by same-sex intercourse. Worse, to borrow an image from Lever's contribution to the racial profiling debate, the policy risks giving these prejudices the "official seal" of the nation's highest medical authority.[87] Finally, as in the profiling case, these harms are not necessarily limited to those who are directly affected by the relevant exclusion; the policy may also indirectly threaten gay men who have no desire to donate blood, or who are unaware of the policy, through its effects on wider social attitudes.

This cursory analysis does not come close to allowing us to draw a moral conclusion about sexual history exclusions. There is no way around the fact that such a verdict requires an assessment of the actual costs of abolishing or forgoing the exclusion, in terms of additional expense or increased risk of disease transmission. All of the parties should be able to agree that some additional costs would be worth paying, and others would not. But the foregoing may help to clarify the direction that the analysis should take, and in particular how the moral considerations on the pro-abolition side of the ledger should be understood.

As in the profiling case, unfairness in who is *selected* for a benefit or burden is probably not the heart of the matter. Nor is the problem simply that the exclusion employs a generalization or stereotype that will not prove correct in many cases. Rather, the moral case against the exclusion rests primarily on the harm it does, which requires close attention to the social meaning of the discriminatory policy, preexisting attitudes towards the group affected, and the qualitative experiences of the people who are discriminated against. These, I suggest, are the proper starting points from which to undertake a moral assessment of a practice of statistical discrimination that does not manifest disrespect.

Conclusion

I have offered a conceptual analysis of discrimination, an account of indirect discrimination, a theory of what makes paradigm cases of wrongful discrimination intrinsically wrong, and an example of how we might assess the morality of discrimination where that objection does not apply. Rather than summarizing the whole book here, let me conclude by highlighting a connection between two of its parts, and then try to distill its overall message.

First the connection. In general, the approach I have taken may foster the impression that the moral analysis of discrimination must proceed on two parallel tracks. Some discrimination is intrinsically wrong, on account of the disrespect it manifests. In other cases discrimination is bad simply because of its harmful effects—and I have tried to sketch out, by way of an extended example, the sorts of considerations that are relevant in making this determination. But these inquiries are, in fact, very closely related. We have already noted one intersection between the two forms of analysis: among the deleterious contingent effects of some discrimination is that it fosters conditions that give rise to acts of basic disrespect along the same lines. Another connection, though, is more fundamental. Whether acting in a certain way manifests disrespect for some people in the first place has a great deal to do with what one understands the effects of one's action to be.

We considered this point briefly in Chapter 3 with regard to the distinction between conventional and basic disrespect. If you don't know that spitting on people is taken as a sign of disrespect, and your ignorance is itself not a consequence of disrespect for anyone, then your spitting on someone does not manifest an attitude of basic disrespect. But if you *do* know what spitting on someone means, then your disregard for the harms of violating the convention means that your action does manifest such disrespect, even if your *aim* is not to show disrespect for the person you spit on.

Much the same analysis applies to support for social policies, although the inference is less clear-cut. Consider the example of racial profiling again. I argued in Chapter 6 that such profiling is normally unjustified in light of its harmful effects. A proponent of profiling could certainly dispute this conclusion: perhaps I have misapprehended the magnitudes of certain harms, or the alternatives are less effective than I have assumed, and so on. But if she does not doubt my conclusion about the policy's effects in good faith, that is significant to how we should understand her support for profiling. If she endorses the policy anyway, that is, we would be entitled to suspect that her support rests on discounting the harm to those who will be injured, in which case it does manifest basic disrespect for them, and is intrinsically wrong on that account.

We would still not be *certain* of this, or should not be, because she could support profiling on the basis of some freestanding principle that implies that it is required notwithstanding its harmful effects. In that case, as long as she sees the harm done as appropriately regrettable, she might not be failing to accord the due normative significance to the interests of the people affected, even if her chosen principle is ultimately unsound.[1]

In general, however, the state of our knowledge about the world plays a crucial role in determining whether certain discriminatory actions, as done by us, manifest a failure to treat some people respectfully as persons. One effect of close analysis of the contingent effects of an action or policy, then, and of publicizing the conclusions, is to add to the moral stakes confronting a decision-maker. Such analysis forces her to choose not only whether to adopt some given course of action, but also, simultaneously, whether to respect all of the persons affected as beings of genuine and equal value.

What, then, is the overall conclusion of the book? At bottom, it may be simply that discrimination is not a phenomenon to which we can or should adopt a unitary stance, but a gross category that subsumes many different kinds of acts, which are troubling in different ways and to different degrees. There is value in distinguishing rather sharply between discrimination and the construct of "indirect discrimination," for instance, since these are really quite different phenomena. Moreover, some cases of discrimination are not in any way bad. Among those that *are* bad, some are immoral regardless of their effects, because they make manifest a failure to recognize some of the discriminatees as persons; whereas others are simply bad because they are harmful.

Then, among those cases of discrimination that manifest disrespect, some are especially egregious, because they involve contempt for the moral standing of the discriminatees rather than a simple failure of recognition. In addition, not all discrimination that disrespects someone as a person does so by way of the *same* failure of recognition, for personhood itself involves different attributes. Failing to treat people as individuals and failing to treat them as beings of equal value are both ways of disrespecting them as persons, and each is characteristically involved in some forms of wrongful discrimination, but they offend against the discriminatee's standing as a person in different ways.

This theoretical edifice is somewhat more labyrinthine than I'd like. But we shouldn't expect a theory that is more elegant than the underlying structure of the phenomena—and this is an area where our thinking could stand for a bit more complexity. The vigor of public opposition to wrongful discrimination reflects a precious and hard-won point of consensus, but it does seem to have come at the expense of intellectual clarity about exactly what is objectionable, why it is, and the different degrees of badness that may be involved in different cases. Racial profiling may be wrong, for instance, without being racist. Sex discrimination motivated by unconscious biases may be wrong, and wrong independent of its circumstantial effects, but not *contemptuous* in the way that classic cases of misogyny are. And discriminatory preferences for certain types of people, with respect to choices where self-interest is rightly regarded as paramount, are sometimes not wrong at all. As a whole, then, I hope this book makes a modest contribution toward clarifying the predicament facing those of us who are quite sure that we're against wrongful discrimination, but remain uncertain just what that commits us to, and why.

Acknowledgments

I have been fortunate to benefit from the insights of many people in grappling with the issues explored here. My greatest substantive debts are to my wonderfully supportive and generous dissertation supervisors, John Broome and Cécile Fabre. I could not have completed this project without their steadfast support and their many contributions. I am particularly indebted to John Broome for supervising my work in moral philosophy from the beginning of my time at Oxford.

In revising the manuscript, I have benefited greatly from the trenchant comments of John Gardner and Kasper Lippert-Rasmussen, who served as the examiners for the dissertation, as well as those of anonymous reviewers for Oxford University Press. For comments and discussions about different facets of this project, I am also very grateful to Bruce Ackerman, Larry Alexander, Tamar Gendler, Tarun Khaitan, Jed Lewinsohn, Lev Menand, Scott Shapiro, Reva Siegel, Gideon Yaffe, and especially Deborah Hellman, whose generous support and critical commentary has been indispensable in bringing this project to fruition.

I am also indebted to the community in Oxford that supported and collaborated in my efforts to understand discrimination from a philosophical point of view, including participants in the Applied Ethics Discussion Group and the Jurisprudence Discussion Group. I am especially grateful to Sherif Girgis, William MacAskill, Adam Sandel, and Joseph O'Shea for talking through with me various of the arguments developed here. In addition, I gratefully acknowledge the funding support of the Rhodes Trust. An earlier version of Chapter 5 was published as Chapter 10 of *Philosophical Foundations of Discrimination Law* (Deborah Hellman & Sophia Moreau eds., Oxford University Press, 2013).

Finally, I thank my parents, Judy and Roy, and my wife, Amy, who have made my interests and projects their own and, in so doing, have made it possible for me to pursue them.

Endnotes

Introduction

1. Grainger PLC v. Nicholson, [2009] UKEAT 0219_09_0311 (climate change); Hashman v. Milton Park (Dorset) Ltd, [2011] ET 3105555/2009 (fox-hunting).
2. For examples and discussion, see Post (2000) and Rhode (2010, 126–34).
3. The recent literature includes Lippert-Rasmussen (2013), Moreau (2010), Horta (2010), Hellman (2008), Lippert-Rasmussen (2006a), Arneson (2006), Blum (2002), Cavanagh (2002), Wasserman (1998), and Alexander (1992).
4. See, e.g., Khaitan (2015) and the work collected in Hellman & Moreau (2013).
5. See, e.g., Fiss (1976); Sunstein (1994); Bagenstos (2003, 857–9).
6. I explore this problem of "normative misalignment" in the specific context of age discrimination claims in Eidelson (2013).
7. King (1962, 119).

Chapter 1

1. Wasserman (1998, 805).
2. A recent example of this approach is Sophia Moreau's "What is Discrimination?" (2010), in which the title question is taken to be a moral one.
3. This definition is from Merriam-Webster (http://www.merriam-webster.com/dictionary/discrimination).
4. Hitchens (2001, 110).
5. See Bertrand and Mullainathan (2004).
6. A symmetric definition could be given for discrimination *in favor of* someone, but I omit that here for clarity. I developed this definition by imposing successive modifications on the very helpful baseline offered by Lippert-Rasmussen (2006a). I highlight one of the key distinctions between my account and Lippert-Rasmussen's—how each regards social salience—below. Perhaps the most basic difference, however, is that Lippert-Rasmussen's formula only presumes to determine whether some instance of differential treatment *is* discrimination, not whether it is discrimination on the basis of some specified trait P. (In his recent book, Lippert-Rasmussen does extend the definition in this way. See Lippert-Rasmussen (2013, 13–53).)

7. This linguistic device is not peculiar to discrimination: when I say "a theft robbed me of my money," for instance, I mean that the theft was a robbery, not that the theft itself *committed* a robbery in the way that a thief does. Janet Radcliffe Richards (1985) offers a contrasting view, which takes discrimination as primarily a quality of rules with derivative application to acts committed by individual agents.

8. As a methodological aside, this is the sort of morally mundane example that I find it useful to employ in working out what kind of connection between a trait and an instance of differential treatment makes for discrimination on that basis, but which we could not use if we limited discrimination to wrongful conduct (or, for that matter, to distinctions on the basis of socially salient traits, an issue I discuss below).

9. Except when we are explicitly comparing direct and indirect discrimination, I will often refer simply to "discrimination," meaning direct discrimination.

10. Other links on the chain will come not too early but too late, though confusion is much less apt to arise as to those cases.

11. Something like this dynamic may obtain in practically all cases of race discrimination, which are describable both as discrimination on the basis of race and as discrimination on the basis of skin color, or facial features, etc. (with these latter traits playing the role of name in the résumé case).

12. The concept of discrimination is more expansive in this regard than Kwame Anthony Appiah's (2005, 68) related notion of "treatment-as": "To treat someone as an L is to do something to her in part, at least, because she is an L (where 'because she is an L' figures in the agent's internal specification of her reasons for the act)."

13. See generally Crenshaw (1989).

14. For discussion of this distinction and its significance in anti-discrimination law, see Gardner (1998, 180–6).

15. See Gendler (2012).

16. Gendler (2012). This "R-A-B" complex amounts to what Gendler terms an "alief." See generally Gendler (2008).

17. Krieger (1995, 1242).

18. Altman (2011).

19. For evidence about gender dynamics in American classrooms, see, e.g., Sadker & Sadker (1994).

20. Shin (2010).

21. It also implies that most ordinary discrimination on a given basis will be structural discrimination on that basis as well. This may be infelicitous, but it makes sense insofar as the point of the category is to relax one of the necessary conditions for discrimination.

22. I offer an example of such a case below at p. 53.
23. For contrasting definitions, see Muigai (2010, 3), Pincus (1996, 186), Altman (2011), and the range of positions canvassed by McCrudden (1982) (examining both "institutional" and "structural" discrimination).
24. Altman (2011) is an example.
25. Lippert-Rasmussen (2006a, 169).
26. Cf. Wasserman (1998, 807): "[G]roups that can be subject to discrimination ... generally have deep social significance: their members are perceived and treated differently in a variety of important respects by the larger society."
27. Altman (2011).
28. Lippert-Rasmussen (2006a, 169).
29. See, e.g., Sack (2011).
30. The latter is prohibited by the Equality Act 2010. Personal convictions about climate change and opposition to fox-hunting have each recently been accepted as "philosophical beliefs" for the purposes of the prohibition. See Grainger PLC v. Nicholson, [2009] UKEAT 0219_09_0311 (climate change); Hashman v. Milton Park (Dorset) Ltd, [2011] ET 3105555/2009 (fox-hunting). Discrimination on the basis of union membership is prohibited in the Trade Union and Labour Relations (Consolidation) Act 1992. The law itself does not use the word "discrimination" in this case, but it is widely described as such: see, e.g., Ewing (2003) and Lewis & Sargeant (2004, 244).
31. See "Letters: Barring Smokers From the Workplace" (2011). The language of "discrimination" is also invoked in some state laws that prohibit such employment practices. See, e.g., CONN. GEN. STAT. ANN. § 31–40s (Connecticut); IND. CODE §§ 22-5-4-1 et seq. (Indiana).
32. Thus I disagree with Lippert-Rasmussen that "[a]lmost all groups on whose behalf the charge of being discriminated against is voiced are socially salient groups," or that "it appears that only one kind of discrimination does not involve a socially salient group," viz., genetic discrimination by insurance companies (2006b, 826).
33. Lippert-Rasmussen (2006a, 168).
34. This possibility is noted by Raz (1986, 254).
35. I revisit this question below at p. 168.
36. Two exceptions are Radcliffe Richards (1985, 64–6) and Lippert-Rasmussen (2006a, 170).
37. Lippert-Rasmussen notes the related possibility of a view of the *badness* of discrimination according to which discrimination is bad "when it does not harm the discriminatee overall, provided that it harms him in

some particular dimension" (2006a, 177). Importantly, however, what I am describing here is a view about what makes something discrimination against someone, not what makes an instance of discrimination against someone bad.

38. Woodward (1986, 811).

39. I consider the connections among racism, disrespect, and wrongful discrimination much more closely in Chapter 3.

40. In fact, I think it would be reasonable to say that the journal discriminates against her in the dimension of according respect as well as in the dimension of paper acceptance. In any case, the key point here is that it is her interest in being treated with respect that makes the differential treatment in each of these dimensions discrimination *against* her.

41. I assume here that Alfred and Betty are both being treated with respect in this case.

42. For a formal statement of this view endorsed by several Christian evangelical leaders in the United States, known as the "Danvers Statement," see Council on Biblical Manhood & Womanhood (1988).

43. I discuss when discrimination on the basis of preferences for role ideals constitutes wrongful discrimination in Chapter 4.

Chapter 2

1. The EU Racial Equality Directive, for example, specifically defines "indirect discrimination," as does the Equality Act 2010 in the United Kingdom. The parallel notion in the United States is known as discrimination "based on disparate impact," as, for example, in Title VII of the Civil Rights Act, 42 U.S.C. § 2000e–2(k).

2. France (1910, 95).

3. The example derives from Alexander & Cole (1997).

4. It bears noting as well that while the *university* can be described as discriminating on the basis of racial-makeup-of-region, it may well be that individual officials who are applying the rule adopted at the first stage—which might simply instruct them to disfavor a certain named region—are, considered as individual agents, discriminating only on the basis of region as such.

5. Art. 2(2)(b). A structurally similar definition is given in British law. See Equality Act 2010, s 19(2). In the United States, an "unlawful employment practice based on disparate impact" is defined similarly in Title VII of the Civil Rights Act, 42 U.S.C. § 2000e–2(k).

6. McCrudden (1985, 84).

7. Schauer (2011).
8. Bentham (1931, 425–7).
9. See, e.g., Eyer (2012, 1276–9).
10. Bentham (1931, 426).
11. Gardner (1996, 364–5).
12. And set aside the fact that pregnancy receives special protection under the law in many jurisdictions.
13. McCrudden (1985, 87).
14. McCrudden (1985, 90).
15. Waldron (1985, 96).
16. McCrudden (1985, 87).
17. Hampson v. DES, [1989] ICR 179. For discussion, see Gardner (1996, 362).
18. Gardner (1996, 365).
19. Moreau (2010, 176).
20. Moreau (2010, 169).
21. Moreau (2010, 155–6).
22. A similar principle is suggested as a means of unifying direct and indirect discrimination by Altman (2011), and the same concerns could be raised about that proposal.
23. Age Discrimination in Employment Act of 1967, 29 U.S.C. § 623(a)(2).
24. See Smith v. City of Jackson, Miss., 544 U.S. 228, 235–36 & n.6 (2005) (plurality opinion) (recognizing disparate impact cause of action); *id.* at 249–51 (O'Connor, J., concurring in the judgment) (denying disparate impact cause of action).
25. A claim about type causation posits a connection between two properties in general (e.g., smoking causes cancer). A claim about token causation, by contrast, concerns the etiology of a particular event (e.g., John's smoking caused his cancer). Specifying the conditions for type and token causation, and the nature of the connection between the two, is a difficult problem.
26. Raytheon Co. v. Hernandez, 540 U.S. 44, 52 (2003).
27. A similar tension is reflected in *Watson v. Fort Worth Bank & Trust*, 487 U.S. 977, 994 (1988), concerning the application of Title VII of the Civil Rights Act of 1964. A plurality of the Supreme Court asserted that:

    Once the employment practice at issue has been identified, causation must be proved; that is, the plaintiff must offer statistical evidence of a kind and degree sufficient to show that the practice in question has caused the exclusion of applicants for jobs or promotions because of their membership in a protected group.

"Because of their membership in a protected group" would certainly seem to suggest that the distribution of group membership must be causally connected to (rather than simply correlated with) the pattern of results. But in fact the Court may have simply run together the question whether a disparity is properly attributable to the challenged criterion (rather than, say, chance) with the distinct question whether the disparity actually arose "because of" some individuals' membership in a protected group. Indeed, in the same case, three other Justices stressed that "the disparate impact caused by an employment practice is *directly* established by the numerical disparity," and that "[t]he plaintiff in such a case already has proved that the employment practice has an improper effect; it is up to the employer to prove that the discriminatory effect is justified." *Id.* at 1004 (Blackmun, J., concurring in part and concurring in the judgment). In a recent case involving housing discrimination, the Supreme Court stressed the importance of a "robust causality requirement," but apparently understood this requirement to pertain to the connection between a defendant's policy and the challenged racial disparities. Texas Dept. of Housing and Community Affairs v. Inclusive Communities Project, 576 U.S. __ (2015) (slip op. at 20).

28. Matt Cavanagh likewise suggests, on somewhat different grounds, that "if all you really object to is that different kinds of people have different chances, it is an unnecessary distraction to use the word 'discrimination'" (2002, 199).

29. Much of this evidence is surveyed by Heckman & Masterov (2007).

30. Brest (1976, 14–15) offers an instructive discussion of such "racially selective indifference" more generally.

31. Young (1990, 194–8).

32. Kary (2010).

33. Kaplan ultimately prevailed based on the Equal Employment Opportunity Commission's failure to introduce credible statistical evidence of a racial disparate impact. See EEOC v. Kaplan Higher Ed., 748 F.3d 749 (6th Cir. 2014).

34. Fiske & Ladd (2004, 99).

35. Walford (1997, 61).

36. McCrudden (1982, 304–5).

37. Waldron (1985, 94).

38. Perhaps, for instance, both prohibitions help to ensure that people will have the adequate range of valuable options needed to live autonomous lives. See Gardner (1998, 182–3). Cf. Khaitan (2015, 117–37).

39. EU and UK law are similar in this respect: see the Racial Equality Directive above, and the definition of indirect discrimination in terms of "protected characteristics," such as race, in Equality Act 2010 s 19(3). For an example of a race-based indirect discrimination case with a white plaintiff, see *Meditz v. City of Newark*, 658 F.3d 364 (3d Cir. 2011). In *Meditz*, the plaintiff challenged the city's ordinance that preferred city residents for hiring, alleging a disparate impact on white non-Hispanics who were part of the relevant labor market but were under-represented within the city limits. The court of appeals reversed the lower court's summary judgment for the city and remanded for more careful consideration of the statistical evidence.

40. I don't mean to imply here that the results would necessarily be objectionable if they *did* reflect direct discrimination on behalf of women or racial minorities; that is a separate question.

41. Ricci v. DeStefano, 557 U.S. 557 (2009).

42. Some of this history is described in Justice Ginsburg's *Ricci* dissent. See *id.* at 608–11.

43. See Allan and Bazelon (2009); U.S. Census Bureau (2011).

44. See *Ricci*, 557 U.S. at 609–10.

45. Johnson v. Transportation Agency, Santa Clara Cty., 480 U.S. 616 (1987).

46. 557 U.S. at 579–80.

47. See Schmidt (2007, 22).

48. Title VII specifically makes it unlawful "to adjust the scores of, use different cutoff scores for, or otherwise alter the results of, employment related tests on the basis of race." § 2000e–2(*l*). Perhaps this would preclude my suggestion here—though that depends on the construction given to "on the basis of race." It should be clear in any case that my proposal does not constitute direct discrimination against anyone on the basis of race.

49. Primus (2010, 1350).

Chapter 3

1. Lippert-Rasmussen (2006a, 174).

2. Lippert-Rasmussen (2006a, 174).

3. Arneson (2013, 87) offers a similar assessment of "[c]ontemporary ordinary commonsense morality" on this point.

4. Might the very fact that she is rejected unfairly, or out of animus, make her worse off—even if it has no material or experiential effects on her? Perhaps. But then what makes her worse off is not a contingent effect of

the action, but some intrinsic feature it has. So a proponent of such a view stands with the conventional wisdom, and outside the family of views with which I am contrasting it, on the point that I am suggesting distinguishes them.

5. Goddard et al. (2014).

6. In fact, the *total* effects of this behavior may not be as trivial: the reduced tendency of cars to stop for black pedestrians may invite riskier crossing behavior, which might in turn contribute to explaining the higher rate of pedestrian fatalities among black men. See Goddard et al. (2014).

7. See, e.g., Alexander (1992), Hellman (2008), Shin (2009), and Cavanagh (2002) (appealing to "contempt" rather than "disrespect").

8. Cavanagh (2002) and Arneson (2006) speak of "contempt" and "animus" respectively as explaining what is intrinsically wrong with some discrimination. I classify them in this group although they do not use the language of disrespect. Alexander (1992) does appeal to disrespect, and understands it in terms of beliefs about a person's moral worth.

9. Darwall (1977, 38).

10. Darwall (2006, 120).

11. Arneson (2006, 782).

12. See McIntyre (2009).

13. See Anderson & Pildes (2000, 1511); their example is adapted from Korsgaard (1996, 75 n.58).

14. Anderson & Pildes (2000, 1511).

15. Anderson & Pildes (2000, 1509–10).

16. Callousness, too, might better be seen as involving the failure to be moved by the reasons given by certain other attitudes, rather than as a reason-giving attitude in its own right.

17. The claim I am making here is broadly in line with Raz's suggestion that "respecting people is... neither a feeling, nor an emotion, nor a belief.... It is a way of conducting oneself, and more indirectly, of being disposed to conduct oneself towards the object of respect" (2001, 138). But I am suggesting that whether one conducts oneself in the relevant way does crucially depend on one's practical deliberation; respecting people is not a *thinly described* way of conducting oneself.

18. Here I follow Raz (2010, 284–5).

19. See Lippert-Rasmussen (2006a, 176; 2011, 56–7); Hellman (2008, 154); Shin (2009, 171–2).

20. See Scanlon (2008).

21. Scanlon (2008, 22).

22. Scanlon (2008, 124).

23. Scanlon (2008, 46).
24. Scanlon (2008, 73).
25. Scanlon explicitly distinguishes meaning in his sense, which concerns the agent's actual reasons for action, from conventional meaning (2008, 52–3).
26. Scanlon (2008, 46).
27. Scanlon (2008, 59–62).
28. Scanlon (2008, 27–8).
29. Scanlon expressly allows that an action's being good or bad may depend on the attitudes or intentions it manifests even if the action's permissibility does not (2008, 25).
30. This commitment is perhaps most clearly exemplified in the doctrine of double effect. But whereas double effect is centrally concerned with intentions, I have in mind features of the agent's deliberation more generally—such as according weight to certain considerations in deciding what to do—that are not simply a matter of what she intends.
31. For a fuller critical evaluation of Scanlon's proposal, see Lillehammer (2010).
32. This category roughly parallels the sense in which Darwall suggests that one can "'be respectful' of something without having any respect for it" (1977, 40–1). Similarly, Leslie Green writes that "[e]xpressions of respect can be accompanied by feelings of contempt" (2010, 219).
33. Glasgow employs a similar example for different purposes (2009, 83).
34. One might wonder whether there are some "moral gestures" whose meaning is rooted not in convention but in universal human responses, and whether spitting on someone might be one of them. As I mean to use it, though, the idea of "conventional" disrespect embraces all judgments of disrespect that rest directly on how acts of the type in question are generally *understood*. That the origins of the ascribed meaning may trace in part to biological predispositions is not, on this view, important to how an allegation of disrespect should be classified. Moreover, the "conventional" label is appropriate even in such cases, for it remains true that social convention could displace rather than ratify an innate aversion, and the act's being understood as disrespectful in the relevant sense thus still depends on what the social conventions are. Indeed, even in the case of spitting on someone, it seems that the gesture's meaning varies by culture, whatever the pre-cultural "default" may be (if it makes sense to speak in such terms at all). For example, in cultures concerned with the "Evil Eye," spitting on a person can be important to breaking or avoiding a curse, rather than a mark of disrespect for her. See, e.g., Stein (1974). I am grateful to an anonymous reviewer for raising this issue.

35. Raz writes: "[S]ince, and to the extent that, we should avoid hurting people, we have reason (though not a reason of respect) to avoid conduct which will hurt through being perceived as disrespectful, whether or not it is" (2001, 171–2). I take this reason to be a reason of respect after all, or at least importantly related to one. Respect for persons, as I have construed it, enjoins one to take the prospect of hurting them as a reason against an action. On the other hand, that hurting someone is disrespectful may not be the only thing counting against it.

36. I have in mind Hellman (2008) and Shin (2009), discussed below. Both offer avowedly "expressive" theories of the morality of discrimination, or, in Shin's case, of "unequal treatment."

37. Anderson & Pildes (2000, 1512–13).

38. Hellman (2008, 33).

39. Hellman (2008, 30).

40. Hellman (2008, 35).

41. In order to demean a person, according to Hellman, one must both express a certain kind of disrespect for her and stand in a particular power relation to her (35). The second condition is discussed below.

42. Hellman (2008, 35–6).

43. Hellman (2008, 40).

44. See esp. 27–30; 169–70. Hellman clarifies that her theory "is not *conventional* in the sense of acquiescing to or validating conventional practices," because practices that are conventionally accepted may nonetheless have conventional meanings that render them demeaning (45). I agree, but I mean to question why there is intrinsic moral significance to these conventional meanings in the first place.

45. I am grateful to Deborah Hellman for helpful discussion of this point.

46. Hellman (2008, 35).

47. I am grateful to Deborah Hellman for discussion of this point as well.

48. Shin (2009, 162).

49. Shin (2009, 166).

50. Shin (2009, 167).

51. They can equally be described as cases in which a person's interest in being treated with respect is among the specific interests in terms of which she is treated comparatively worse by differential treatment in a material dimension.

52. I return to this point below at p. 163.

53. Glasgow (2009, 81).

54. This is very plausible, I think, once we observe that much discrimination that embodies role-based disrespect—such as a failure to recognize the

authority that comes with being a police officer, but only when the officer is female—is derivative of more basic disrespect for the discriminatee's equal standing as a person.

55. Glasgow (2009, 81).

56. I borrow the helpful schema of "P-based" and "P-ist" discrimination from Lippert-Rasmussen (2006a, 168), though I understand "P-ist" differently than he does. It also bears noting that an analysis of "P-ist" discrimination in terms of disrespect does not capture ordinary usage perfectly. Sometimes to say that a practice is "ageist," for instance, is simply to say that it discriminates on the basis of age, without any necessary implication that it is disrespectful or even objectionable. But I think this usage is misleading and nonstandard.

Chapter 4

1. The obvious difference between these cases, of course, is that although classical music may be good, there may be nothing that is good or bad *for* classical music, except in an extended or metaphorical sense.

2. See, e.g., Garza (2014).

3. My understanding of these particular attachments and the nature of their value is shaped by Raz (2001, 10–40).

4. Frankfurt (1999, 151). Frankfurt's formulation is correct, in my view, as applied to the concern we afford to different people's interests. But it could also be read to imply a wholesale embrace of what I call the "relevant-difference view" below, which I reject.

5. Brest (1975, 48).

6. Shin (2009, 153).

7. Shin (2009, 153).

8. Frankfurt (1999, 153).

9. Garcia (1996, 259).

10. Garcia (1996, 264).

11. As does Glasgow's treatment of racism. See Glasgow (2009, 82–3).

12. Alexander (1992, 158–61).

13. Cavanagh (2002, 166, 176–7).

14. Lippert-Rasmussen (2006a, 182–4).

15. Lippert-Rasmussen (2006a, 183).

16. See, e.g., 17 Corpus Juris Secundum: Contempt § 6.

17. Glover (2000, 343) (emphasis added).

18. In other settings, of course, gender-based disrespect does indeed target women's equal value. Consider, for instance, the edict issued by the

Afghan Ulema Council declaring that "[m]en are fundamental and women are secondary" (Levinson 2012).

19. I am grateful to an anonymous reviewer for pressing me to clarify this point.

20. For overviews and evidence of the behavioral effects of implicit bias, see, e.g., Greenwald et al. (2009) and Jost et al. (2009). For helpful philosophical treatments of implicit bias, see Gendler (2011) and Holroyd & Sweetman (forthcoming).

21. Gendler (2011, 44).

22. Goddard et al. (2014).

23. Alexander explicitly allows that "differential concern" may be "detached from judgments of differential moral worth," a distinction he employs to explain the permissibility of "personal loyalties and commitments" (1992, 162). So it is clear that the differential concern itself does not constitute (or always indicate) the judgment in question.

24. Alexander (1992, 182–3; 181).

25. Frankfurt (1999, 153).

26. For discussion of these issues, see, e.g., Holroyd (2012); Madva (2013).

27. Madva (2013, 6).

28. Holroyd & Kelly (forthcoming).

29. In considering implicit bias here, I have posited a kind of unconscious differential concern for people's interests (i.e., literal "bias"). In fact, however, the evidence argues for disaggregating implicit bias into distinct evaluative and stereotyping components with their own psychological mechanisms (Amodio & Devine 2006; Holroyd & Sweetman (forthcoming); but see Madva & Brownstein 2013). These forms of bias are revealed in different tests (the "Evaluative IAT" and the "Stereotyping IAT") and predict different behaviors. For our purposes, it is significant that a person's degree of concern or responsiveness to another's interests is neither the same as her affective preference for the other (tested, for instance, by desire to befriend the other), which is predicted by "implicit evaluation" scores, nor the same as her tendency to form judgments about the other's character (tested, for instance, by evaluations of a writing sample), which is predicted by "implicit stereotyping" scores. On the other hand, implicit differential concern is surely a real and significant phenomenon (as the crosswalk study suggests), whether it has roots in one or both of these other tendencies or in something else. I discuss implicit stereotyping in Chapter 5.

30. Alexander (1992, 160).

31. Again, the same basic approach is reflected in Cavanagh (2002, 166–80).

32. This is not intrinsic to the nature of these traits, but an observation about the realities of the world we live in. There could be a world in which racial differences form the basis of communities structured such that their members could have attachments of genuine normative significance to one another, similar in kind to attachments within families. There may even be some such communities in our world. But, without giving a full theory of how particular attachments gain normative standing, I think it is clear that the category of "white people," in our society, is far too thin and broad to bear that sort of weight.

33. Arneson expresses doubts about his qualified defense of this view, which expressly assumed a deontological framework, in later work. See Arneson (2013, 90–1).

34. Arneson (2006, 787).

35. Lippert-Rasmussen (2006a, 180).

36. Arneson (2006, 792).

37. Arneson (2006, 791–2).

38. This is an instance of the sort of (intrinsically) benign preference-based discrimination I discuss in the next section. It might take a range of forms. For example, Glenn Loury identifies "internal institution building, mutual affirmation, and selective association" as among the elements of "the collective mobilization toolkit on which an historically oppressed, racially stigmatized population must draw" (2002, 98).

39. Alexander (1992, 160) likewise suggests that "[a]ny 'ties' I feel towards the white race,...to the extent they produced anti-black bias, would most likely be based on an ideology of black moral inferiority."

40. Greenwald & Pettigrew (2014, 2).

41. Lippert-Rasmussen (2006a, 180).

42. Glasgow highlights this as a virtue of a disrespect-based account of racism as well (2009, 83).

43. Dworkin (1978, 234).

44. Dworkin's distinction has been criticized, and it may not prove ultimately viable. See, e.g., Ely (1983). But I employ it here only as a helpful expository device. My view does not rest the moral status of an act of discrimination on whether it is motivated by an external or a personal preference.

45. I considered the possibility that policies undertaken in pursuit of this preference do not constitute discrimination at all, because they are premised on mutual complementarity, above at p. 37.

46. Alexander (1992, 149).

47. Barbaro (2011).

48. I borrow this example from Alexander (1992, 166).
49. Loury (2002, 98–9).
50. Cf. Dovidio et al. (1997).
51. Emens (2009, 1377).
52. For fuller discussion of this issue, see Loury (2002, 99–100).
53. Recognition of some form of this dynamic, and concern about it, has been an important engine of *opposition* to school integration in the United States. The day after the Supreme Court's decision in *Brown v. Board of Education*, 347 U.S. 483 (1954), for instance, a Mississippi newspaper editorialized that "White and Negro children in the same schools will lead to miscegenation. Miscegenation leads to mixed marriages and mixed marriages lead to mongrelization of the human race." See Siegel (2004, 1483–4).

Chapter 5

1. Alexander (1992, 169).
2. Alexander (1992, 170–1).
3. Alexander (1992, 193).
4. Arneson (2006, 788).
5. Scanlon (2008, 70).
6. I adapt this example from one of Hellman's (2008, 143).
7. See Hellman (2008, 143).
8. Kawakami et al. (2000).
9. Blair et al. (2001). Gendler (2008) offers an instructive discussion of this and other research as it bears on issues in philosophy of mind.
10. See, e.g., Correll et al. (2007).
11. Miller (1999, 168–9).
12. The idea figures prominently in the rhetoric of courts enforcing antidiscrimination guarantees. See, e.g., Miller v. Johnson, 515 U.S. 900, 911 (1995) ("At the heart of the Constitution's guarantee of equal protection lies the simple command that the Government must treat citizens as individuals, not as simply components of a racial, religious, sexual or national class." (quoting Metro Broadcasting, Inc. v. FCC, 497 U.S. 547, 602 (1990) (O'Connor, J., dissenting)); Missouri v. Jenkins, 515 U.S. 70, 120–1, (1995) (Thomas, J., concurring) ("At the heart of [*Brown's*] interpretation of the Equal Protection Clause lies the principle that the government must treat citizens as individuals, and not as members of racial, ethnic, or religious groups."); Arizona Governing Comm. for Tax Deferred Annuity & Deferred Comp. Plans v. Norris, 463 U.S. 1073,

1083 (1983) ("Title VII requires employers to treat their employees as *individuals*, not 'as simply components of a racial, religious, sexual, or national class.'" (quoting City of Los Angeles, Dep't of Water & Power v. Manhart, 435 U.S. 702, 708 (1978)); Parents Involved in Cmty. Sch. v. Seattle Sch. Dist. No. 1, 551 U.S. 701, 730 (2007) (invoking "our repeated recognition that '[a]t the heart of the Constitution's guarantee of equal protection lies the simple command that the Government must treat citizens as individuals, not as simply components of a racial, religious, sexual or national class'"). A similar principle is expressed in Regents of Univ. of California v. Bakke, 438 U.S. 265, 318 (1978) (holding that an affirmative action program must "treat[] each applicant as an individual in the admissions process").

13. Miller (1999, 168).

14. Blum (2002, 79). Blum acknowledges that "being treated as an individual is indeed an important value," but contends "it is seldom what is at stake in potential contexts of discrimination." See also Levin (1992, 21–4), Cavanagh (2002, 187–93), Schauer (2003, 19), Arneson (2006, 787), and Lippert-Rasmussen (2011) (offering a "revisionist" rather than "nihilist" take on the idea).

15. This point is elaborated especially clearly by Schauer (2003).

16. Lippert-Rasmussen (2011, 54).

17. It is open to Lippert-Rasmussen to respond that, since he does not take treating people as individuals in his sense to be morally required in all cases, the dissonance in this example is due to the applicant's *complaining* that he hasn't been treated as an individual, when in fact there is no ground for complaint there. I will argue below that treating people as individuals *is* morally required. But anyway I think the counterexample retains its force if we simply ask whether the school has failed to treat the applicant as an individual—I don't think it has—setting aside the morality of its doing so.

18. Scanlon (2008, 117–18).

19. Dworkin (1988, 110).

20. For example in Gerald Dworkin (1988, 85–149) or in Wolff (1970).

21. For example in Raz (1986, 369–99) and in Ronald Dworkin (1985, 181).

22. Feinberg (1989, 27).

23. Raz (1986, 369).

24. Dworkin (1988, 34).

25. Raz (1986, 370).

26. Raz (1986, 370) calls them "only very indirectly related," whereas Waldron (2005) suggests that influential accounts of each have important features in common.

27. Raz (1986, 204).
28. Dworkin (1988, 32).
29. Benn (1988, 91).
30. Some version of this distinction is drawn by each of Gerald Dworkin (1988, 31), Raz (1986, 372), and Feinberg (1989, 28). Feinberg identifies two further senses of "autonomy" as well, referring to an ideal of character and a kind of sovereign authority.
31. I assume that autonomy is a matter of degree. See Raz (1986, 373).
32. Raz (1986, 374). In fact, as Raz presents his view, lacking adequacy of choice is one way of lacking the *capacity* for autonomy. But he says he is using "'capacity' in a very wide sense" (372). I will use it more narrowly. Normally to say that someone is autonomous, in the sense of a capacity rather than a realized condition, is to say that he has the *internal constitution* appropriate for autonomy, as the prisoner does. On Raz's account, however, this is only one of three conditions that are jointly required for the "capacity" for autonomy (or for satisfying the "conditions of autonomy"). I don't think this terminological difference matters much.
33. Raz (1986, 372).
34. Dworkin (1988, 18–20; 108).
35. This suggestion draws on Frankfurt's (1971) influential account of the connection between second-order reflection and our concept of person-hood. Dworkin (1988, 31–2) also argues for a close connection between the capacity for autonomy and the concept of a person.
36. Dworkin (1988, 32).
37. The sculpture example may suggest a more controversial stance on issues in aesthetics than I intend. Without wandering too far afield, I believe my suggestion about this case is consistent with the view, associated with New Criticism, that "the design or intention of the author is neither available nor desirable as a standard for judging the success of a work of literary art." Wimsatt & Beardsley (1987, 367). The argument supposes only that respect for me as the author of the work necessitates attending to the significance of what I *did*, not to what I may have intended in doing it.
38. See Lippert-Rasmussen (2011, 51).
39. I use "predict" loosely, since what is being predicted may sometimes be in the past, but unknown to the agent making a judgment about it. Anyway, in this case the prediction concerns the future.
40. Here I draw on Frankfurt's (1971) influential account of the connection between freedom, second-order reflection, and our concept of personhood.

A similar idea animates Wasserman's (1991) theory of the morality of relying on statistical evidence in legal settings, discussed below.

41. Lawrence Blum (2004) has offered an incisive philosophical account of stereotyping that develops a similar claim, arguing that "[s]tereotyping involves seeing individual members through a narrow and rigid lens of group-based image, rather being alive to the range of characteristics constituting each member as a distinct individual" (272).

42. I take the example from Arneson (2006, 788). He ends up attributing the wrongfulness of this romantic racial ideology to the abolitionists' failure to apply "reliable and epistemically nondefective rules and procedures" to black people.

43. Gardner (1998, 171).

44. Gardner (1998, 170–1).

45. Gardner (1998, 171).

46. Gardner (1996, 366–7). Another relevant comparison is to Sophia Moreau's contention that wrongful discrimination denies us "freedoms to deliberate about and decide how to live in a way that is insulated from pressures stemming from extraneous traits of ours." Moreau (2010, 147). As I have formulated it, however, the autonomy account does not demand that those pressures be relieved so much as that they be counterbalanced under certain conditions.

47. See Walton (1989). I came to Walton's essay by way of Randall Kennedy's helpful discussion of related but different issues (1997, 157–8).

48. The ad itself is available online from the Museum of the Moving Image (http://www.livingroomcandidate.org/commercials/1988/willie-horton).

49. Walton (1989).

50. For discussion of this objection to much racial discrimination, see Thomas (1992, 31).

51. Perhaps this sort of failure is *less* bad than a case in which one ignores the person's autonomous choices altogether and bases a decision on his or her other demographic qualities. That seems plausible to me, but I will not pursue it here.

52. This point is developed by Gardner (1998, 178 n.23).

53. Dworkin (1985, 190).

54. One recent example is Sophia Moreau, who says "it seems important to protect us from the costs of being of one sex rather than another in part because this trait is unchosen" (2010, 156). Moreau also argues that different traits might be treated as grounds of discrimination for different reasons.

55. Cohen (1981, 627); see also Cohen (1977, 74).

56. Wasserman (1991, 942-3).
57. Wasserman (1991, 943) (emphasis added).
58. Lippert-Rasmussen (2011, 53).
59. Compare Feinberg's suggestion that autonomy, understood as a capacity, "is determined by the ability to make rational choices, a qualification usually so interpreted as to exclude infants, insane persons, the severely retarded, the senile, and the comatose, and to include virtually everyone else" (1989, 28).
60. I am grateful to Gideon Yaffe for suggesting a version of this example.
61. Appiah (1990).
62. See Gendler (2011, 43); Devine & Elliott (1995, 1144-6).
63. For discussion of blameworthiness and implicit bias, see p. 109.
64. See, e.g., Lippert-Rasmussen (2006a, 169); Cavanagh (2002, 155-6); Wasserman (1998, 807); Arneson (2006, 796); Koppelman (2006, 811-12).
65. Koppelman (2006, 812).
66. See, e.g., Lippert-Rasmussen: "[My] formula refers to discrimination for and against for [sic] different, *socially salient groups* for the following reason. An employer might be more inclined to hire applicants with green, rather than brown or blue, eyes. This idiosyncrasy might not amount to discrimination in the sense that interests us here, even though, obviously, the employer differentiates between different applicants" (2006a, 169, internal citation omitted).
67. Cavanagh (2002, 155).

Chapter 6

1. See Thomas (1992) on the role of self-presentational behavior in profiling.
2. Chan (2005).
3. Crowder (2010).
4. Cf. Strauss (1986, 114-15).
5. Keteyian (2009).
6. These arguments against profiling are surveyed and developed by Harcourt (2004).
7. The philosophical literature on racial profiling is mainly composed of three exchanges. One was launched by Michael Levin (1992), and includes contributions by Thomas (1992), Pojman (1993), Cox (1993), and Adler (1993). More recently Risse and Zeckhauser (2004) renewed interest in the topic: their article serves as a focal point for contributions

by Lever (2005), Lippert-Rasmussen (2006c), Levin (2007), and Risse (2007). Finally, the *Journal of Ethics* devoted a special issue to the topic in 2011, with new contributions from several of these writers as well as others.

8. Versions of this distinction are drawn in a number of court opinions, including *Brown v. City of Oneonta*, 221 F.3d 329 (2d Cir. 2000), and *Monroe v. City of Charlottesville, Va.*, 579 F.3d 380 (4th Cir. 2009). I give examples from the academic legal literature below. Within the philosophical literature, the most systematic engagements with this distinction are offered by Thomsen (2011, 95–9) and Applbaum (1996). The distinction is also noted by Lippert-Rasmussen (2006c, 191). But often profiling is simply defined so as to encompass both practices alike. Risse and Zeckhauser, for instance, define racial profiling as "any police-initiated action that relies on the race, ethnicity, or national origin and not merely on the behavior of an individual" (2004, 136).

9. Banks (2001, 1084–5) discusses several examples; see also Harris (2002, 152).

10. Banks (2001, 1082).

11. Lever (2007, 20); see also Lever (2011, 63).

12. See Tanovich (2004, 318).

13. Risse & Zeckhauser (2004, 140).

14. This prescription does not take account of the compelling moral and prudential reasons why one would not want to allocate scrutiny this way. The purely prudential reasons against profiling—that is, reasons that tell against employing it even if crime prevention is one's sole goal—are explored in depth by Harcourt (2004).

15. Gross & Livingston (2002, 1415).

16. Thomson (1986, 205).

17. Thomson (1986, 203). Richard Schmalbeck criticizes this claim, arguing that the frequency distribution of cabs is causally relevant in this case (1986, 232–3). I am sympathetic to that view, but the resolution of that debate is not essential to the discussion here.

18. Thomson (1986, 203).

19. David Wasserman makes a similar point about cases in which a "'causally relevant factor' operating in the defendant" is still insufficient to render evidence "individualized" (1991, 952).

20. Hitchcock (2001, 361).

21. By contrast, Frej Klem Thomsen suggests that we understand "profiling" very broadly, as essentially the use of epistemic proxies in policing (2011, 98). He then recognizes a kind of "testimonial profiling," encompassing

cases in which the relevant probabilistic information is rooted in a witness description of a suspect. This is structurally analogous to my view, insofar as he is in effect distinguishing among different kinds of component effects. But casting them all as profiles may obscure the distinction between inferences that are mediated by the ascription of a disposition to commit a crime-type and those that are not. That, I will suggest, is important to understanding the putative moral significance of the distinction between profiles and suspect descriptions.

22. Shogenji (2003).
23. See Banks (2001, 1104-6).
24. Applbaum (1996, 151).
25. See, e.g., Gingrich (2009).
26. Compare Kennedy's argument that "governments should, if necessary, increase taxes across the board," discussed below (1997, 158-61).
27. Durlauf (2006, F415).
28. Kennedy (1997, 158-61).
29. Lippert-Rasmussen (2006c) considers the significance of this situation to the justifiability of racial profiling in depth.
30. Durlauf (2006, F415).
31. For discussion of this idea, see Arneson (2004).
32. Colb (2001).
33. Kennedy (1997, 160).
34. Cf. Lippert-Rasmussen (2007, 397-8).
35. Herbert (2010).
36. Thomson (1984, 128-9).
37. Thomson (1984, 129).
38. Jonathan E. Adler (1993) has also noted the analogy between racial profiling and the Red Cab case and suggested that explanatory relevance might bear on the moral permissibility of racial profiling.
39. Thomson (1984, 129).
40. Levin (2007, 33-4).
41. Levin (2007, 34) considers and rejects this objection as well.
42. Boylan (2008, 5).
43. See Schmalbeck (1986, 232-3) for an argument that it is not.
44. See the note on the preceding page for one sketch of what that connection might look like.
45. Risse & Zeckhauser (2004, 141).
46. Risse & Zeckhauser (2004, 148-9).
47. I return to the moral significance of publicity in profiling below at p. 215.

48. Thus Lever (2005, 104) argues that "fear of violence and of death at the hands of the police—not just feelings of hurt, resentment and distrust—are likely to be among the harms of profiling in a racist society, and to occur even when the police officer one is dealing with appears to be polite and considerate."

49. Risse & Zeckhauser (2004, 146).

50. Risse & Zeckhauser (2004, 147).

51. Risse & Zeckhauser (2004, 148).

52. Risse & Zeckhauser (2004, 149).

53. Risse & Zeckhauser (2004, 148).

54. Risse & Zeckhauser (2004, 149).

55. Risse & Zeckhauser (2004, 149).

56. Risse & Zeckhauser (2004, 146).

57. Risse & Zeckhauser (2004, 149).

58. Risse & Zeckhauser (2004, 152).

59. Risse & Zeckhauser (2004, 169).

60. Some aspects of their argument do strongly suggest this first reading. In a response to critics meant to clarify these and other issues, for instance, Risse asserts this principle:

> A utilitarian policy maker should count as costs of policy P only costs specifically incurred through imposing P, not costs that also arise in the process of implementing P but that are plausibly seen as caused by underlying socio-economic conditions rather than by P itself. (2007, 10)

The notion of costs that "arise in the process of implementing P" clearly suggests costs that are causally due, if not to P, then to the implementation of P, or to the process of implementing P. So Risse's principle really does call for discounting some such costs on account of the fact that these costs are "plausibly seen as caused by"—or as Risse and Zeckhauser put it in the original article, "largely caused by"—background facts about racism in society. As I've said, this is mistaken: every harm that will come about if we decide on and implement P, but which would not come about if we did not, should be counted against deciding on and implementing P.

Moreover, at another point in his response to critics, Risse argues for his approach by criticizing a hypothetical alternative under which "utilitarians went about assessing the costs of any practice that might be a reminder or focal point of underlying racism by counting as costs all consequences in whose causal explanation appear both that practice and underlying racism" (2007, 14). But that is just what utilitarians *should* do. Similarly, they should count as costs of my introducing the second chemical into the room all consequences in whose causal explanation appear both that act and underlying facts about the context in which it will be released, including the vulnerability induced by the ambient toxic substance.

How could Risse object to this approach? He warns that "the overall harm done by racism, no matter how large, will be massively overstated" (14). Risse writes:

> This is so because plenty of separate practices would be associated with underlying harm, but the overall harm caused by all these practices must be aggregated from the harm associated with these practices individually, which leads to an overall much bigger amount of harm than what is associated with the underlying racism of society. In other words, there would be less harm associated with racism in society overall than with the aggregate of individual practices that constitute social interaction in society, which is absurd. (14)

I am not sure exactly what to make of this, and as Risse says, "[i]t would take large efforts in the metaphysics of harm to make this train of thought precise." What this objection may reveal, however, is that Risse thinks of an expressive harm as a kind of mere reflection of the harmfulness of the states of affairs in virtue of which it is harmful. In this respect, calling it an expressive *harm* may be something of a misnomer; perhaps it is rather an *expression of* a harm, but not necessarily itself harmful at all. If this were so, it would indeed be wrong to multiply the harm to which an expression refers—in this case, the "harm associated with racism in society overall"—by the number of times or ways it is expressed.

But if this interpretation of Risse is right, it is his understanding of expressive harm that is faulty—or, equivalently, his classification of the harms of racial profiling as expressive harms in his sense. The belief that one has been singled out on account of one's race is harmful *because of* background facts about the social meaning of race, but this harm is not *redundant with*, or a mere reflection of, the other harms that are due to those same facts. Durlauf (2006, F409) reads Risse and Zeckhauser this way and advances a similar objection.

61. Risse (2007, 10).
62. For instance, this reading is inconsistent with Risse's objection to "counting as costs [of a practice] all consequences in whose causal explanation appear both that practice and underlying racism" (2007, 14). If he meant what I suggest here, presumably he would instead object to counting all consequences in whose causal explanation appears underlying racism, full stop.
63. Risse & Zeckhauser (2004, 149).
64. Harris (2002, 96). This remark also recalls Anthony Walton's essay, and complements the autonomy account advanced in Chapter 5: what is

disrespectful about forming judgments about people on the basis of race is, at least in part, that this *disregards* "everything you've accomplished in your life, everything you've worked for."

65. Lever (2005, 97).
66. See Archibold (2010). Several provisions of the law were struck down by the U.S. Supreme Court in *Arizona v. United States*, 132 S. Ct. 2492 (2012). Others were left standing, including a provision requiring police to make a "reasonable attempt . . . to determine the immigration status" of those they stop or arrest on other grounds if "reasonable suspicion exists that the person is an alien and is unlawfully present in the United States." Ariz. Rev. Stat. Ann. § 11–1051(B) (West 2012).
67. See, e.g., Hellman (2008, 21–5).
68. Wasserman (1996, 117) similarly notes that many of the reference classes on account of which people might be scrutinized—such as being at an opera where a gunshot was fired—are distinguished from racial generalizations by their transience.
69. See Gil-White (2001).
70. Gil-White (2001, 534).
71. Kennedy (1997, 154).
72. Loury (2002, 61).
73. Mullen & Hu (1989, 234).
74. Loury (2002, 62).
75. Wasserman (1996, 117).
76. Lever (2005, 107).
77. Risse & Zeckhauser (2004, 154).
78. Risse & Zeckhauser (2004, 154–5).
79. Risse & Zeckhauser (2004, 155) (emphasis in original).
80. Seifert (2004, 471).
81. White House Commission on Aviation Safety and Security (1997).
82. Indeed, this view implies that, from the moral point of view, the debate *about* racial profiling may be important in much the same way as profiling itself. If racial profiling is morally troubling essentially because of the message it sends, then pundits who clamor for profiling on television in the aftermath of each terrorist incident could do as much damage as racial profiling itself—conducted discreetly, without political fanfare—would.
83. The United Kingdom moved from a lifetime ban to this one-year policy in 2011. See Gallagher (2011). A similar change is pending in the United States. See U.S. FDA (2014).

84. Joint United Kingdom Blood Transfusion Services and Tissue Transplantation Services Professional Advisory Committee (2007).
85. Risse & Zeckhauser (2004, 147).
86. Dunning (2009).
87. Lever (2005, 106).

Conclusion

1. The argument here parallels a suggestion I made earlier concerning discrimination in pursuit of particular role ideals, when these are seen by the discriminator as rooted in weighty moral convictions. See p. 120 above.

References

Adler, J.E. 1993. Crime Rates by Race and Causal Relevance: A Reply to Levin. *Journal of Social Philosophy* 24:176.

Alexander, L. 1992. What Makes Wrongful Discrimination Wrong? *University of Pennsylvania Law Review* 141:149.

Alexander, L., and K. Cole. 1997. Discrimination by Proxy. *Constitutional Commentary* 14:453.

Allan, N., and E. Bazelon. 2009. The Ladder. *Slate*, June 25, 2009, http://www.slate.com/id/2221250/

Altman, A. 2011. Discrimination. In *The Stanford Encyclopedia of Philosophy (Spring 2011 Edition)*, edited by E.N. Zalta.

Amodio, D.M., and P.G. Devine. 2006. Stereotyping and Evaluation in Implicit Race Bias: Evidence for Independent Constructs and Unique Effects on Behavior. *Journal of Personality and Social Psychology* 91 (4): 652.

Anderson, E. 2012. Epistemic Justice as a Virtue of Social Institutions. *Social Epistemology* 26 (2):163.

Anderson, E.S., and R.H. Pildes. 2000. Expressive theories of law: A general restatement. *University of Pennsylvania Law Review* 148 (5):1503.

Appiah, K.A. 1990. Racisms. In *Anatomy of Racism*, edited by D.T. Goldberg. Minneapolis: University of Minnesota Press.

Appiah, K.A. 2005. *The Ethics of Identity*. Princeton: Princeton University Press.

Applbaum, A.I. 1996. Response: Racial Generalization, Police Discretion, and Bayesian Contractualism. In *Handled with Discretion*, edited by J. Kleinig. Lanham, MD: Rowman & Littlefield.

Archibold, R.C. 2010. Arizona Enacts Stringent Law on Immigration. *The New York Times*, April 23, 2010, http://www.nytimes.com/2010/04/24/us/politics/24immig.html

Arneson, R.J. 2004. Luck Egalitarianism Interpreted and Defended. *Philosophical Topics* 32 (1/2):1.

Arneson, R.J. 2006. What Is Wrongful Discrimination? *San Diego Law Review* 43:775.

Arneson, R.J. 2013. Discrimination, Disparate Impact, and Theories of Justice. In *Philosophical Foundations of Discrimination Law*, edited by D. Hellman and S. Moreau. Oxford: Oxford University Press.

Banks, R.R. 2001. Race-based suspect selection and colorblind equal protection doctrine and discourse. *UCLA Law Review* 48:1075.

Bagenstos, S.R. 2003. "Rational Discrimination," Accommodation, and the Politics of (Disability) Civil Rights. *Virginia Law Review* 89:825.

Barbaro, M. After Roasting, Trump Reacts In Character. *The New York Times*, May 1, 2011, http://www.nytimes.com/2011/05/02/nyregion/after-roasting-trump-reacts-in-character.html

Benn, S.I. 1988. *A Theory of Freedom.* Cambridge: Cambridge University Press.

Bentham, J. 1931. Principles of the Penal Code. In *The Theory of Legislation*, edited by C. K. Ogden, translated by R. Hildreth from E. Dumont. London: Kegan Paul, Trench, Trübner.

Bertrand, M., and S. Mullainathan. 2004. Are Emily and Greg More Employable than Lakisha and Jamal? A Field Experiment on Labor Market Discrimination. *The American Economic Review* 94 (4):991.

Blair, I.V., Ma, J.E., and A.P. Lenton. 2001. Imagining Stereotypes Away: The Moderation of Implicit Stereotypes through Mental Imagery. *Journal of Personality and Social Psychology* 81 (5):828.

Blum, L. 2002. *"I'm Not a Racist, But..."*: *The Moral Quandary of Race.* Ithaca: Cornell University Press.

Blum, L. 2004. Stereotypes and Stereotyping: A Moral Analysis. *Philosophical Papers* 33 (3):251.

Boylan, M. 2008. Racial Profiling and Genetic Privacy. *Center for American Progress*, https://cdn.americanprogress.org/wp-content/uploads/issues/2008/03/pdf/racial_profiling.pdf

Brest, P. 1976. Foreword: In Defense of the Antidiscrimination Principle. *Harvard Law Review* 90 (1):1.

Cavanagh, M. 2002. *Against Equality of Opportunity.* Oxford: Clarendon Press.

Chan, S. 2005. In New York, It's Open Bag or Find Exits. *New York Times*, July 23, 2005, http://www.nytimes.com/2005/07/23/nyregion/23york.html

Cohen, L.J. 1977. *The Probable and the Provable.* Oxford: Oxford University Press.

Cohen, L.J. 1981. Subjective Probability and the Paradox of the Gatecrasher. *Arizona State Law Journal* 1981 (2):627.

Colb, S.F. 2001. The New Face of Racial Profiling. *FindLaw's Writ*, October 10, 2001, http://writ.news.findlaw.com/colb/20011010.html

Correll, J., et al. 2007. Across the Thin Blue Line: Police Officers and Racial Bias in the Decision to Shoot. *Journal of Personality and Social Psychology* 92 (6):1006.

Council on Biblical Manhood & Womanhood. 1988. The Danvers Statement on Biblical Manhood and Womanhood, http://cbmw.org/core-beliefs/

Cover, T.M, and J.A. Thomas. 1991. *Elements of Information Theory*. New York: Wiley.

Cox, C.B. 1993. On Michael Levin's 'Responses to Race Differences in Crime'. *Journal of Social Philosophy* 24 (1):155.

Crenshaw, K. 1989. Demarginalizing the intersection of race and sex: A black feminist critique of antidiscrimination doctrine, feminist theory and anti-racist politics. *U. Chicago Legal Forum* 1989:139.

Crowder, S. 2010. Arizona Governor Signs Controversial Immigration Bill. *Hannity (Fox News)*, April 23, 2010, http://mediamatters.org/mmtv/201004230053

Darwall, S. 1977. Two Kinds of Respect. *Ethics* 88 (1):36.

Darwall, S. 2006. *The Second-Person Standpoint*. Cambridge, MA: Harvard University Press.

Devine, P. G., and A. J. Elliott. 1995. Are racial stereotypes really fading? The Princeton trilogy revisited. *Personality and Social Psychology Bulletin* 21 (11):1139.

Dovidio, J.F., et al. 1997. On the Nature of Prejudice: Automatic and Controlled Processes. *Journal of Experimental Social Psychology* 33 (5):510.

Dunning, J. 2009. Gay blood ban to be reviewed. *The Lesbian & Gay Foundation*, October 26, 2009, http://lgbt.foundation/news/gay-blood-ban-to-be-reviewed/

Durlauf, S.N. 2006. Assessing racial profiling. *Economic Journal* 116:F402.

Dworkin, G. 1988. *The Theory and Practice of Autonomy*. Cambridge: Cambridge University Press.

Dworkin, R. 1978. *Taking Rights Seriously*. London: Duckworth.

Dworkin, R. 1985. *A Matter of Principle*. Cambridge: Harvard University Press.

Eidelson, B. 2013. Comment: Kidney allocation and the limits of the Age Discrimination Act. *Yale Law Journal* 122:1635.

Ely, J.H. 1983. Professor Dworkin's External/Personal Preference Distinction. *Duke Law Journal* 1983 (5):959.

Emens, E. 2009. Intimate Discrimination: The State's Role in the Accidents of Sex and Love. *Harvard Law Review* 122:1307.

Eyer, K.R. 2012. That's Not Discrimination: American Beliefs and the Limits of Anti-Discrimination Law. *Minnesota Law Review* 96 (4):1275.

Ewing, K.D. 2003. The Implications of *Wilson* and *Palmer*. *Industrial Law Journal* 32 (1):1.

Feinberg, J. 1989. *The Moral Limits of the Criminal Law Volume 3: Harm to Self*. Oxford: Oxford University Press.

Fiske, E.B., and H.F. Ladd. 2004. *Elusive Equity: Education Reform in Post-Apartheid South Africa*. Washington, DC: Brookings Institution Press.

Fiss, O.M. 1976. Groups and the equal protection clause. *Philosophy and Public Affairs* 5 (2):107.

France, A. 1910. *The Red Lily*. In *The Works of Anatole France in an English Translation*, edited by F. Chapman, translated by W. Stephens. New York: John Lane Company.

Frankfurt, H. 1999. *Necessity, Volition, and Love*. Cambridge: Cambridge University Press.

Frankfurt, H. 1971. Freedom of the Will and the Concept of a Person. *Journal of Philosophy* 68 (1):5.

Fricker, M. 2007. *Epistemic Injustice: Power and the Ethics of Knowing*. Oxford: Clarendon Press.

Gallagher, J. 2011. Gay men blood donor ban to be lifted. *BBC News*, Sept. 8, 2011, http://www.bbc.com/news/health-14824310

Garcia, J.L.A. 1996. The Heart of Racism. In *Race and Racism*, 2001, edited by B. Boxill. Oxford: Oxford University Press.

Gardner, J. 1989. Liberals and Unlawful Discrimination. *Oxford Journal of Legal Studies* 9 (1):1.

Gardner, J. 1996. Discrimination as Injustice. *Oxford Journal of Legal Studies* 16 (3):353.

Gardner, J. 1998. On the Ground of Her Sex(uality). *Oxford Journal of Legal Studies* 18 (1):167.

Garza, A. A Herstory of the #BlackLivesMatter Movement by Alicia Garza. *The Feminist Wire*. Oct. 7, 2014, http://thefeministwire.com/2014/10/blacklivesmatter-2/

Gendler, T.S. 2008. Alief in Action (and Reaction). *Mind & Language* 23 (5): 552.

Gendler, T.S. 2011. On the Epistemic Costs of Implicit Bias. *Philosophical Studies* 156 (1):33.

Gendler, T.S. 2012. Between Reason and Reflex: Response to Commentators. *Analysis* 72 (4):799.

Gil-White, F.J. 2001. Are Ethnic Groups Biological "Species" to the Human Brain? *Current Anthropology* 42 (4): 515.

Gingrich, N. 2009. On Terrorism it's Time to Know, to Profile, and to Discriminate. *Human Events*, December 30, 2009, http://www.humanevents.com/article.php?id=35025

Glasgow, J. 2009. Racism as Disrespect. *Ethics* 120 (1): 64.

Glover, J. 2000. *Humanity: A Moral History of the Twentieth Century*. New Haven: Yale University Press.

Goddard, T., et al. 2014. Racial Bias in Driver Yielding Behavior at Cross-walks. National Institute for Transportation and Communities, http://ppms.otrec.us/media/project_files/NITC-SS-733_Racial_Bias_in_Driver_Yielding_Behavior_at_Crosswalks.pdf

Green, L. 2010. Two Worries about Respect for Persons. *Ethics* 120 (2):212.

Greenwald, A.G., and T.F. Pettigrew. 2014. Malice Toward None and Charity for Some: Ingroup Favoritism Enables Discrimination. *American Psychologist* 69 (7):669.

Greenwald, A.G., et al. 2009. Understanding and Using the Implicit Association Test: III. Meta-Analysis of Predictive Validity. *Journal of Personality and Social Psychology* 97 (1):17.

Gross, S.R., and D. Livingston. 2002. Racial profiling under attack. *Columbia Law Review* 102 (5):1413.

Harcourt, B.E. 2004. Rethinking Racial Profiling: A Critique of the Economics, Civil Liberties, and Constitutional Literature, and of Criminal Profiling More Generally. *University of Chicago Law Review* 71:1275.

Harris, D.A. 2002. *Profiles in Injustice: Why Police Profiling Cannot Work.* New York: New Press.

Heckman, J., and D. Masterov. 2007. The productivity argument for investing in young children. *Review of Agricultural Economics* 29 (3):446.

Hellman, D. 2008. *When is Discrimination Wrong?* Cambridge: Harvard University Press.

Hellman, D., and S. Moreau, eds. 2013. *Philosophical Foundations of Discrimination Law.* Oxford: Oxford University Press.

Herbert, B. 2010. Jim Crow Policing. *The New York Times,* February 1, 2010, http://www.nytimes.com/2010/02/02/opinion/02herbert.html

Hitchcock, C. 2001. A tale of two effects. *The Philosophical Review* 110 (3): 361.

Hitchens, C. 2001. *Letters to a Young Contrarian.* Cambridge: Basic Books.

Holroyd, J. 2012. Responsibility for Implicit Bias. *Journal of Social Philosophy* 43(3):274.

Holroyd, J., and D. Kelly. Forthcoming. *Implicit Bias, Character, and Control.* In *From Personality to Virtue: Essays in the Philosophy of Character,* edited by J. Webber and A. Masala.

Holroyd, J., and J. Sweetman. Forthcoming. The Heterogeneity of Implicit Bias. In *Implicit Bias and Philosophy,* edited by M. Brownstein and J. Saul.

Horta, O. 2010. Discrimination in Terms of Moral Exclusion. *Theoria* 76 (4): 314.

Joint United Kingdom Blood Transfusion Services and Tissue Transplantation Services Professional Advisory Committee. 2007. Prion

Associated Diseases. http://www.transfusionguidelines.org.uk/dsg/wb/guide
lines/pr004-prion-associated-diseases

Jost, J.T., et al. 2009. The existence of implicit bias is beyond reasonable
doubt: A refutation of ideological and methodological objections and
executive summary of ten studies that no manager should ignore. *Research
in Organizational Behavior* 29:39.

Kary, T. 2010. Kaplan Higher Education Sued for Race Discrimination. *The
Los Angeles Times*, December 22, 2010, http://articles.latimes.com/2010/
dec/22/business/la-fi-kaplan-sued-20101222

Kawakami, K., Dovidio, J.F., Moll, J., Hermsen, S., and A. Russin. 2000. Just
Say No (to Stereotyping): Effects of Training in the Negation of Stereo-
typic Associations on Stereotype Activation. *Journal of Personality and
Social Psychology* 78 (5): 871.

Kennedy, R. 1997. *Race, Crime, and the Law.* New York: Random House.

Keteyian, A. 2009. Behind the Abdulmutallab Security Breach. *CBS News*,
December 28, 2009, http://www.cbsnews.com/stories/2009/12/28/cbsnews_
investigates/main6031469.shtml

Khaitan, T. 2015. *A Theory of Discrimination Law.* Oxford: Oxford University Press.

King, M.L. 1962. The Ethical Demands for Integration. In *A Testament of
Hope: The Essential Writings and Speeches of Martin Luther King, Jr.,*
edited by J.M. Washington (1986).

Koppelman, A. 2006. Justice for Large Earlobes! A Comment on Richard
Arneson's "What Is Wrongful Discrimination?" *San Diego Law Review* 43:809.

Korsgaard, C.M. 1996. *The Sources of Normativity.* New York: Cambridge
University Press.

Krieger, L.H. 1995. The content of our categories: a cognitive bias approach
to discrimination and equal employment opportunity. *Stanford Law
Review* 47 (6):1161.

Letters: Barring Smokers From the Workplace. 2011. *The New York Times*,
February 16, 2011, http://www.nytimes.com/2011/02/17/opinion/l17smok
ing.html

Lever, A. 2005. Why racial profiling is hard to justify: A response to Risse and
Zeckhauser. *Philosophy & Public Affairs* 33 (1):94.

Lever, A. 2007. What's Wrong with Racial Profiling? Another Look at the
Problem. *Criminal Justice Ethics* 26:20.

Lever, A. 2011. Treating People as Equals: Ethical Objections to Racial
Profiling and the Composition of Juries. *Journal of Ethics* 15:61.

Levin, M. 1992. Responses to race differences in crime. *Journal of Social
Philosophy* 23 (1):5.

Levin, M. 2007. Comments on Risse and Lever. *Criminal Justice Ethics* 26:29.

Levinson, C. 2012. Afghan Women Seen Losing Ground. *Wall Street Journal*, March 6, 2012, http://online.wsj.com/news/articles/SB1000142405297020 4276304577265341368406930

Lewis, D., and M. Sargeant. 2004. *Essentials of Employment Law* (8th edn). London: Chartered Institute of Personnel and Development.

Lillehammer, H. 2010. Scanlon on Intention and Permissibility. *Analysis* 70 (3):578.

Lippert-Rasmussen, K. 2006a. The badness of discrimination. *Ethical theory and moral practice* 9 (2):167.

Lippert-Rasmussen, K. 2006b. Private discrimination: A prioritarian, desert-accommodating account. *San Diego Law Review* 43:817.

Lippert-Rasmussen, K. 2006c. Racial profiling versus community. *Journal of Applied Philosophy* 23 (2):191.

Lippert-Rasmussen, K. 2007. Nothing Personal: On Statistical Discrimination. *Journal of Political Philosophy* 15 (4):385.

Lippert-Rasmussen, K. 2011. "We Are All Different": Statistical Discrimination and the Right to be Treated as an Individual. *Journal of Ethics* 15:47.

Lippert-Rasmussen, K. 2013. *Born Free and Equal?: A Philosophical Inquiry into the Nature of Discrimination*. Oxford: Oxford University Press.

Loury, G.C. 2002. *The Anatomy of Racial Inequality*. Cambridge: Harvard University Press.

Madva, A. 2013. *Implicit Bias, Moods, and Moral Responsibility*. (Unpublished).

Madva, A., and M. Brownstein. 2013. *The Blurry Boundary between Stereotyping and Evaluation in Implicit Cognition*. (Unpublished).

McCrudden, C. 1982. Institutional discrimination. *Oxford Journal of Legal Studies* 2:303.

McCrudden, C. 1985. Changing Notions of Discrimination. In *Equality and Discrimination: Essays in freedom and justice*, edited by S. Guest and A. Milne. Stuttgart: F. Steiner Verlag Wiesbaden.

McIntyre, A. Doctrine of Double Effect. In *The Stanford Encyclopedia of Philosophy (Fall 2009 Edition)*, edited by E. N. Zalta.

Medina, J. 2013. *The Epistemology of Resistance: Gender and Racial Oppression, Epistemic Injustice, and Resistant Imaginations*. Oxford: Oxford University Press.

Miller, D. 1999. *Principles of Social Justice*. Cambridge: Harvard University Press.

Moreau, S. 2010. What Is Discrimination? *Philosophy & Public Affairs* 38 (2):143.

Muigai, G. 2010. Remarks of United Nations Special Rapporteur on contemporary forms of racism, racial discrimination, xenophobia and related intolerance (as delivered). In *Intergovernmental Working Group on the Effective Implementation of the Durban Declaration and Programme of Action, 8th session*, United Nations Office of the High Commissioner for Human Rights, http://www2.ohchr.org/english/issues/racism/rapporteur/docs/IGWG8_18102010.doc

Mullen, B., and L. Hu. 1989. Perceptions of ingroup and outgroup variability: A meta-analytic integration. *Basic and Applied Social Psychology* 10 (3):233.

Pincus, F.L. 1996. Discrimination Comes in Many Forms: Individual, Institutional, and Structural. *American Behavioral Scientist* 40 (2):186.

Pojman, L.P. 1993. Race and Crime: A Response to Michael Levin and Laurence Thomas. *Journal of Social Philosophy* 24 (1):152.

Post, R. 2000. Prejudicial Appearances: The Logic of American Antidiscrimination Law. *California Law Review* 88(1):1.

Primus, R. 2010. The Future of Disparate Impact. *Michigan Law Review* 108:1341.

Raz, J. 1986. *The Morality of Freedom*. Oxford: Clarendon Press.

Raz, J. 2001. *Value, Respect, and Attachment*. Cambridge: Cambridge University Press.

Raz, J. 2010. On Respect, Authority, and Neutrality: A Response. *Ethics* 120 (2):279.

Richards, J.R. 1985. Discrimination. *Proceedings of the Aristotelian Society, Supplementary Volumes* 59:53.

Risse, M. 2007. Racial Profiling: A Reply to Two Critics. *Criminal Justice Ethics* 26:4.

Risse, M., and R. Zeckhauser. 2004. Racial Profiling. *Philosophy and Public Affairs* 32 (2):131.

Rhode, D.L. 2010. *The Beauty Bias: The Injustice of Appearance in Life and Law*. Oxford: Oxford University Press.

Sadker, M., and D. Sadker. 1994. *Failing at Fairness: How America's Schools Cheat Girls*. New York: C. Scribner.

Sack, K. 2011. Virginia to Ask Supreme Court to Rule on Health Law. *The New York Times*, February 3, 2011, http://www.nytimes.com/2011/02/04/health/policy/04virginia.html

Scanlon, T.M. 2008. *Moral Dimensions: Permissibility, Meaning, Blame*. Cambridge: Harvard University Press.

Schauer, F. 2003. *Profiles, Probabilities, and Stereotypes*. Cambridge: Harvard University Press.

Schauer, F. 2011. Bentham on Presumed Offenses. *Utilitas* 23 (4):363.

Schmalbeck, R. 1986. The Trouble with Statistical Evidence. *Law & Contemporary Problems* 49:221.

Schmidt, P. 2007. *Color and Money: How Rich White Kids Are Winning the War Over College Affirmative Action.* New York: Palgrave Macmillan.

Seifert, J.W. 2004. Data mining and the search for security: Challenges for connecting the dots and databases. *Government Information Quarterly* 21 (4):461.

Shin, P.S. 2009. The Substantive Principle of Equal Treatment. *Legal Theory* 15:149.

Shin, P.S. 2010. Liability for Unconscious Discrimination? A Thought Experiment in the Theory of Employment Discrimination Law. *Hastings Law Journal* 62:67.

Shogenji, T. 2003. A condition for transitivity in probabilistic support. *The British Journal for the Philosophy of Science* 54 (4):613.

Siegel, R.B. 2004. Equality Talk: Antisubordination and Anticlassification Values in Constitutional Struggles over *Brown. Harvard Law Review* 117:1470.

Stein, H.F. 1974. Envy and the Evil Eye Among Slovak-Americans: An Essay in the Psychological Ontogeny of Belief and Ritual. *Ethos* 2 (1):15–46.

Strauss, D.A. 1986. The Myth of Colorblindness. *Supreme Court Review* 1986:99.

Sunstein, C.R. 1994. The Anticaste Principle. *Michigan Law Review* 92:2410.

Tanovich, D.M. 2004. Moving beyond Driving While Black: Race, Suspect Description and Selection. *Ottawa Law Review* 36:315.

Thomas, L. 1992. Statistical Badness. *Journal of Social Philosophy* 23 (1):30.

Thomsen, F.K. 2011. The Art of the Unseen: Three Challenges for Racial Profiling. *Journal of Ethics* 15:89.

Thomson, J.J. 1984. Remarks on causation and liability. *Philosophy & Public Affairs* 13 (2):101.

Thomson, J.J. 1986. Liability and Individualized Evidence. *Law & Contemporary Problems* 49:199.

U.S. Census Bureau. 2011. State & County QuickFacts, http://quickfacts.census.gov/qfd/states/00000.html

U.S. Food and Drug Administration. 2014. FDA Commissioner Margaret A. Hamburg's statement on FDA's blood donor deferral policy for men who have sex with men, December 23, 2014, http://www.fda.gov/NewsEvents/Newsroom/PressAnnouncements/ucm427843.htm

Waldron, J. 1985. Indirect Discrimination. In *Equality and Discrimination: Essays in Freedom and Justice,* edited by S. Guest and A. Milne. Stuttgart: F. Steiner Verlag Wiesbaden.

Waldron, J. 2005. Moral Autonomy and Personal Autonomy. In *Autonomy and the Challenges to Liberalism: New Essays,* edited by J. Christman and J. Anderson. Cambridge: Cambridge University Press.

Walford, G. 1997. Privatization and Selection. In *Affirming the Comprehensive Ideal*, edited by R. Pring and G. Walford. London: Routledge.

Walton, A. 1989. Willie Horton And Me. *The New York Times*, August 20, 1989, http://www.nytimes.com/1989/08/20/magazine/willie-horton-and-me.html

Wasserman, D.T. 1991. The Morality of Statistical Proof and the Risk of Mistaken Liability. *Cardozo Law Review* 13:935.

Wasserman, D.T. 1996. Racial Generalizations and Police Discretion. In *Handled with Discretion*. Lanham, MD: Rowman & Littlefield.

Wasserman, D.T. 1998. Discrimination, Concept of. *Encyclopedia of Applied Ethics* 1:805.

White House Commission on Aviation Safety and Security. 1997. *Final Report to President Clinton*, http://fas.org/irp/threat/212fin~1.html

Wimsatt, W.K., and M.C. Beardsley. 1954/1987. The Intentional Fallacy. Reprinted in Joseph Z. Margolis, ed., *Philosophy Looks At The Arts* (Philadelphia, PA: Temple University Press, 1987).

Wolff, R.P. 1970. *In Defense of Anarchism.* New York: Harper & Row.

Woodward, J. 1986. The non-identity problem. *Ethics* 96 (4):804.

Young, I.M. 1990. *Justice and the Politics of Difference.* Princeton: Princeton University Press.

Index

Primus, Richard 66
Principle of Insufficient Reason 8, 98
problem of statistical evidence 134,
 158–9, 181–2, 192–3
proxy discrimination, *see* statistical
 discrimination
psychology:
 regarding ingroup favoritism 114
 regarding outgroup homogeneity 212
 regarding racial groups as natural
  kinds 210–11
 see also implicit bias

racial discrimination 4, 17, 20, 43–4,
 55–7, 59, 63–4, 71, 72–3, 87, 96,
 108, 113–14, 153–5, 161–2; *see also*
 racial profiling; racism
Racial Equality Directive 45, 48
racial profiling 9–10, 170, 173–219, 225
 belief-dependent harms of 198–200,
  205, 218
 distinguished from suspect
  descriptions 178–86
 non-belief-dependent harms
  of 200–1, 205, 219
 significance of publicity in 215–19
 see also Harm Argument (against
  racial profiling)
racism 2, 8, 10, 32, 57, 75, 92–3, 97, 101,
 122, 163–4, 169, 203–7, 213–15,
 218; *see also* racial discrimination
Radcliffe Richards, Janet 18n.7, 31n.36
Raytheon Co. v. Hernandez 54n.26
Raz, Joseph 30n.34, 79n.17, 79n.18,
 85n.35, 98n.3, 129, 139–41
recognition, *see* disrespect
Red Cab case, *see* problem of statistical
 evidence
relevant differences (wrongful
 discrimination as failure to attend
 to) 98n.4, 99, 134–5
religion, as cause of discrimination 37;
 see also role ideals
religion, discrimination on basis of 53,
 56, 65, 123, 137, 191
respect, *see* disrespect
responsibility (of person for a trait that
 is basis of discrimination) 158,
 189–90, 191–2; *see also*
 mutability
Ricci v. DeStefano 40, 60–6

Risse, Mathias 180, 196, 199, 202–5,
 215, 220
role ideals 116–20, 224n.1; *see also*
 preferences

Scanlon, T.M. 80–3, 131, 136
Schauer, Frederick 46, 134n.14, 134n.15
"screening off" condition 185
second-class status, *see* subordination
second-order discrimination 40–4,
 45–7, 49–51, 57, 65
self-definition, *see* autonomy
separate but equal treatment 36–8
sex discrimination 23–4, 28, 37,
 48–51, 59, 107, 116–17, 131–3,
 145–8, 174, 225; *see also* sexism
sexism 2, 8, 10, 34, 75, 92–3, 107, 163–4;
 see also sex discrimination
sexual orientation, discrimination on
 basis of 56, 77, 117–20, 219–21
Shin, Patrick 24, 89–90, 99
shooter bias 132
Smith v. City of Jackson, Miss. 53–4
social meaning, *see* conventional
 meaning
social priming 131
social salience 9, 26–30, 168–9, 210
special attachments 97–8, 111–13
statistical discrimination 1–2, 9, 72, 135,
 170, 173–7; *see also* generalizations,
 discrimination on basis of; problem
 of statistical evidence; racial
 profiling
statistical evidence, *see* problem of
 statistical evidence
stereotypes, *see* generalizations,
 discrimination on basis of
stigma 32, 43, 108, 118, 167, 169, 177,
 197–8, 201, 205–10, 221
structural discrimination 24–6, 54
subordination 2, 3, 71, 87–8, 96–7
suspect descriptions:
 distinguished from profiles 178–86
 morality of 186–7, 209–10
symmetry 58–60, 112–14

terrorism 137, 175–6, 180–3, 187, 189,
 202, 210, 219n.82
*Texas Dept. of Housing and Community
 Affairs v. Inclusive Communities
 Project* 54n.27